BREAKING BORDERS

TRAVELS IN PURSUIT OF AN IMPOSSIBLE RECORD

JAMES ASQUITH

Published by James Asquith

Copyright © James Asquith, 2016

Cover design by Lieu Pham, Covertopia.com
Layout by Guido Henkel

INTRODUCTION
The Road to Anywhere

I heard a saying many years ago that stuck with me and evolved my way of thinking: "The life you have led doesn't need to be the only life you have." Traveling around the world became a distinctive life choice for me, and it was my liberation. My journey was not just about the desire to see the world, it was the need for escapism, for a very real adrenaline rush of danger. Consequently, loneliness and solitude were emotions that became mine to cherish and adapt around.

The date is July 17, 2013, and I am standing in front of the very last border crossing, the final frontier, for lack of a better expression. "Welcome to The Federated States of Micronesia," a rather obscure and remote island in the depths of the mid-Pacific. But I didn't feel the emotions of success and accomplishment I had thought I would as I approached my 196th country. No grandiose triumphant feelings for something I had strived to achieve over the last five years. No relief or fulfilment, and certainly not the very undeniable realization that the most significant part of my life had come to its objectified end.

Anyone who tells you they are wildly happy and unconstrained while traveling the farthest corners of the globe without anyone to share these memories is lying to you, and potentially, without even realizing it, lying to themselves. Traveling can be lonely, and it really is a learning experience and an escapism reflex, as it was for me. I was unquestionably happy, but I certainly wasn't in the most content place I could imagine.

For anyone that has ever traveled solo and sat for that quiet moment by themselves on a deserted beach or perched on a secluded cliff edge: can you honestly say there was not a part of you thinking, "I'm captivated, but I want to share this with those people important to me?" My best memories are the ones I shared, and although I will cherish the loneliest memories as my own, that seclusion comes with profound and deep-seated human emotions that were the very reason I embarked on doing something different. A journey that was mine to keep forever, but one that would have been worthless without the people that were with me along the way, both in person and subjectively. I have looked out across every ocean, climbed mountains, wandered deserts, pleaded for my sanctuary and experienced the fall of dictators, but most importantly I have met some of the most incredible people who have made me smile, laugh and even cry. Many of their names were never known to me, but the most paramount element of my journey across the world was the people. Some of them I may never see again, and some are not a part of my life anymore, but their influence was insightful, and without sharing these memories throughout my voyage, it would have seemed almost inconsequential and meaningless. I have made new friends across the world, and even those who I will not see again, sometimes out of choice, were still unique in shaping my adventure and becoming a part of my story, that culminated in officially becoming the youngest person to travel to every sovereign nation in the world as I crossed the 196th border.

A lot of people ask me how I could afford to venture around the whole world and, granted, if you want to see as many varied aspects as possible, there are occasions where traveling is not a cheap hobby; there were times where I felt disgusted with how much money I had spent on letters of invitation and visas, sometimes spending as much as $500 on documents before I had even booked a flight or place to stay.

I had always asked for money at Christmas and birthdays, and worked little jobs whenever I could, from washing cars with my friends from the age of 11 to working in bars when I was older. I managed to accumulate a decent savings account, and put this to work on the stock market during the financial crisis in 2008/9, making enough money to begin my travels independently.

I was incredibly lucky and, to be honest, it felt more like chance at the time. I didn't have much idea of what I was doing, and this money would only complement my travels. I never traveled for any longer than a few months at a time, and kept a job when I returned to London between travels to pay for my next adventure.

My father was a pilot for BMI and later for British Airways, which was obviously a colossal influence on my aspirations to travel, but also in assisting—when I was lucky enough—to fly to many destinations with my dad for often reduced rates. In addition to getting much inspiration from my father, my mother regularly talked about her experiences growing up in various places around the world, from Hong Kong to Germany, and I guess the desire to travel was in my blood.

So we go back to 2008. I had already begun to be influenced by Alex Garland, as many young travelers are with his far reaching depictions of paradise. His ideas began to remonstrate with my situation and the journey I would embark on, specifically the concept of why we become infatuated with people and objectives. As is so often the case, there was a picturesque and ideal aspiration that I believed was all I had been looking for in life, in respect to exactly how I hoped my life would progress, but this idea of captivation became too obscure when life did not work out how I had hoped. I had become almost reliant on this improbable objective of unattainable happiness, and so I craved an escape from the situation. Was it an endeavor for attention? The more dangerous and off-piste the better? Possibly.

Something in my mind triggered then and there when a relationship did not work out, and although it was initially meant to be to escape the situation, the act of travel became my obsession. We all have vices and addictions, and traveling became my default craving. I learnt how to actually achieve what I wanted, and without hesitation, if the opportunity was there, I would just book a ticket and go. Sure, there are always obstacles, and if I was to compile a do and don't list for many of my trips, such as to Afghanistan when it was an active war zone, then I would have achieved nothing, and I certainly wouldn't have traveled to every country in a dynamic and ever-changing world within five years. What will the world look like in another five years, where will and won't be safe? Who knows quite honestly. It is perhaps foolhardy, and naïve, but just buy the ticket... and go.

CHAPTER 1
Bangkok

In March 2008 I booked my very first ticket to go to Mombasa, Kenya for three months. I had never left Europe before, except for when I visited the U.S. as a child with my family, and booking the trip to Mombasa garnered the reaction I was looking for. I had no idea what I was doing, and everyone was desperate to talk the naïve 19-year-old out of this, which only made me more determined. Ironically, I never actually went to Mombasa, and have still never been there to this day (which I should really do as it seems like where this journey began—without ever starting).

Instead of traveling to Mombasa on my own, I was convinced to join two of my best friends on a part of their gap year. So my very first expedition headed to the ever-popular backpacking melting pot of Southeast Asia which began with two of my best friends, Jack and Chris. There was a large element of relief to traveling for a vast period of time with people that I knew, and for anyone thinking of embarking on travel around the world out of their comfort zone, I would highly recommend making that first trip with others, not to mention creating memories to cherish with your friends. I had known these guys for nearly 10 years at the time, and in hindsight, taking this journey with the people who will remain in my life forever and who later became best men at my wedding was instrumental in developing my obsession and my desire for further travel. I am not so sure I would have necessarily picked up the so called "travel bug" embarking on a solo debut trip to Mombasa.

I remember that first journey like it was yesterday. Shopping around for that first backpack, buying the cheapest one, against the advice of the shop assistant who'd assured me I would catch the travel bug and use this very backpack for years to come. I shrugged off that advice and still bought the cheapest backpack—incredibly, it nevertheless survived all those countries and continents! A lot of people have since asked me if I had set out to become the youngest person to visit every country in the world. I think back to this moment whereby I bought my first (and only!) backpack, believing the trip ahead would be my only adventure, and the answer is certainly no. I guess I just got carried away over time, but more on that later.

So there we were, three pale English boys dumped in the hectic metropolis of Bangkok. Before arriving in Thailand, we had flown via Mumbai, India, where I naïvely ordered an ice cream from a street vendor. This was clearly going to be a very steep learning curve for me as the vendor "created" a new flavor ice cream by simply dunking his dirty finger into the bowl and mixing two scoops together. This was certainly not the type of hygiene we were used to, and we would clearly have to adapt quickly. Oh, and I mustn't forget the ice cream wafer falling on the ground. That was seemingly not a problem either, as the wafer could be reused it seemed, so it got placed back into my ice cream. Already I had stepped into a deeply unfamiliar environment away from everything I was used to in London. That fact very soon obtrusively struck me with the pungent smell of what could only be described as a mix of unidentified cooking meat, sewerage and sex as we landed in Bangkok. Combine this setting with the unapologetically booming music, and seemingly half of the city attempting to sell us anything and everything—from unlimited drinks to t-shirts, hookers, hookers with dicks (advertised as both large and small) and drugs I had never even heard of.

Welcome to the prominent and audacious Khao San Road.

So many travelers start and finish their journeys on this small stretch of tarmac in Bangkok. This is the ground zero of scams, but like so many who have come here before and will continue to come here in the future, you will always have a story to tell. Be it attending a "ping-pong show", whereby an army of women who seemingly have machine guns for vaginas relentlessly fire ping-pong balls at your head, with an alarmingly pin point aim; or witnessing your friend sporting a paper origami-type hat, that has been "constructed" by a female performer using only her private parts. OK, fine, that "friend" was actually yours truly.

Bangkok can certainly become sordid. It is shameless and it sells that sleazy vibe, but those types of crude and obnoxious entertainment are acceptable only here. And truth be told, I got to experience a very different side of Bangkok when I returned for Songkran a few years later with my now wife, Elena. She has been with me for so much of my journey and was present at that final frontier in Micronesia. Bangkok (and Thailand

11

as a whole) is a crazy place, but I would highly recommend visiting during Songkran, the celebration of Thai New Year, when the friendliness and openness of the locals truly peaks.

Elena and I had planned to go for a nice dinner on the evening of Songkran only to find that you could not move anywhere in Bangkok without being pelted, smeared and simply drenched in paint and water. All colors. It didn't matter if you were young or old, you were targeted by water balloons and multi-colored varnish. We tried to avoid it for a while, but this was absolutely fruitless. We finally gave in to the fact dinner would not materialize, and I gave in to my inner childish self. I bought myself a twin set of "master-blaster series 5" water cannons, which seemed to do the trick and gave us endless hours of fun. There I was finding vantage points to fire water into the faces of people I didn't even know—the same people who didn't know me but had dispatched paint into my hair moments earlier.

Afterward, we returned to the magnificent Lebua hotel where we were staying and was popularized in the movie "The Hangover 2." We were dripping with water and paint, and armed with water guns in the elevator with everyone else dressed to go to the posh bar on the top floor. They all looked horrified!

This was a very different experience to having "ladyboys" (the Thai slang for transvestites) chase me down Khao San Road five years earlier, but it was equally as amusing. Chris and I had almost lost Jack to one of Bangkok's many, and at times very aggressive, ladyboys, who we had convinced ourselves, was a girl (despite the big hands and prominent Adam's apple, which should have been a dead giveaway). This particular individual had developed quite an obsession for Jack one evening at a bar where towers of beer were consumed in copious volumes. We had misplaced Jack at some point during the partying that night, and had to curb crawl our taxi with the door open, shouting for him in the area around Khao San Road that was overflowing with revellers. We presumed he was mid-way through being sexually assaulted until, out of nowhere, he jumped in and ducked down, shouting, "Go go go." It was like being in a really trashy horror-movie-turned-comedy. Moments later, the taxi stopped and, as we were all crouched down in the back seat, giggling like the kids we were at the time, the door slowly opens and we were greeted by the individual with: "Jack, I can see you." It felt like a game of chase, and only got worse when we decided to hide in our shower on the 6th floor of the hostel. Soon after, we heard the clicking of high heels ascending the stairs and the shower curtain was pulled open (we still hid with our hands over our heads like we could not be seen). How had she found us again? What was her objective? There were more questions than answers here but for now we had to ask the security guard to remove her. What a bizarrely fascinating introduction to Bangkok this had been! I never did find out exactly what happened that night, but this individual just would not give up chasing Jack.

Essentially, Bangkok and Khao San Road in particular are amazing places, although appropriately inexplicable at times, and downright crazy—that night ended with paying tuk-tuk drivers (the little motorbike taxis that are both visually and audibly symbolic of Southeast Asia) to allow Jack, Chris and I to drive them in their own tuk tuks in a drunken role reversal, and I was later picked out as a "volunteer" to eat the banana that had been inside a woman's vagina at a ping-pong show (I categorically never ate it). And that was while we were all intermittently caught in the crossfire of ping-pong balls fired at our eyes from this same multi-tasking vagina!

The debauchery of the capital aside, there are some amazing places to see nearby, from the dark history and sobering nature of visiting the Bridge on the River Kwai to the controversial proximate tiger sanctuaries. Although there is much debate about the conditions these magnificent cats live in, the particular sanctuary we visited seemed to care tremendously about the animals. I personally thought it was a truly amazing experience, being able to bottle feed the baby tiger cubs and to continue the day washing, walking and witnessing the sheer power of the larger beasts that live there.

CHAPTER 2
The Islands of Thailand

From the hectic metropolis of Bangkok we headed to some of the most beautiful islands in the world—starting with experiencing unbelievable diving in the pristine turquoise waters of Ko Tao, moving on to the amazing sand spit island of Ko Phi Phi Don and its gorgeous and iconic Maya Bay beach, hugely popularized among Southeast Asia's backpackers by Alex Garland's novel "The Beach." These islands are quite simply dazzling.

There is a beach aptly named 'Monkey Beach' close to Phi Phi, where groups of travelers used to stop for a visit as part of the standard tour itinerary. However, nowadays only the bravest and most carefree of guides, those with little concern for health and safety, allow tourists to venture here.

For Jack, Chris and me, Monkey Beach became the scene for what we like to call "the attack of the monkeys." Dozens of these seemingly adorable, but as it turned out, thoroughly aggressive primates, viciously attacked me and Chris after we (kindly) tried to feed them mini bananas. We had to scramble into the sea for safety, as these evil little creatures didn't seem to appreciate our offering. My only other run-in with monkeys took place at another aptly named place later on my travels, Monkey Mountain in Malaysia. Five of them jumped on Elena and bit fairly deeply into her hand, but she was again provoking them with mini bananas, so there seems to be a common theme here.

There is one island that stands above and beyond the rest in Thailand, be it for good or bad reasons and experiences. Many travelers return with stories of debauchery and, indeed, insanity from the island of Koh Pha Ngan—the home of the original Full Moon party. Travelers have a pre-conceived concept of the wild antics that occur here: sipping concoctions from buckets on the beach, doused in face paint and dangerously playing with various measures of fire while being barely sober enough to stand. And many of these notions happen to be true. Revellers let go of their inhibitions on this island, and there are many places around the world similar to it; say, for example, Bourbon Street in New Orleans and Ibiza. Yet Koh Pha Ngan is truly unique. It is grubby and disarrayed and, as most Thai people will agree, not illustrative of Thailand at all.

There are usually scams around every corner for the unsuspecting tourist on this island, or those simply too drunk to suspect, but it remains a strange right-of-passage for backpackers in this region to experience the debaucheries of Koh Pha Ngan. I was certainly naïve about it and, after staying on the island for a week, I knew it was time to leave—or maybe I simply couldn't drink any more alcohol. My encounters were blurred to say the least. I have memories of us three fools buying a lot of fireworks (not that we had any experience with them, and yes, despite all the warnings we should maybe have avoided this) and attempting to put on our very own firework spectacle on the beach. Sure, it seemed great at the time, but our display was probably shit, illustrated by all the locals shaking their heads at us. Even the guy that sold us the fireworks appeared distinctly unimpressed. I also remember running around for several days with an Australian girl I had met, following her like a lapdog, believing I had found an island romance. We got together a few times and all seemed well until I saw her at a UV party kissing some guy in an overly tight "wife beater" with drinks buckets apparently glued to each hand. This is how this place was; there was no order or sanity, and you were lucky to get out unscathed. Or that could just have been me! Karma may have pursued when that same group of girls all had their clothes stolen on the beach whilst skinny dipping in the sea the following evening, but compared to some stories you hear, such as undercover police officers selling drugs as entrapment during the full moon party, it seemed relatively tame, although unfortunate.

However, my strangest memory came from the actual night of the full moon. Boat loads of people transfer from neighboring islands, desperate to get a piece of the party but not wanting to subject themselves to the obscurity of staying on the party island. Nonetheless, on the night of the full moon party, no one was taking the boats out from Koh Pha Ngan, just arriving, except for one idiot. Yes, I ended up inexplicably cradling a baby shark (that had already been killed) on a beach in Koh Samui, a two-hour boat ride away. I was so drunk on copious buckets of whatever alcohol they had been distributing with their Thai Red Bull (that is lethal), that I lost my friends on Pha Ngan, and somehow got upset outside a restaurant that was selling baby shark. They had the shark on ice outside the restaurant, and come what may, in my completely irrational state, I paid 2,600 Thai baht so no one else could eat this poor shark, then hopped on the first boat out of there. To this day, I cannot explain what motions were running through my head or what I hoped to achieve, but, like many who go to Koh Pha Ngan, or hope to go, these are the kinds of idiotic but memorable stories you can come away with.

From there it was onward to the ever-popular destination of Phuket on a rickety wooden overnight boat, whereby the three of us huddled together on the bottom deck through tumultuous waves during an almighty thunderstorm. It was a terrifying experience and one I genuinely thought I wouldn't live through. The waves continually crashed into the sides of this ancient wreck of a boat, sending passengers flying into the air during a hideous eight-hour ordeal against nature. This was only to be compared through personal experience with the boat crossing between Dar es Salaam and Zanzibar, which unfortunately claims many lives every year. My experiences of Phuket are not the most insightful. Twice I have visited, and both times I accomplished very little, despite being signed up to the Phuket health service while bed ridden and tended to by copious amounts of Thai nurses who were uncontrollably giggling while sticking injections in my ass.

Illness or no illness, there was rarely time to sit still on this journey, and we moved onwards...

CHAPTER 3
Cambodia and Laos

We went overland from Bangkok to Siem Reap, Cambodia on the now well-documented 'Tourist Scam Bus'. If unaware, this bus costs marginally less than the 'standard' service, yet takes about three times longer, taking passages that I couldn't possibly refer to as roads, with potholes similar in size to that of small meteor craters. Conveniently for the drivers' friends, the bus also arrives in Siem Reap (or, rather, some outer suburb where life barely exists) at about 1 A.M., with almost everyone on the entire bus, the driver included, clenching their backs in pain. However, conveniently, the driver's friends were waiting for us, willing to put us up in the most relatively overpriced and atrocious accommodation across town.

My advice would be to pay marginally more to drive on something that actually resembles a road if ever taking this journey. We refused the accommodation offers and trekked around with our backpacks to find better value. Back then, it cost 2 USD a night (for three people) to stay in a shack with no windows where you will get eaten alive by mosquitos and have the added perk of a pet cockroach on your pillow, so it is also probably worth paying a marginal amount extra for somewhere else.

I have traveled in both luxury and, contrastingly, on a very tight shoestring budget before, but sometimes it is amazing how much further an extra dollar or two can get you, and this was certainly one of those instances. Terrible lodging issues aside, we awoke a matter of hours later to see one of man's most spectacular creations—Angkor Wat.

This is the largest religious building in the world, and it looked remarkable in the golden light of dawn, the majestic temples reflected in the lake. Returning back to this spectacular destination a few years later with my wife was like looking after an uncontrollably excited child that had been overly inspired by Lara Croft, climbing through the temples and crevices. Cambodians, in my experience, are some of the friendliest people in the world. They have turned their most recent bleak history around remarkably; on this note, a trip to the killing fields from Phnom Penh is a most exceptionally sobering experience.

You will also find some very questionable and relaxed gun laws (and unethical options at the point of consumerism relating to gun use in Cambodia). Picture this setting: it is Khmer New Year day, a national holiday, and most businesses are closed, so carrying, let alone firing, only handguns, on this particular day was "strictly" prohibited. After being convinced to hop into the back of a local's pick-up truck and driven into the middle of nowhere to a farm, Elena and I found ourselves quite literally firing through all of our spending money as we purchased more and more rounds and magazines of ammunition. Semi-automatics, rocket-propelled grenades, even anti-aircraft guns (!) were all readily available—and we definitely tried our best to fire them all! It was even possible to wield a flame-thrower, however, considering the gas canisters and general assembly of this weapon suggested that it pre-dated the 70s, we agreed that this would not be the day we exploded in a burning hot fireball all in the name of fun.

I did previously witness others pay the very controversial $200 fee to fire an RPG at a cow. Yes, that's right, in Cambodia, it is possible to pay a relatively measly sum of money to blow up a live farm animal with a grenade launcher, and it is both horrifying and disgusting. However, I did take great pleasure in watching some imbecile hand over his $200, only to then watch his grenade sail straight over the stone-faced cow, ultimately exploding about 30 meters behind it, with little more than a simple "moo" from the cow by way of reaction. Another $100 later, and the guy had missed again. By this time, I thought the cow had managed an unlikely escape, but it was later explained that this exercise is quite a gimmick with an impossibly misaligned scope to almost ensure the cows survival, to likely be sold back in the market later that day.

So during our later visit during Khmer National day, Elena decided she wanted to fire handguns, but we were just shooting into thin air on this occasion. This was, as I said, "strictly" prohibited on their national day. We were told this was "impossible," at first, but as so regularly seems to be the case, that little bit of extra money seems to go a long way here. We were told that it was possible to buy a "special permit" to allow us to use handguns on this particular day. So off the young Cambodian boy drove on his motorbike, across the dirt field. He returned minutes later with a big grin emblazoned across his face, one hand on the handlebar while waving a handgun frantically in the air with the other. After he witnessed that this lax enforcement of the rules seemed to amuse us, he removed the safety and shot haphazardly into the sky while still driving through the field. For a country that had so very recently been subjected to one of the worst genocides of modern times, this was astonishing to see, but I can genuinely say I didn't feel unsafe once during my time in Cambodia.

Back to 2008 and onwards to Laos we ventured, where my most vivid memory is that of the ever-popular tourist stop of Vang Vieng—an extremely bizarre travelers melting pot that has very little in common with Laotian culture. It is formed around one street populated by cafés with beds designed solely for the weary backpacker, and showing episodes of popular US sitcoms on repeat, day and night. Combine that with Westernized food menus, and isolated cafés that serve peculiar edible drug concoctions such as weed milkshakes, opium coffees and shroom pizzas, and after a few days when the initial excitement has worn off, the excessive debauchery really starts to grate on you.

Our main reason for going to Vang Vieng was going tubing down the Nam Lik river rapids. If white water rafting type activities are foreign to you, as they were to me at the time, tubing can be a fairly daunting adventure, especially if rainfall was heavy in the preceding days. The experience began with us following the signs from the town into the wilderness, walking barefoot and dressed in nothing but our swimming trunks. When we reached the river, a kid no older than 16 threw us rubber rings similar to those you might use to meander down a 'lazy river'. It's certainly worth getting your hands on one that hasn't been patched up with duct tape. Rings in hand, off we went down the rapids. They were anything but a 'lazy river'.

We made the journey down these rapids the first day the experience re-opened following a forced two-week closure period following the deaths of a young couple. To make matters worse, the locals had told us that they had never before seen the rapids so fierce—this was the result of extraordinarily heavy rains in the past fortnight. I won't lie: I was terrified. We were young and foolhardy, and despite the obvious dangers, we thought that we were invincible at this time of our lives. As I travelled around the world more, I certainly assessed these types of situations more prudently.

The difference between the Nam Lik rapids and most other river rapids is that here tubing is not a simple journey from A to B; it is more like a journey from A to H, but in no particular order, with allegedly necessary stops at variously scattered riverside bars that will ply you with Lao Lao, the local spirit (I still have no idea what this drink is made from, but the dead scorpion marinating at the bottom of the bottle should have been the first warning sign). Each bar attempts to coax you out of the cold water with promises of singalongs around the fireplace to warm those of us stupid enough to be attempting this.

But the most bizarre feature is the various activities at each bar. These ranged from rope swings directly into the rapids to zip-lines where the objective is to let go from 40 feet, falling into the raging river below and very likely cutting your leg open on the rock. The luckier ones just emerge with their arms flailing about 100 feet downriver, trying to stay afloat.

Despite the dangers involved in these conditions, it was tremendous fun, and sure Jack, Chris and I came away with a few war wounds, but it was a great experience. Well, it was a great experience until I ended up so intoxicated from the vile scorpion spirit drink that I got separated from the group, and there I was, all by myself, floating on the calm part of the river, procrastinating, wondering where the rapids end. All the locals said there would be a "big red cross sign" where the rapids ceased to be "fun," and under no circumstances was anyone to journey beyond this point (they stopped just short of saying you would die, while laughing). So, I looked out for this enigmatic sign while traveling right down the middle of this river, and it should be noted that actually moving yourself from the center to the river bank took quite some effort, such was the immense strength of the rapids. Abruptly, the elusive sign appeared—precisely the opposite of what had been described: a tiny obscure green circle that was smartly placed partially behind a fucking tree, where green leaves were aplenty (I am also colorblind, so this was a further hindrance).

By the time I realized this petite sign was in fact the finishing point, and I was done cursing at the wind, I used all my strength to get toward the river bank. The rapids were the strongest they had been throughout the journey at this point, and in this situation the enraged rapids in the distance looked morbid. I had the ring around my head and I was swimming as fast as I could to almost just stay stationary and not be swept down the rapids, but they were too strong. I let the ring go, and all seemed fine as a group of young boys, who looked like they knew these rapids well, jumped in with ropes and rafts. I would be plucked from the water and be saved it appeared. To my bemusement, they were actually only retrieving their rubber ring and seemed to think I would somehow find my own way out of this perilous situation. Eventually, as I got closer, a local guy extended a large stick and pulled me from the water with only one cut down my leg and abandoned shoes. He could see I was panting with exhaustion, but he simply asked where his rubber ring was! I genuinely thought I was going to die there. Maybe I over-exaggerated in the moment, or maybe they have just witnessed worse situations, but the summary was that no one seemed to care, and despite the late drama, it was a great experience.

After luckily leaving Laos with my life, we moved East to complete probably the most popular backpacker circuit in the world: Thailand, Cambodia and Laos. The next stop would be my last with Jack and Chris: Vietnam.

CHAPTER 4
Vietnam

Vietnam has a special place in my heart as we spent nearly two months in the small town of My Tho, south of Ho Chi Minh City as volunteers, building a house under the supervision of an exceedingly controlling and bossy local woman. She would come out while we took a lunch break and wave her broom at us, telling us to get back to work on her house, and she'd instruct us exactly how she wanted things changed. When you are not used to working manual labor outside in 38 Celsius in the monsoon season, a lunch break is fairly necessary, but when you get told she doesn't like how we put the roof on after battling to construct it with very little clue what we were doing, it almost felt ungrateful.

Attempting to integrate with the local (and completely alien) culture and customs of this tiny town was a challenging experience for us as white Westerners. At first, we received only very weary looks from locals, since My Tho is located quite far off the traditional tourist trail but after a short period of acclimation, the true friendly and warm spirit of the Vietnamese prevailed. After hearing our British accents, the common nickname shouted in our general direction was "hey, you, David Beckham", often followed by offerings of ghastly eel soup.

Walking home after work each day was seldom boring, as it seemed half the town wanted to invite us into their homes for dinner (sitting on the mini plastic chairs that everyone seemed to use as a staple part of their furniture, and which are designed for young children). There were some nights where we would stop for three or four dinners, and it felt rude to ever refuse the heartfelt invitations.

Linguistic communication was at a bare minimum, but this really illustrated how simple body language can go a very long way. Alcohol was aplenty as was the laughter, but the food was certainly questionable; dog was obviously a popular item on the menu here, and it became difficult to avoid it. Some of the conditions we saw the animals were living in were utterly disgraceful. I saw some families keep dogs that were barely alive and almost disabled as they would hack pieces of meat off the dogs as and when they required them. The idea behind this extremely inhumane and vile practice is to keep the meat as fresh as possible.

Steamed chicken was on the menus as well, but this was also not my favorite dish as most of the feathers were still present on the tasteless meat. Yet by far the worst dish I was served, anticipated to be chicken, turned out to be cat. This was truly revolting and consisted mostly of cartilage and bone, certainly something I would never recommend.

It was not until the last day, after nearly two months in My Tho that I discovered a cosy little restaurant that served egg and fries for breakfast. It was situated down an alleyway just opposite the house we were staying in, so I was infuriated not to have found it earlier. This place would have made the culinary experience here bearable and a little more diverse.

The amateur crash course in Vietnamese construction could not have come at a worse time, as it was monsoon season. The building process regularly seemed to be one step forward, two back. It took us a week to dig foundations, only for them to then be entirely consumed with rainwater as we were about to start laying the brickwork. So there we were, refusing to give up, bare footed, deep in trenches of mud-water, helplessly trying to remove the water with buckets quicker than the clouds above could deposit it. We had all sorts of exotic creatures and bugs as our companions in the cavities of the foundations and inevitably on us; our Swiss army knife was regularly used to remove creatures attempting to burrow under our skin. However, Mother Nature apparently always triumphs, and a day rarely passed where we felt that we had prevailed over the elements.

I suppose it was for the best when we did finally leave. I felt we had outstayed our welcome by this point, as tensions broiled over in the shared house where we stayed.

One of the other volunteers had taken quite a liking to Jack and, in the final week after she had intoxicated herself to quite absurd levels, essentially attempted to sexually assault him. Again, there seems to be a continuing theme here with aggressive advances towards Jack, and after she petulantly but amusingly left chili power in our pillows, our vengeance was to go to the local supermarket and buy four of the largest crabs I have ever seen to leave in her bed. It's safe to say she metaphorically hit the roof and we rapidly vacated the house soon after. This all happened at the time when construction of the house was complete, less a few windows, but relationships had reached new lows. It was time we moved on. After two months in tough conditions with virtually inedible food we had finally reached breaking point, hence resorting to petulant pranks as our only source of entertainment.

Onwards we traveled, northwards through Vietnam. Similar to nearby Cambodia, Vietnam is an immensely spectacular country considering the relatively recent atrocities that had occurred here. Few sights are more sobering than the displays at the War Remnants Museum in Ho Chi Minh City: jars containing unborn babies—victims of napalm attacks—as well as copious amounts of other graphic, moving accounts of the effects of chemical weapons.

From here we visited the Cu Chi tunnels where you can follow in the footsteps of Vietnamese troops who moved underground in their intricately small passages. This is quite daunting for those who suffer from claustrophobia, and I certainly felt very sweaty and anxious underground. Despite rapid progress in Vietnam, this remains a country that bears the scars of war, and the contrast in attitudes of the people in the north of Vietnam is evident, where there was certainly increased hesitation toward Western-looking tourists compared to the South. Many Vietnamese in the North still ride around on their motorbikes wearing old army helmets, often dispatching hostile stares. Personally, I much preferred the south of the country, but the north has the remarkable and enticing Halong Bay, which is a must-see during any trip to Vietnam. Wending through the gargantuan rock formations on a tiny boat was fascinating, while the numerous quaint floating bars dotted throughout the bay (a seemingly typical feature of water activities in Southeast Asia) afford explorers the chance to truly savor these otherworldly views together with a relaxing drink during a memorable sunset.

My most vivid memories of Vietnam are attached to Nha Trang, a small coastal town with very friendly locals excluding a small handful which we will come onto later. The majority of people were wonderful, as with the rest of Vietnam, and there were some beautiful settings, such as that of the Sailing Club, where I spent many a day sipping a beer looking out at the water. It was in Nha Trang that Chris and I had a real argument for the first time in nearly 10 years of friendship.

We had rented a motorbike, and naturally, my reckless, excited, 19-year-old self took pleasure in driving the bike with maniacal extremeness. My taking of the bends was outrageous to say the least, and despite Chris's pleas on the back of the bike, the intensity wasn't reduced. The three of us had purchased an acoustic guitar that had been with us since Thailand that we named Petchi (after the road of the very first hostel we stayed at in Bangkok), and this guitar had traveled all around with us, picking up wooden carvings in its bodywork along the way. You can therefore understand Chris's sheer anger when the guitar went flying off the back of the bike, most likely due to my reckless driving, but a few dents did nothing to stop Petchi's adventure. However, we were quick to smooth things over, and what better way to do it than at the Sailing Club. We were fascinated at how relatively cheap the drinks were there, so, between two of us, we ordered the entire cocktail menu of over 70 drinks. The waiters seemed shocked and continued to march out cocktails two by two over the course of several hours. We could barely stand by the end of this and likely only got through about 35 between us, but this still seemed like a good effort.

Contrary to the fantastic memories from the Sailing Club, there was a group of locals that genuinely had me fearing for my life when I later returned to Nha Trang a few years later. There was a military themed bar in Nha Trang (which was seemingly run by the local Vietnamese mob). And it had an ex-army 4x4 outside, the type with the windscreen that folds down onto the hood (I have never understood the reasoning for that). Now, I had met a nice guy called Dan on my travels, and Dan must have weighed 110 kg, and he insisted on posing for a photo on the hood of this jeep. I'm not saying this action didn't deserve some form of punishment, but Dan hadn't realized there was a windscreen that was folded down until the clear "crack" sound resonated. A group of angry looking Vietnamese locals immediately appeared. This is where things got a little strange as the owner of the bar interrupted what looked like something that could have turned out as a savage beating. He invited us and the travelers we were with downstairs for a drink. This felt like drinking in an evil lair, and the kind of scene you see before someone gets killed in a Hollywood movie. He asked how much we thought was fair to pay for the windscreen, which turned out to be more of a rhetorical question since he later had his henchmen march Dan to an A.T.M. to pay $300 for it. After forcing us to pay for the drinks, we were told that there were now no hard feelings, and he invited us back the following night to a party. We reluctantly agreed to this, but soon after walking just one street away, we immediately returned to our hostel, packed our bags and got the first bus out of town that same night. We were later told by others who remained at the hostel that there was an enraged group of what they claim was over 20 men with bats waiting outside this bar the following evening, and it can only be assumed this displeased display was for us.

Backpacking around Southeast Asia was my first independent trip, and it will forever remain a truly memorable experience. Still, I was young and so naïve back then; many of the actions we took and arrogance we displayed throughout our journey deserved to be punished at times. When I have since returned to Bangkok and seen those pale skinned and excited teenage backpackers setting out on their maiden voyage, it certainly brings back adolescent memories. You will make mistakes, that is a natural part of growing up, but hopefully, as happened the more I travelled, you will learn from these mistakes. Back then, I didn't think I would catch the traveling bug as markedly as I clearly did. Jack and Chris were both influential in forming my love of travelling, and although future trips would vary in their format and fun, I wanted to continue this journey. Our first adventure was crazy at times and we did immature things that one does when they travel. Jack and I got our eyebrows and tongues pierced for example, on a drunken night out which would have shocked Chris more if we hadn't have walked in on him shoving a toothbrush down his throat in an attempt to vomit after some strange illness. It was these types of funny stories and memories that I will cherish forever. Very soon after returning home, it was time to take the plunge and book my first solo trip and, almost immediately, I repacked my bags and headed to Egypt.

CHAPTER 5
Egypt, Lebanon and Syria

The Middle East has a completely different culture to anything I had ever experienced, and it has its own dangers, wholly unlike those I had learnt to be wary of in Asia. This segment of my travels became a steep learning curve, both in terms of my growing up emotionally and in acquiring greater respect for the countries I was visiting. My trip to Egypt became illustrative of how I used travel as an escape too, as there was a girl back in London that I was in a relationship with (and it wasn't going particularly well with us), so I had used this travel as an escape, and subsequently she broke up with me.

I was in Cairo in February 2009 when Khan al-Khalili market became the tragic setting of a deadly terrorist bomb blast. Incredibly, when I visited this immense market just days later, life had largely seemed to return to normal, with the bustling and lively market operating as one would expect. Unlike watching the news on TV from the safety of your home, being there was an educational experience that meant you had to be aware of the issues around the world, and when I visited Luxor and the

Hatshepsut Temple here soon after, it was prudent to also remain educated about recent terrorist attacks in the Valley of the Kings—the dangers all became very real to me on this trip.

Again, there were many first experiences for me in Egypt, from smoking shisha—which has now become a tradition for me during any trip to the Middle East—to riding camels in the desert with the Pyramids of Giza as the spectacular backdrop. The laid back nature of Egyptians was something special and it seemed amazing to me that guards with heavy machine guns would have no problem allowing you to pose for pictures with them and their guns, for a price of course—everything has a price here too.

This trip taught me a lot about patience and the combination of being able to judge and trust people as, of course, the guy that stands out can be seen as the easy target, so before jumping into the wrong car, judgement calls always need to be made, which is something that was a very important lesson to me later in my travels.

After several days of traveling solo, I met up with a friend from university in Egypt, who was nicknamed Prince. I traveled from Cairo to Alexandria, to Luxor and to the popular resort destination of Sharm el-Sheikh, and being able to experience local customs and cultures with someone who can speak the language and introduce you to the local aspects of everyday life, became something I would crave on my future travels. After this introduction to Arabic culture, I was keen to return to this part of the world as soon as possible. The next time my father flew to Beirut, I boarded the plane with him. Being on a plane piloted by my father was always a surreal and amazing experience.

Beirut is often described as the melting pot of culture in the Middle East, and I can vouch for the truth of this description. Beirut was much more cosmopolitan than most other Middle Eastern cities, with bars and clubs lining the coast. However, when I visited Lebanon, there were also reminders of the trouble in the region, illustrated by entire shells of buildings and apartment blocks that had been reduced to rubble, previously subjected to rocket attacks from Hezbollah I was told. But these topics remained understandably sensitive to discuss with locals as I tried to understand more.

I eventually adapted to the multitude of bizarre local customs and socially acceptable patterns of behavior. Western and Middle Eastern cultures are worlds apart, but the most noticeable differences to me were the little ones, such as it being completely acceptable to smoke absolutely everywhere, airport toilets included, and it being absolutely taboo to flush paper down the toilet for the fear of causing an unpleasant blockage. I had waved goodbye to Western breakfasts of eggs and cereals, replacing them with Middle Eastern breads and humus with copious amounts of olive oil on everything, and it was fantastically immersive. Sounds that are at first unfamiliar, such as the call to prayer at 5 A.M. every day, became normal, and, in a strange way, I missed them when I moved on from the region.

Jews, Christians and Muslims live peacefully side by side in the cosmopolitan melting pot of cultures and religions in Lebanon. The one thing you can almost never 'obtain', so to speak, as a Westerner here, are the women. They are among the most beautiful in the world, as they are in Iran too, but as I was told by a local, "You can look all you want, and sometimes they may look back and smile, but as a white Westerner, you cannot touch."

Beyond the beating heart of Lebanon and downtown Beirut, there is so much to see in this country, from the spectacular ruins at Heliopolis to the stunning Jeita Grotto, where you can get a boat through this system of caves. There are parts where due to the sheer depth and vast nature of these caves they are only partially visible to the human eye.

The one commonality across this part of the world is the extreme dislike members of the military have of photographing government buildings—and the difficulty is that some of the more attractive looking buildings happen to belong to the government. In addition, there seems to be an infinite number of ministries with their buildings sprawled everywhere. I found this out the hard way in neighboring Syria.

Syria has obviously become an exceptionally hard country to travel to in recent times. The situation was far more stable when I visited. Nevertheless, everywhere I turned in Damascus I felt as though government personnel were watching, and this paranoia turned out to be partly warranted. I always knew Syria would be tricky to visit after previously unsuccessfully attempting to cross overland at the Lebanese border without a visa. Who knew that visas were necessary in my early and inexperienced stages of traveling? After some aggressive prods away from the border guards with their guns, which shook me up at that stage as it was the first time I had experienced this, I turned back with my tail between my legs. Things would get a lot worse for me at border crossings in the future, and a few prods from a man with a machine gun seem quite timid looking back now.

I had my first experience of obtaining a visa at the Syrian embassy in London and again, although not pleasant, there were far worse to come, but I was more prepared at this stage for Syria being a slightly different beast in the Middle East. After a long and repetitive interview from an aggressive official at Damascus Airport who spat in my face every time he spoke, I finally entered Syria. But now what? Foolishly, I thought it would be similar to other countries I had visited, in that I could just rock up at the nearest hostel and exchange stories about the Middle East with fellow travelers, but alas, there were no hostels. After hours of driving around, I ended up in a dark basement room in what seemed to be a graveyard. Yes, an actual graveyard. There were no lights anywhere, and the soundtrack (in addition to the call to prayer) seemed to be one of a massacre somewhere in the vicinity of my hotel. I could only hear banging, smashing and screaming, but when you are clearly the outsider, you just remain quiet in those situations. I can honestly say though, that when I began to explore Syria, the people were incredibly hospitable, and I regularly had people coming up to me at the thriving and vibrant markets from Damascus to Palmyra thanking me for coming to Syria.

I visited Aleppo briefly as well, and like areas I have since been to in northern Iraq, it is truly saddening to see the state of these cities now, ravaged by airstrikes and war. They are filled with amazing people who deserve so much better. My only real issues in Syria came from government officials and the aforementioned consequences of taking photos. I was quite innocently (or so I thought) taking some pictures in Umayyad Square in Damascus when a whole wrath of shouting in Arabic came wailing in my direction. To put it into perspective, this "square" was more of a roundabout with a busy road that these men screaming in my direction like hyenas had to cross to get to me. I was oblivious to the shouting as I learnt to ignore random noises in the Middle East; it was a common feature of such passionate people. If I were to turn around in shock every time I heard shouting, I would look like a scared tourist all the time. But it just so happened that this time it was indeed directed at me because, apparently (how was I to know), there happened to be a government building in the background of my shot—likely it would have been the Ministry of Traffic or something as overly bureaucratic.

There I was, snapping pictures, and I noticed that the locals were trying to get my attention. Before I knew it, I had several military personnel run through the traffic toward me, grab both of my arms and take my camera, followed by a car screeching to a halt with several more of these similarly dressed gentlemen donning ear pieces quickly exiting the vehicle. At first I thought I was being kidnapped, but a few pointing jabs toward the building followed by "government, government, not allowed picture," I thought my problems were going to be of wholly a different nature.

However, after one of them removed the battery from my camera and kept it, they all disappeared as quickly as they had swarmed upon me. Yes, that's right, the battery. Not the memory card. I think there may have been some confusion from them as to which part performed which function, but the photo of whatever that building may have been still sits with me today. The only other country in the region where I have encountered unwanted attention from the government or perhaps "secret service" personnel was in Iran.

CHAPTER 6
Iran, Bahrain and Kuwait

Getting the right visa for Iran was a long and arduous process, as this was during the so-called Arab Spring. Suspicions and tensions were high. After finding a sympathetic lady in Tehran through the internet who would "sponsor" my visit (which constituted vouching for my presence, then obtaining a further letter of invitation and showing all of my bank account details to illustrate I would not seek refuge in Iran), I believed I had everything in place to receive the coveted Iranian visa at the embassy, but this was not so. I sat for a whole day at the embassy and was subsequently told to leave as they would not give me a visa due to not having justifiable grounds to visit Iran by myself. However, on the advice of the lady in Tehran, who explained how Iranians were fantastic and kindhearted people, and would not only eventually give up if I demonstrated resolve and was that much of a nuisance but would find my perseverance almost endearing, I persisted.

I tried again the next day, sitting in the embassy until it closed, but alas, on the third day of trying, begging and pleading, with a wry smile, the embassy worker ordered me to hand over my passport and told me to collect my visa the next day. I was still apprehensive, but success ensued, and days later I was in Iran. I was sure I was being followed from the moment I stepped out of the airport, but the difference in Iran is that the Ministry of Intelligence are anything but subtle, posting suited men in sunglasses in the very dimly lit hotel lobby and situating some more just meters from my room. I had nothing to hide, and this became the norm for me after a day. I guess I had my own little security detail as long as I did nothing wrong.

On arriving at the Laleh Hotel in Tehran, I was told—in fact ordered—by the rather elderly hotel manager, to sit and wait in the lobby and not to check in. This seemed strange, but I went with it, as in Iran it is uncommon to go against the advice of one's elders. So about 15 minutes passed, and he approached with a big beaming smile and introduced his son Keyvan, explaining how we are the same age, how Keyvan had brought his car and, as I am the guest, I was to explore the city with his son. Initially skeptical, I went along with this, and we are still friends today. I got to explore this fascinating country like a local, and I can honestly say that Iran is one of my favorite countries in the world. If you manage to filter through the embassy warnings and Western propaganda, this country is spectacular with so much to offer in terms of beauty and nature, not to mention the ancient Persian heritage. Yes, there are some strict rules in this country, which I may not necessarily agree with, but you need to respect them as a visitor, and I can say that from all the late night discussions I had had in coffee shops, smoothie bars and pizzerias, the young population of Iran wants progressive change, and are incredibly intelligent and open-minded.

To illustrate, there is a 15-story building in Iran with a large mural of the U.S. flag down the side, where the stripes transform into bombs. Scrawled across it reads, "Down with the U.S.A." I tried to pose for a picture in front of this rather bizarre mural, but received a lot of strange looks. Was it because I looked American? No. A group of Iranians approached and explained how they detested this graffiti and wanted it removed. They loved the U.S.A., and they talked about Hollywood and New York City with a passion. Peace and progress is what the youth of this country wants, and they are not afraid to express that.

Another amazing thing about Iran is the throwback feeling. Time seems to have stopped here, which is a feeling very similar to the one I had when I visiting Cuba in 2012. Credit cards were useless due to sanctions, and so it was necessary to carry wads of cash into the country. Combining this with the Iranian etiquette of taroof—which ranged from bizarre customs such as politely refusing more food as it was dumped onto your plate to refusing a cup of coffee several times before accepting it—you have a very unique country indeed.

Traveling to Iran meant difficulties for me later on during this trip as I traveled to Bahrain from Iran at a time when governments were being toppled across the region, and many in Bahrain blamed Iranian funded involvement. I was, to be honest, unaware of this at the time, and I had heard wonderful things about the small nation of Bahrain from expats who called it home. However, I saw an entirely different side to this country during my first attempted visit.

I was actually looking forward to a few home comforts in Bahrain, and after a relatively easy visa free process at immigration, the officer opened my passport to a new page and picked up the stamp, inked it and could only have been millimeters from stamping my entry when I opened my big mouth.

"Oh, this is a much easier process than in Iran," I nervously joked to break the awkward silence. What was I thinking?

The stamp came to a grinding halt, and the officer discovered the recent Iranian entry visa that he had previously missed. At first I had no idea what was going on, but after 10 hours in a cell type room, I began to realize what was happening. I went through the range of emotions from playing innocent to getting angry and shouting as Westerners breezed through immigration, to being remorseful and then pleading. But nothing whatsoever worked. More hours passed, and I was simply told to go back to London, get a fresh new passport with no Iranian visa in it, and then I could return to Bahrain, as if that was no big deal. It seemed highly illogical and overly bureaucratic to me, but they refused to budge on the issue. As happened in several other destinations, it was up to me at my own expense to book a ticket and find my way out of the departure lounge that they had later generously constrained me in, but at least this was a vast improvement on the cell.

My best option was traveling onwards to neighboring Kuwait. I did later return to Bahrain, trembling with anticipation as I walked up to the very same immigration desk, and that time I swiftly passed through without saying a word. I was growing up, and began to learn that sometimes saying nothing at all was for the best.

Bahrain turned out to be everything I had by then expected: a largely pointless offshoot of Saudi Arabia, with a few malls, a lot of Western influence—a decent place to stop for a day or two, but no more. The one highlight was visiting the Tree of Life—a very unassuming tree in the middle of the desert where nothing else seems to grow and where there are otherwise very little signs of life. The tree is unique, but it is now being damaged extensively by tourist graffiti carvings, and ultimately, it is still just a tree, but worth a visit off the beaten track if in Bahrain.

Kuwait turned out to be very similar to Bahrain: hot, dusty, a lot of camels, and a large Western influence in the form of malls and hotels. Then again, it was a very comfortable stopover destination. After experiencing an unusual flight delay due to a sandstorm, I arrived in Kuwait to almost zero visibility, and spent the next day roaming around with scarves across my head to protect from the harsh sand that scathed my face.

The main aim of my visit there was to enter Iraq without a pre-arranged tourist visa, as this was almost impossible to obtain at the time. More pressingly, there was still armed conflict in the country. Was I stupid? Perhaps. But I was intrigued to visit, and wanted to try and get to Basra. A large element of my thinking was, contrastingly, a lack of thinking, and it was the adrenaline of the unknown, unexplored and even the dangerous that motivated me to do this. The day before I attempted to enter Iraq, I visited the famous Kuwait towers, which largely served as a propaganda museum denouncing the Iraqi invasion of Kuwait in 1990, with images that illustrated the "barbaric" destruction of air conditioning units and "even destroying" the toilets, but provided very little mention of the thousands of lives lost. It is difficult to explain in words, but priorities in terms of wartime propaganda seem highly disjointed here.

CHAPTER 7
Iraq

I set out on the now infamous "highway of death" from Kuwait City toward Basra, which was even then littered with wrecked and burnt out armored vehicles and tanks. This had been the scene of intense cluster bombing of retreating Iraqi armed forces in 1991 and galvanized some of the most recognizable images from this war with charred human remains and thousands of vehicles. As mentioned, traces of this are still vaguely visible today, and the morbid nature of the surrounding scenery should have been a warning sign for me to turn back.

I was dropped off at the Iraqi border alone, with nothing but a small backpack, my passport and a few dollars to my name as the driver returned to the relative safety of Kuwait City. I was met by several members of the armed forces who instructed me to turn back. After I became the victim of extortion from Iraqi border personnel, the guard finally agreed to let me pass into Iraq without a visa, but he would keep my passport—no stamp, no proof of entry.

At this point in my travels I didn't yet have the objective of visiting every country in the world, so I would later find myself returning to the north of Iraq to the autonomous region of Kurdistan to obtain the required stamp needed to prove I had visited Iraq. In addition to every single government advising against all travel to Iraq, I got one final token warning from the immigration officer that I shouldn't enter Iraq. Then he took my passport and, with a smug smile, which conveyed the message that he did not think I would be returning, and allowed me to enter Iraq.

So, there I was, I had stepped foot in Iraq, but there was nothing.

It was silent.

No activity, no one who could give me a ride, and so I waited, and waited a little more.

Eventually one of the worst kept sedans I had ever seen screeched toward the border with some very loud Arabic music booming from this rusting wreck. The man inside, who called himself Mo, asked where I wanted to go. "Basra" I said.

He let out a laugh and said, "Come, I take you."

Usually I like to assess my options and take the safest route possible, but in this situation, quite frankly, this was my only option. So we drove a little, and I wondered whether this guy had conveniently been tipped off to turn up there for me. Kidnappings were rife, but that was not my only concern. The further we drove, wave after wave of military convoys sped past us in a hurry.

"See? All flat land," Mo explained to me. "Nowhere to go, easy for ambush this road."

The amount of burnt out military wrecks seemed to increase in number, and Basra seemed a long way off still. Helicopters zoomed over our heads at low altitude, and it became apparent we were also viewed as a threat to the military, in a country where suicide bombings against armed forces were on the increase.

Minutes later we saw large plumes of smoke rising in the distance, probably just a couple of miles away, and that was the moment when the adrenaline suddenly turned off and I pulled the rip-cord, this was borderline insanity. We were in a war zone, an obvious target to just about anyone, and I didn't even know what I was going to do when we arrived in Basra. We turned back, which seemed to please Mo, so long as he was getting paid and it seemed like an age to get back to the Kuwait border, but it passed without incident.

A couple of years later I finally returned to Erbil, the capital of Iraqi Kurdistan, in the north of the country. This had been planned slightly more diligently, and I stayed at the best hotel in the city—for security reasons, even though, at the time, it was a relatively safe enclave in Iraq. This was a beautiful and friendly city. Unfortunately, it has now been negatively affected by insurgency and several years of instability, like so many other areas in Iraq.

Kurdistan also had huge wealth and massive oil reserves, which led to great income inequality, and with that came a very unusual situation for me in my hotel. There I was, relaxing, reading a paper in the lobby when out of the corner of my eye I saw an Iraqi guy who looked a similar age to me. It was not an unfamiliar situation to be simply stared at in certain places for looking different, with people sometimes just wanting to talk and perhaps take an interest in what I was doing or practice their English maybe. But this guy seemed a little unusual, and he stared with a smirk on his face.

After doing my best to pretend I hadn't seen him, he still sat down next to me and asked why my glass was empty. This seemed very mundane, but perhaps it was an ice breaker. I told him I was waiting for another drink, at which point he jumped up and began screaming at the staff in Arabic, waving his hands and demanding they bring me a new drink. He then calmly sat down and simply asked me, rather crudely, "How much money do you earn?"

For many reasons, this is not something I would discuss with just anyone, but in this instance in particular my immediate thoughts were that I could become a kidnapping target, so I avoided answering the question.

He continued to persist, and on what must have been his tenth attempt at asking me, I finally just gave him a number, and he burst into laughter. For one reason or another he clearly didn't believe me, but he proceeded to ask me how much I thought he earned.

This seemed very petulant at this stage, and I really didn't care, but I entertained him and started blurting out random numbers. The answer was that he had supposedly earned $50m last year from oil, and he was 22 years old. He could also tell I didn't believe him, so he shouted to the reception. A staff member then brought over his room bill, which was for multiple rooms and spanned a two-week period. The bill was somehow running at $100,000. He then told me everything during my stay, including my room, would be on his tab.

I didn't want to owe anyone anything, but after refusing this offer several times, I simply gave up. But it's safe to say that, when I checked out, my total bill amounted to zero.

Maybe these kind of cocksure conversations over the previous two weeks had been the reason his bill had ballooned so excessively and disproportionately in the first place, but the take-away conclusion is simply one of confusion on my part. It felt like accepting blood money, as I am sure his activities were not completely transparent, but it was a very unusual and perplexing encounter on my travels in the south of Iraq. This was also an illustrative reminder to never judge a book by its cover, I guess (despite spending much time getting the cover of this book right, because no matter what, we naturally do have an instinct to make judgmental first impressions!).

CHAPTER 8
Yemen and Afghanistan

The only other countries in this region where I felt equally, if not more unsafe, were Yemen and Afghanistan.

Firstly, Yemen has been one of the world's most unstable countries for many years now, and the capital, Sana'a, is regularly subjected to suicide bombings. Every government advises against any travel whatsoever to Yemen. Most embassies have closed down and diplomatic staff have been withdrawn. Getting a visa was nigh on impossible, but I received help via the internet from a local man with a very small travel company who offered to vouch for me as a family friend. This meant sending me all sorts of documents in advance to allow me to board the flight. They obviously came at a hefty fee, and once he had ushered me off the plane (that's right, the lack of security meant he could somehow be waiting right beside the plane door, with a cigarette in hand, may I add, less than one away meter from the airplane). His objective was to hand me the relevant hand stamped documents from the Ministry of the

Interior to allow me through immigration and he was swiftly gone soon after leaving me to my own devices.

Visas aside, getting into Yemen was a nightmare, to say the least. It required traveling to Eritrea in the Horn of Africa, and only when there could I turn up and purchase a paper ticket for a charter flight in person which then twice got canceled before I made it to Yemen. This felt like traveling in the 1980s. Even some countries that receive very few tourists and are perhaps very underdeveloped have some form of skeleton transport links at least. It's as though after decades of civil war most countries have cut all ties with Yemen. From my travels around the world, I would certainly say that the two most 'forgotten' countries are Yemen and Somalia, but more about my difficulties through Somalia later.

I stayed at apparently the safest property in Yemen, with huge boulders blocking the entrance at the bottom of the hill so that trucks couldn't drive through (apparently this tactic had been used before by suicide bombers). The actual hotel was placed at the very top of the hill, and I was kindly warned by a staff member that we were still in danger of RPG attacks here. Brilliant. It was only weeks before my visit that a suicide bomber blew himself up in Tahrir Square I was told by locals, yet it was like nothing had happened in Sana'a when I visited, and these instances are now so frequent that they are rarely reported in Western media. Buildings in this square still had blood stains on them and there were large charred patches on the ground where the bomb had exploded. The most concerning aspect in Yemen is that no one is safe, with virtually no embassies left and suicide attacks being so commonplace. This coupled with the storming of hotels and kidnapping of foreigners, there literally felt like nowhere to hide.

I certainly cannot claim to be an expert on Yemen as my stay was brief, just a couple of nights, and every activity I enjoyed revolved more around safety. Every little aspect appeared to be a threat, from simply seeing a fuel tanker parking by the main market and watching locals flee, dragging me through the crowds with them as they appeared more aware of unforeseen dangers, to the very real situation of seeing security forces open fire on a car that did not stop at a road block in the city. This was not something I stuck around to witness the conclusion of, but it was utterly terrifying and happened so rapidly. The saddest part was that this had probably not even been a threat at all, just a common mistake that ended in deafening gunfire and the high likelihood of a loss of a life. This is illustrative of a country on edge, one that has been for many years. The sense of relief when I did finally leave (after several more canceled flights) Yemen was tremendous, and witnessing something such as a man walking through the metal detectors at the airport smoking a cigarette without any contest from authority is a strange representation of the breakdown of governance in this country. Yet I sincerely hope I will get the chance to explore more of Yemen one day, as my grandad has told me many remarkable stories about the time he spent living in Aden many decades ago.

My journey into perhaps the last unstable country in the region, Afghanistan, was attempted overland from the border of Uzbekistan. The timing of my visit was again less than ideal, as I aimed to travel to Mazar-i-Sharif in the north of the country, which had seen a military base attacked and bombed by terrorists just weeks before. As with Yemen, the paperwork and logistics undertaken to organize the tour took far too much time and effort to be scrapped at this point.

As you may be aware, there is a "no man's land" between many borders, usually increasing in size between where you leave one country and enter the next depending on how unsavory the political and military backdrops are. I was not aware of just how large this particular no man's land would be. After a long drive through Uzbekistan, I crossed the border with relatively few issues, and then stepped onto a barren abyss where there was absolutely nothing except a dirt track leading the way. I must have walked on this road for a couple of miles. I crossed bridges and even passed houses in the no man's land until I finally found a sign saying "Welcome to Afghanistan" in English, Arabic and Russian—a testimony to how long this country has been subjected to occupation and wars.

By this point I was sweating and dehydrated and was happy to be offered water with no questions asked by members of the U.S. Army, who had copious amounts of personnel at this border, flanked by armed vehicles and tanks aplenty. Their first and obvious question was, "What the hell are you doing here?" The soldiers did not actually seem suspicious of me in any way, which was strange considering this was still an active military zone. They went above and beyond the friendly welcome as they posed for photos with me atop their tanks. Once I explained what I was trying to achieve (by this point visiting every country in the world had become a potential objective for me although I wasn't sure if it was possible), they even offered to give me to a ride to Mazar-i-Sharif in the back of one of their armored vehicles. I actually jumped at the chance (and the free security,) and on arriving in the city I did not stray out of sight of them. I had a long walk around and got a kebab and tea for lunch, but the capability to see more without taking a wild and reckless personal risk was limited.

Problems began when I attempted to leave Afghanistan; this was without doubt the worst and most aggressive extortion I have been subjected to. Technically, this happened as I attempted to re-enter Uzbekistan. The actual exit from Afghanistan was a long and arduous process because, upon my entry into the country border control had stamped my passport with a stamp in French. There was now evidently confusion as to the translation of the French name of the month of my entry, March, which some officers seemed to think translated to May. Therefore, it appeared as though I had spent three months in Afghanistan thus overstaying my visa. The translation issue led to much debate, and the expression "too many cooks in the kitchen" comes to mind, as there were perhaps a dozen immigration officers arguing over it, including the very same officer that had stamped my passport that very same morning. I cannot imagine many travelers make that border crossing on foot on any given day, but it was one of those situations that, in this instance, I was fairly confident would solve itself as I had done nothing wrong, so I just let them argue among themselves until they had exhausted the issue.

I was eventually allowed to leave Afghanistan, and after another trek back through "no man's land" to the Uzbekistan border I was understandably met with a certain degree of skepticism from border officials. You know those obscure customs forms you have to fill in sometimes? They're mostly outdated now, but in countries where they still exist, most people don't pay much attention to them, particularly when you are asked to disclose the exact amount of cash you are carrying. Additionally, cash was essentially my only source of funding on this journey as using credit cards was nigh on impossible in this region, so USD was my lifeline.

On re-entering Uzbekistan, I said I was carrying $300, which was (unknown to me) then compared to my form from previously exiting Uzbekistan where I had stated I had $250. This was met with suspicion from the Uzbeks, or maybe they just thought it was their lucky day to extort cash. With these mismatches, I had my entire belongings searched—every page of every book, every crevice of every pocket and sock, only stopping short of a full rectum examination. It turned out that I had $800 on me, which was mostly my emergency cash reserve, but for obvious reasons didn't want to declare this to begin with to prevent potential extortion and corruption.

However, my mistake was not remembering exactly what I had declared on entry, which led to a long interview of how I had seemingly "made" money in Afghanistan. This was corruption at its proudest, as it was explained—rather lectured—to me how anything above the original $250 would be kept by them. It was plain daylight robbery, and I couldn't easily contain or accept my emotions. I got increasingly angry and voices were raised as I argued this outrageous decision with the "sergeant" of this particular outpost. Although I was sure the decision wouldn't change, I could not just let them rob me because of a simple mistake.

Within seconds, the sergeant pulled out his hand gun and forced it to my head. I froze. He could obviously see the fear on my face. I had never been in this situation before, and after the soldier clearly stated how this scenario would play out, the issue was closed to debate. Their rules were the rules, and his henchmen with their AK-47s did not stand down through another patronizing speech about how he was a good person and these were the rules. Then, in another peculiar twist, he offered me a shot of vodka and a cigar, with which I obliged. It was clear I had little element of choice in these surroundings and, to be honest, I needed them at that point.

After essentially having stolen from me, the sergeant then offered to put me up for the night in his own home; it was almost as though he was desperate to have his power trip persist. I declined, insisting I had other plans and journeyed into neighboring Tajikistan at the earliest possible opportunity, my wallet now considerably lighter. The lack of funds naturally hindered my (strange) experience in Tajikistan, but more on that later.

CHAPTER 9
Jordan, Israel and Saudi Arabia

I had conquered Afghanistan, Yemen and Iraq, but the daunting challenge of entering Saudi Arabia on a tourist visa still lay ahead. Firstly, however I journeyed to Jordan and Israel. This particular trip began in Amman in Jordan, where I met a broad shouldered U.S. Marine named Tom on the flight, who was on his way home from duty in Afghanistan. Tom had a deep Southern accent and a dark sense of humor, and together we traveled to Petra during his stopover. Petra is a fascinating archeological site in the Jordanian desert dating back to 300 B.C.

Petra, just like Angkor Wat and Machu Picchu, is a truly breathtaking man-made structure, and before arrival there is excitement of that first sighting of the classic picture postcard shot. Perhaps it was the time of year I visited (March), but I found Petra to be one of the less crowded UNESCO World Heritage sights. A little bit of energy goes a long way here, as it is seldom regulated and patrolled, so climbing up rocks surrounding the various hiking trails can get you some great pictures across the canyons and even better aerial views of Petra below. You may even encounter the odd mountain goat and donkey along the way that has somehow managed to navigate its way onto a seemingly inaccessible ledge. Ample and exhausting hiking was followed by a traditionally Arabic finale—relishing strong local coffee and shisha at a little café perched atop this wondrous heritage site.

Amman is a fairly quiet city compared to other Middle Eastern capitals, but my experience of it was not drama free. The evening we returned from Petra, Tom and I ended up taking a turn down a secluded alleyway, only to find our way swiftly blocked off by a group of aggressive looking men. When we looked back, a couple more men impeded our way through the alleyway. Let me help you visualize this. Tom was stacked and had probably been in a lot worse situations than this, being a Marine, so when he told me to keep walking, I followed his lead. We were soon confronted, and his reply to being told to hand over his wallet was a simple, "Fuck off," despite being surrounded by five men. As the closest one to Tom pulled a knife, and before another word was muttered, Tom knocked him to the floor, looked at me with a nod, and we continued walking with barely another movement from the others left standing. All I could think was, "I'm with that guy," and in a particularly adrenaline enthralling moment, I had barely played a role at all!

Tom's masterful resolution of this precarious situation got me wishing I could have him accompany me on my travels all over the world, but alas, his leave had come to an end, and I was on my own once again as I arrived in Israel. By this point, my passport was tightly packed with an array of various stamps, including those from Iran. This caused a lot of questions on entry from a few Israeli kids with guns, younger than me. In a country where national service is obligatory it is commonplace to see baby-faced soldiers.

Israel is fierce when it comes to monitoring its borders, and once I had entered the country, it felt like a relatively safe enclave. Still, I am not a fan of Tel Aviv; while it might have some great parties and be the home to some very beautiful women, and despite its fantastic beachside location, I found the city to be decidedly soulless.

That being said, I did thoroughly enjoy the old city of Jerusalem, with its beautiful cobbled streets and synagogues that are blinding when the sun shines off their golden domes at an obscure angle. After a quick stop at the Wailing Wall, I was off to float around in the Dead Sea. This actually seemed like the most popular social hangout spot in Israel, with big groups of bikini-clad women and military personnel (which seemed to be any guy under the age of 23 in Israel) having abandoned their military greens, hugging almost every spare speck of sand around the shore. On arrival in Israel I had to get a special piece of paper stamped for my entry that I could later remove from my passport, showing no evidence of entry, as my next destination was Saudi Arabia, which certainly wouldn't permit me entry with an Israeli entry stamp.

Since all my persistent efforts to obtain a tourist visa for Saudi Arabia had proved to be fruitless, I instead booked the longest and most convoluted set of connecting flights (which totaled 48 hours) that eventually transited through the Saudi capital, Riyadh—all in the hope that I would be allowed to exit the airport once I got there. I was previously told by the embassy in London that leaving the airport without a visa "might" be possible on arrival, but I was skeptical to say the least. Upon landing, I was indeed allowed to exit the airport, but unfortunately, my passport was kept by immigration officers who refused to stamp it. However, when I explained to one of the younger officers what I was trying to achieve—traveling around the world—I instantly saw his face light up with excitement. Sometimes seeing that kind of passion for something that may not be directly relevant to another person, but means everything to you, is really quite inspiring and heartwarming.

He took me into a side-room and told me to wait. Minutes later, he returned, grabbed my arm and practically dragged me through the airport alongside himself, as though I was his pet dog, flashing his badge at any security checkpoint along the way. Once we were outside the terminal building, he handed me my passport with a fresh visa and entry stamp in it, then looked at me and said, "Welcome to Saudi Arabia, my friend!" I had a beaming smile on my face and gave him a hug as he wished me safe travels. Unfortunately, like with so many other people who played pivotal roles in my journey, I cannot recall his name. I will likely never see him again, but I will always remember him, and others like him, with gratitude.

I only stayed in Riyadh for a couple of days, and I would certainly like to see more of Saudi. Yet my impressions of this country are fairly similar to those of Iran; the younger population is very smart and desire change, particularly the abolition of the more rigid laws of Saudi Arabia. To illustrate some of the very different ways in which this country thinks, not only do they have a "magic police," which does exactly as you might assume—preventing apparent witchcraft, which is strictly against the law—but it is also possible to "buy innocence" here. Sometimes referred to as blood money, there are certain prices you can pay to rid you of justice, and the amount varies depending on the severity of the alleged crime. You can even buy insurance that will pay for your innocence if you commit a crime, provided you have kept up with your premium payments!

From the unusual laws of Saudi Arabia, it was to the extreme opulence of the U.A.E. and, in particular, to the playground of the rich and famous—Dubai, a city like no other.

CHAPTER 10
U.A.E, Qatar and Oman

Native Emiratis constitute only 15% of Dubai's population and the city itself is a buzzing and cosmopolitan cultural mix where the beaches are lined with day clubs that rival those of Ibiza, and almost every week a brand new exclusive bar is opening somewhere in this city.

Is Dubai a little soulless? Undoubtedly, and it's a place that people love to hate. Thirty years ago there was barely anything here than desert, but, similar to Las Vegas (which some would also argue has little soul), Dubai is a guilty pleasure. The trick is to just embrace it for what it is. From even the Dubai police driving Lamborghini Aventadors and other super cars, to vending machines which dispense gold—almost everything here is part of an extraordinary display of wealth, an unapologetic paragon of hedonistic pleasure. You can bungee jump off a crane, ski down an indoor slope (in the middle of the desert), or spend $20,000 a night for a suite at the Burj Al Arab, the world's only seven-star hotel.

I do think the food in Dubai is spectacular, and there is an inherent, healthy rivalry between restaurants, whereby establishments are always competing with each other to be the tallest, largest, most expensive or all of those combined. Some of my most memorable gourmet experiences in this city was traversing the elaborate canal system of the Madinat Jumeirah hotel on a little wooden boat to the spectacular Pad Thai restaurant, and savouring a five course meal at the Burj Al Arab, with each course served in a different one of their sublime restaurants, starting in the Al Muntaha restaurant at the top of the tower, and eventually making my way down to the Al Mahara restaurant, which is located below water level and serves real gold leaf atop your dessert.

I have ridden seaplanes, helicopters, quad-bikes, sand boards and camels through the desert here. Dubai truly is an adults' playground. Don't forget to check out the water parks, particularly Aquaventure at Atlantis, especially if you are a big kid at heart!

I travelled on to Abu Dhabi, the capital of the U.A.E.; this city felt a little more mature and sophisticated than Dubai (despite still having raucous beach bars and water parks). Everyone in the U.A.E. is impeccably polite and well mannered; I must admit that I rather enjoyed being called 'Mr. James' everywhere I went (most likely because my surname was unpronounceable to the locals).

The U.A.E., together with Qatar and Oman, are leading the way in the Gulf region, particularly in terms of development, and it's a great introduction to Arabic culture for anyone wanting to explore this part of the world while wanting to remain aligned with Western comforts.

Qatar, like the U.A.E., boasts a large expat population. You can get almost anything you would commonly see on the shelves in Europe in this incredibly gas-rich sovereign nation. The overwhelming majority of leisure activities here are centered around the indoors, malls and the like, since temperatures in summer exceed 50 degrees Celsius. Stepping outside, even briefly, is unbearable as you are instantly dumbfounded by the blistering dry heat.

In my opinion, Doha could never compete with Dubai, as it simply lacks the vibrancy and although making a more than pleasant stopover, away from the Corniche, it will never really be any more than a flying visit for me.

Oman is another safe, stable, wealthy and western influenced Gulf state. I spent a while in Muscat; tours are booming here now and I was truly impressed by the sheer amount of luxury desert hotels I encountered while taking a 4x4 ride out into the sand dunes. It is a country that boasts no income tax, almost zero crime and requires individuals to hold a permit for purchasing alcohol, and, as such, is certainly unique. I found the people to be very friendly and the prices to be very high but, then again, with no income tax in Oman, maybe the prices just seemed expensive to a foreigner!

Granted, Oman is not the only country in the region to have no income tax, and Qatar even goes a step further and hands out free water, electricity and health care to Qatari nationals. However, similarly to Qatar, unless you want to take a retreat with absolutely 100% guaranteed sunshine in the desert—which is admittedly becoming ever more popular and there are certainly some truly incredible hotels here, like the Grand Hyatt which occupies a pristine beach—a stop through Muscat is going to be fairly brief.

CHAPTER 11
Brazil

At some point among my intermittent travels through the Middle East, I embarked on a solo trip to South America for five months—a continent that I have come to love deeply, and a place I cannot help returning to.

Patience and a sense of humor go a long way on this continent, since you will inevitably find that many fundamental aspects of day to day life that we take for granted in the western world, such as reliable transportation and people adhering to schedules, are bound to malfunction. And when they do, the only response you will get from those in charge is a shrug of the shoulders. However, the culture, cuisine, architecture and, most importantly, the spirit and emphatic nature of the people who inhabit this continent and are its true heart and soul abundantly compensate for any mundane inconveniences you might experience.

My first exploration of South America began with me boarding a plane headed for Rio de Janeiro at London Heathrow airport; I brought with me a return ticket, Panama City to London, dated some five months later, and absolutely no concrete travel plans in between. This felt incredibly liberating after coming from regions where meticulous visa planning had been the norm—I was backpacking again. I landed in Rio after midnight, and while I now had some traveling experience under my belt, big city problems can always arise if you let your guard down and, furthermore, South America had different dangers of its own. Hence, I was keen to find a like-minded traveler on my flight. Luck had it that I met a German traveler, Felix, with whom I spent the next few weeks traveling through Brazil.

Although Southeast Asia is an incredibly popular backpacking circuit, I would say, from my experience, that Latin America is the most popular solo traveling destination. Therefore, it was only natural for me to cover the various parts of this trip with a multitude of temporary companions.

I had seen and read a lot about Brazil in the media and travel guides, from the carnival spirit to the love of soccer at Copacabana Beach—and it certainly didn't disappoint. Once in Rio, I was thrust into a rambunctious new world of bright colors and extraordinarily tanned people. The passion here resonated from every corner you turned. A couple of us from the hostel made the mistake of accepting the challenge from a group of young boys about half our age (and size) to play a game of soccer on the beach. By the end of it, we were toiling around in the sand, defeated and embarrassed. They gratefully accepted us buying them coconuts to drink as a forfeit. I think this was the first time I'd tried a coconut drink, and it has now become a beach-destination staple for me.

Speaking of soccer, Felix and I soon found ourselves visiting the infamous Maracanã Stadium for a big local match. It was everything we had imagined: the police lined up in riot gear, red flares being set off everywhere, walls of passionate fans blocking roads and chanting. And there we were, the gringos in our vests, in the middle of this heated atmosphere. I don't remember much of the match itself, but what I vividly remember are the events that followed.

I got split up from Felix, so I was walking close to the stadium, attempting to find my way back to common ground, when all of a sudden a car screeched to a halt right next to me, it's horn blasting persistently. After I gave them a completely blank look, the group in the car shouted at me in Portuguese, and then English, "Get in the car now! Quick!"

It was one of those occasions that required a quick and immediate judgement call. I found that the more I traveled, the better I got at being able to assess these types of situations. In this particular scenario, there were two guys and two girls in the car. Was this a clever ploy to make me lower my guard? Were they going to sell my organs (of which I had read some awful stories about before traveling to South America)?

I had no time to think any more about it. I jumped in the car through the door they had invitingly opened for me. As we sped off, they told me to look out the rear window. What I remember seeing was a large group of men with face scarves on and wielding bats or some type of wooden planks, running toward the car. They then slowed in a resigned manner as soon as we drove away.

I was immensely lucky that day. I could have been robbed and "only" got a beating, or it could have been much worse. But what was truly terrifying was that I was the clear and obvious target in this situation. I was saved only by pure luck and the kindness of diligent strangers, and the chance I had taken in trusting them.

In true Brazilian spirit, my saviours later invited me to their home for a family dinner and, of course, I obliged. The following day, I took them all up Sugar Loaf Mountain as a thank you. They had never been and, if you're really lucky, up here you can stand on the edge as clouds rise into and above the mountain while precipitating on you. It's a strange concept, but essentially the clouds are moving through you and it's incredibly unique. The other must-see high point in Rio is, of course, Christ the Redeemer (which is not actually on the same rock as Sugar Loaf Mountain).

Much in this city revolves around its beaches, be it the famous Ipanema and Copacabana, or the spectacular district of Leblon with its incredible street parties, where every night feels like a diminutive version of the notorious Rio Carnival.

When I returned to Brazil with my wife a few years later, it was for the World Cup. We watched all the Brazil World Cup soccer matches on the big screens on Copacabana Beach, and what an incredible and unforgettable atmosphere it was—comparable to a much larger party in Leblon, but on sand, and the party itself was seemingly on steroids! We were wearing Brazil soccer shirts and, in the true spirit of this nation, we were plastered from free drink supplied by the locals who invited us to carry on partying with them afterward.

Half-time and everyone rushed to the Atlantic Ocean to use it as a big communal toilet, no questions asked. When goals were scored, whatever drinks people had in their hands got launched into the crowd. It was a crazy and quintessentially Brazilian atmosphere, and the parties went on all night. From

Samba dancing to Carimbo, we found it, and tried it at least a couple of times in Brazil, although as Elena tells me, I was pretty bad at any form of local dancing.

One thing I would highly recommend doing while in Brazil is a trip into the "favelas" on a "Slum Tour." You will need a guide for this if you don't look distinctly South American. The guides live in these makeshift and traditionally poorer districts. The tours were created as an extra income for these underdeveloped communities that were built on the outskirts of the cities on unclaimed land, usually on hillsides. Although they had a very negative reputation only a decade ago as hotbeds for drugs and for being completely ungoverned and unpoliced communities, they have recently been cleaned up a lot, and are actually home to millions of people in Rio. They are an intrinsic part of the city community. You get to meet some amazing people there, try their food and, above all, you probably get one of the better views of the city from the favelas. A ride on the infamous yellow streetcar to Santa Teresa brings yet another contrast to the favelas in Rocinha below, but both are fantastic settings to walk around.

Getting around South America can be either very simple, or an absolute nightmare. The aviation sector has merged excessively in South America to create, essentially, a duopoly, so there is very little incentive to improve. Flight delays and cancelations are the norm, all the while airfares remain extortionate.

On the other hand, the coach and bus transportation network across this continent is truly spectacular. The journey from Rio to São Paulo takes a mere six hours. There are upgrade options available on the busses beyond the regular seating, where you can pay for a virtually flat bed, and hostesses serve three course meals along with beer and whiskey night-caps, all for less than an airplane ticket. I was travelling around South America on a fairly tight budget and so I only took this upgrade once, although it was totally worth it. I found overland travel to be a magnificent way to explore the continent, seeing a great deal, and taking regular stops in places I would not normally venture to.

Despite being so close, São Paulo is very different to Rio: no beaches, no one strolling the streets in swimwear clutching a surfboard, and a lot—I mean, a lot—of tall buildings, as far as the eye can see, in all directions.

São Paulo is the true definition of a mega-city, the largest in South America in fact, and a wonderful cosmopolitan hub where you can watch free concerts in the parks, integrate with locals over their traditional drink, caipirinha (I had a few too many of these in São Paulo and haven't drunk one since), or simply marvel at the wonderful art and culture this city has to offer.

Again, the Brazilian spirit is abundant here, and little touches just make it that little bit more special. For example, Elena and I had dinner at La Terraza, a wonderful fusion restaurant high above the city, where you can enjoy outdoor cocktails on the terrace 60 stories high while listening to a live band performing rat-pack jazz and blues classics. When we arrived, they enthusiastically placed the Brazilian flag in the middle of our table and our respective national flags at each end. Many drinks later, and it seemed every couple was on the dance floor swinging to Frank Sinatra, and wherever you are the party never seems to end in Brazil.

From São Paolo, I travelled on to the intersection of Brazil, Argentina and Paraguay. Welcome to the thundering Iguazu

Falls, of which each country claims a part. There are four waterfalls that will stand out on bucket lists around the world, and each of them is unique in its own way. Angel Falls in Venezuela is the tallest in the world, but due to its enormous height, the water seems to fade out halfway down in times of low rainfall. Victoria Falls in Zimbabwe and Zambia is surrounded by spectacular wildlife and you can bathe in the Devil's Pool right on the edge of the falls, watching the bravest of giraffe roaming through the water. Niagara Falls has the fantastic boat ride under the falls, and is an attraction more to get the visitor soaking wet.

The thing that makes Iguazu Falls my favorite, however, is not only the surrounding rugged landscape of jungle and rainforest, but the possibility to actually get to the bottom of the falls via walkways. Such is the strength of the falls that the closest paths are regularly closed off as people can quite literally be blown over. There were even some deaths here. But all the walkways are truly spectacular, and the surrounding wildlife on both the Brazilian and Argentinian sides are fabulous. You can also guarantee always seeing at least one rainbow here when the sun is shining.

The first time I visited the falls, I stayed in very rustic tented accommodation, and let me tell you, it was astonishingly freezing at night! The few misconceptions about South America are not only that of the temperature—it fluctuates tremendously, with some areas having very hot days and then dropping below freezing at night, like at Iguazu—but also that of the altitude. It is home to some of the highest capital cities in the world, namely La Paz in Bolivia and Quito in Ecuador, and it is more than feasible to drive from sea level to an altitude of 4000 meters in a day. This can pose altitude sickness problems for many, which was not something that really affected me until it was combined with the extreme temperature fluctuations in Bolivia, but more about that later.

In these tents at Iguazu, we received one bucket of freezing cold water each morning for washing, which was extremely painful. But first, we'd have to scoop out the copious amounts of bugs that had decided to take a dip in the bucket overnight. How things had changed when I returned a few years later with Elena and took a helicopter over the falls, something I had always wanted to do. The aerial view really put into perspective how small and obscure Iguazu Falls looked relative to the vast expanses of rainforest you could see all around, but I was slightly relieved when it was over. I love planes, and flying, but for some reason I do not like helicopters at all. I think the reason is that, unlike a plane that works with physics and is still capable of flying, or at least descending, without engine power, the aptly named god bolt in a helicopter completely defies physics and relies solely on engineering. So although I have seen some fantastic sights from helicopters, I am not a comfortable flyer when you get me in one!

CHAPTER 12
Paraguay, Argentina and Uruguay

I mentioned earlier how buses were the best way to travel around this continent, and I took buses from Rio all the way south through Argentina and up north as far as Ecuador. I had, however, two major setbacks during my bus travel through South America. I was held hostage on a bus in Peru (which I will get to later), but the first came when I left Iguazu in Brazil to travel to Asuncion in Paraguay.

This was a night bus, and the border crossing between the two countries was fairly close to the start of our journey. Imagine my dismay when I woke up on this bus, hours later, in the middle of the night. I asked the lady next to me where we were (in awful Spanish) and she said "Paraguay" as though I had been high on coca leaves or something (which, by the way, all the long distance bus drivers appear to constantly chew here, and this is likely one of the causes of the frequent bus accidents on mountain roads here). In a panic I went to check with the driver, and he confirmed we had crossed into Paraguay. Shit. I had slept through the whole border crossing escapade (and these are usually not simple affairs on this continent in particular as there are regularly multiple checks, especially for drugs and contraband). No one had wakened me, and there I was, cruising along toward the capital of the least visited South American nation with the prospect of having to explain why I had no exit stamp from Brazil, but more importantly, no entry stamp into Paraguay. The gringo that could barely speak Spanish would rarely fare well in this situation, and any story could easily be fabricated by the police force that was largely corrupt in Paraguay. With no British embassy to seek help from, I was a little vulnerable here. I didn't want to keep my situation unannounced for too long, because the longer I left it, essentially being an illegal immigrant in Paraguay, the worse it would likely become.

Next morning over breakfast in a little café, I spoke to an American woman who lived in Asuncion. She advised me to go to the Ministry of the Interior and explain as honestly as possible how this was just an innocent mistake. Despite this seemingly being my only option (except for trying to smuggle myself back into Brazil of course), it was still never going to be straightforward.

After hours of listening to condescending speeches about how bad the situation was for me (accompanied by lots of head shaking) at the Ministry of the Interior), I sat in a hallway while my passport and belongings lay in the room next door. This was exactly what I had expected, it was just the outcome that I was unsure of; I could only assume there was a debate as to how much they could try to extort from me. Then, the unexpected happened. A rather important looking lady in her early 50s walked past me, and obviously, upon seeing my head in hands, inquired (in perfect English) what was wrong. As the situation was unlikely to get much worse, I simply opened up and explained everything. She asked me to come with her, and I ended up waiting by myself in her office.

A little while later, the door to her office opened, and I caught the tail end of her screaming at someone in Spanish back down the hallway. She walked over to me with a beaming warm smile and handed me my passport together with a letter. She explained that she was the First Minister of the Interior, and she had given me a letter with all my details. She read this out to me, explaining how I was allowed to stay in Paraguay for as long as I wished, and if there were any issues, to contact her directly. It was a very strongly worded letter, and to really illustrate her power, she then stamped the letter in front of me.

She explained how she had a son who was a similar age to me, and she hoped that someone would help him if he was in need. It was scenarios like this one that have given me tremendous hope in any kind of grave situation that I have found myself in as, many times, there will always be good people who can and will try to help.

Unsurprisingly, there were still attempts to extract money from me when I tried to leave Paraguay, but when I waved the letter a few times, the boisterous officials in question quickly backed down.

It was onwards to Argentina, a beautiful country with fantastic food and wine. A quick stopover in the town of Rosario, just north of Buenos Aires, also demonstrated the attractive nature of Argentina's people.

Rosario is a university town, where (supposedly) women outnumber men 6 to 1. There are some fun parties to be had here, but like the city of Mendoza in the west, which is great for tasting lots of wine from the Andean region, I found short stopovers to be sufficient, as for me, the real heart of Argentina, is the capital, Buenos Aires.

I had heard many great things about B.A., and predicting that I would love the city, the very first thing I did when I arrived was book my bus ticket out of there. I gave myself a week, although I had met people who had stayed there for months. I wanted to explore more of the continent and, besides, after a while, it seemed eating, drinking and partying on repeat was all the long-staying travelers had achieved, like an indulgent Groundhog Day. I didn't want to slip into a state whereby I was so comfortable in B.A. that a month would pass and I'd fail to explore other areas of the Continent. I met many like-minded travelers in B.A. and took many different trips out of the city, such as a boat to nearby Uruguay with Zoe and Monique whom I had met at the hostel. For all the other great draws of this city, if you have an open mind socially, you will certainly be rewarded with making friends for life here. Speaking of great draws, steak is certainly a big attraction of Argentina, and some of the amazing vintage steak restaurants in the old town are truly unique. One of the standouts for me was La Cabrera, a cosy restaurant where while you wait in line for a table outside under heaters while they serve you never-ending champagne and chorizo. You could fill yourself up before even setting foot in the restaurant! The value here was staggering. For $20 you could get a huge piece of fantastic steak with half a bottle of wine, and the real showstopper: dozens of little pots of various sauces and sides to accompany your steak scattered around your plate. Tastefully decorated interiors and old waiters who had likely been popping corks of vintage reds since before I was born, all add to the ambiance here; the best part is, there are many similar restaurants here.

The striking thing about this city, though, is just how late people eat and when the nightlife begins. I remember my first night in B.A. I was knocking back some beers at the hostel bar at about 10 P.M., asking where everyone was, and the answer I received was—you guessed it—on siesta. Safe to say, I could never quite adapt to this pattern, so I never lasted out at nightclubs as long as the others. Obviously there are some very touristy aspects to B.A., such as the commercialized tango shows. Nevertheless, it is still immensely popular with the locals , and if you're lucky enough you will see Argentinian couples tangoing at local little cafés– my attempt at this with Elena failed spectacularly, and she marched me back to our table after my embarrassing try. Also, watch out for the little guy always walking around La Boca dressed as Diego Maradona, in full Argentina soccer kit doing kick ups. To be fair, it is a slight tourist fad, and he looks more like Maradona in recent years than in his prime, but occasionally, there are some cheesy things you feel like doing on vacation, such as getting your portrait drawn in Times Square, or taking a photo pretending to hold up the Leaning Tower of Pisa, and getting my picture taken with this guy for a few Pesos was precisiely one of those moments.

With fantastic culture, great food and some beautiful architecture, it's understandable that Buenos Aires is referred to as the Paris of the South. This is a city I have always been sad to leave, especially seeing as I have always been able to integrate with locals so easily in what can be both a relaxing and hectic city, depending on your mood or the time of day.

CHAPTER 13
Chile and Bolivia

It was time to head toward Chile, a country I had heard was the most developed and expensive on the continent. At the time, I did not plan on spending too much time there as my finances were beginning to dwindle. Additionally, it was now July, and I had naively packed as though South America were one big Rio de Janeiro type climate zone, so taking some long distance buses through Argentina and Chile on which the heating broke down proved to be slightly painful at times. Instead, I headed north, all the way to the hot beaches of Máncora in northern Peru.

The border crossing from Argentina to Chile was simply sensational; along winding roads through the Andes, with the actual frontier at the very top of a mountain covered by snow. I had come a long way since Copacabana Beach. As I headed further north through Chile, passing through Santiago and the large industrial ports at Antofagasta, the days became warmer, but the nights remained freezing cold. I turned up in the northern town of San Pedro de Atacama after a mammoth 42-

hour bus journey. It was here I linked up with a couple of other travelers and together we journeyed all the way to Cusco in Peru. There was Charles who was a photographer which came in useful across the incredible landscapes, Paul and his girlfriend Jesse, and later Graham who joined us in Bolivia and I went on to travel with in Peru.

Our first course of action from San Pedro was to cross the very harsh Atacama Desert, and subsequently Salar-de Uyuni in Bolivia. This turned out to be a very harsh five-day trip. We hired a guide to drive us across the desert and the salt flats, and soon set off in a banged up 4x4 that barely made it out of the town. Things weren't looking particularly positive, and subsequently the car did break down at least half a dozen times during the trip. On the bright side, we all learnt how to change tires and, toward the end, the juddering of the engine and smoke pouring out of the open hood raised only smiles and sighs followed by, "Ah, again," and we simply got on with it.

The toughest part of this five-day trip were the extremely harsh weather conditions. We experienced +25 degrees Celsius in the daytime with the low lying sun beaming through the side of the 4x4, compounding a magnifying glass effect and making it feel much warmer, then the contrasting -10 degree nighttime temperature. Added to this was the extreme altitude. We drove from sea level to nearly 5,000 meters during the first day. To put this into perspective, it is about half the altitude of a cruising jetliner.

The food the guide provided us was fairly minimal, and with all these factors combined, I felt extremely disoriented after several days into the trip. This was the night we stayed in a 'hut' made entirely of salt. At this point, it was like the sand in the desert had turned to salt—so much salt, everywhere. The ironic thing was, I really wanted salt with the bland food we were served, and yet there wasn't any of the edible variety. I naively tried to hack salt right out of the ground and, although hard to explain, it wasn't as simple a process as you would imagine where you can scrap some up and serve. It simply didn't work and wasn't edible. There I was, staying in a block of salt, my bed was salt, the hole in the ground that was the toilet was cut out of salt, and despite it being -10 degrees, I started walking around outside in just a towel, until I slipped (from the condensation at night that had accumulated on the salt) and passed out slumped on the side of my salt shack until morning. I had never been disoriented like this before, or since. Yet, in between the dizzy spells, the completely flat white salt flats were breathtaking, and spanned for as far as the eye could see. Paired with a clear blue sky, we had spectacular views and even better picture opportunities.

We had hours of entertainment taking photos using the perspective of the landscape, with people in the foreground combined with some of us in the background, 100 meters behind, for example. The perspective meant you could appear tiny and, on photos, be jumping out of your friend's ear, or being crushed under their foot. It was only on the very final day in the Bolivian salt flats when I was struggling so much that the guide finally decided to pull out his 'gourmet trump card'. Somehow, in the middle of the desert, when we had barely eaten for four days, he revealed a mini gas stove and whipped up scrambled eggs, an alpaca steak (which was not as bad as you might think), and Fanta! Unbelievable. The relief (and anger that he kept this all this time) on our faces was evident, and it was a great end to a pretty unique and spectacular trip with a fun bunch of people I had only just met.

It was then time to get away from the copious amounts of salt and to lower ground. Ironically, we ended up in La Paz, the highest capital city in the world, only a few days later. Bolivians are famously not the best looking people in South America (competing with the likes of Argentina and Colombia is tough), but the prices here are among the cheapest on the continent; Bolivia is certainly a must-see country. Money goes a lot further here than in Brazil and Chile, and with it being such a politically unpredictable country, you can always expect the unexpected.

I got caught up in the middle of a political protest in downtown La Paz, which initially passed very peacefully with seemingly harmless chanting and waving of banners. Then, without any warning, this protest suddenly morphed into what could only be described as an outright riot. Like with so many situations that you have never experienced or become accustomed to, it all developed so quickly, after what I can only assume was interference on the part of the riot police who then proceeded to fire tear gas into the crowd. I was on the very perimeter when this happened and tried to get out of there as swiftly as possible, but the side streets were rapidly closed off by baton-wielding police with riot shields. There was no time to think. I had only stepped out to get some lunch when I got entangled in this, where mass anger quickly turned to panic as everyone pushed aggressively to get to apparent safety, with only a few people seemingly intent on bloody fighting with law enforcement. At the next intersection, the riot police split the crowd across different streets, and we were dispersed to go as we pleased. It all ended as abruptly as it had started, and the emotions of the protesters around me quickly turned jovial once again as they reminisced about the short burst of adrenaline they'd just had.

Just days after this incident, I came away from La Paz with yet more unique stories, because this is a city where you can ride alpacas through the streets, find yourself caught up in the middle of passionate impromptu demonstrations. Naturally, being coaxed into a "bar" one lunchtime here led to so much more. Graham and I were searching for a place to get a drink in La Paz one afternoon; when we were invited into a bar (it was actually much more reminiscent of a nightclub), and so we walked upstairs and ordered "dos cervezas."

We briskly drank our beers while daylight screamed through the windows and all the disco lights flashed in time to thumping music. The setting was highly unusual and something just didn't seem right. Moments later, we were asked if we wanted something "special" and after a nervous shrug of the shoulders, which was our polite way of saying, "No, get me out of here," the guy brought over a parcel the size of a small brick and placed it on the table. He pulled out a knife and stabbed the block. The whole thing was cocaine. He walked down the stairs and said, "Enjoy, let me know."

To this day, I'm still not sure if we were mistaken for someone else.

As a few moments went by, we both looked at each other, and without saying a word, jumped up from our chairs and got out of there as quickly as possible. This was not the place we were meant to be.

From getting accidentally caught up in narco activity in the capital one day to taking a small propeller plane out to Rurrenabaque in the Amazon jungle the next, no two days in Bolivia were the same. We seemed to have left civilization behind us as we landed on a cleared grass landing strip and set sail down the river. Everything is just abnormally overgrown there.

Plants, trees and animals are gargantuan compared to what most of us are used to. The locals, particularly in La Paz, love to dispel myths about the Amazon, but pink dolphins? Completely true. Fishing for sardines to then use them as bait for giant pirañas to have for dinner? Well, we experienced that on our first evening. All right, maybe I'm exaggerating—I personally didn't manage to catch any pirañas, but our guide did, and I revelled in his success.

My Amazon experience was brief but quite honestly, I wouldn't bother too much with overly self-protective planning of bug sprays and nets. These insects and creatures will find a way. My advice would be to accept it and stop fighting it. I found inner peace when I abated from trying to fend off every persistent little bastard bug and let nature take its course, which was essentially allowing them to snack on you. Bugs aside, this was a detour I won't ever forget.

CHAPTER 14
Peru

From Bolivia I crossed into Peru, making my first stop at Lake Titicaca—an ancient lake where many inhabitants still live on floating wooden islands; the lake has therefore become a popular tourist attraction. I must admit, as my bus stopped at the shore and the driver announced, "Lake Titicaca," I had doubts about getting off the bus, but I did, despite being the only person to do so. The bus drove off, and I instantly regretted it. I could see the wooden huts from where I stood, and I genuinely had very little interest in staying there for any length of time. It was early in the day, and so I waited for the next bus to come along. And I waited some more. Until eventually, what was probably only an hour or two later, yet felt like days, a bus turned up heading to Cusco, the ancient Inca city which is the starting point for visitors to Machu Picchu. This was perfect, as I was headed there next. However, I never want to go back to that bus stop on the shore of Lake Titicaca again—I can still picture it perfectly years later. There will be some people that loved it, but I was incredibly bored as I had left the group of 4 I was travelling with to see this, so at this point I felt particularly lonely after being with the largest group I had travelled with for months. I instead played catch-up to essentially "put the band back together".

So to my favorite place in Peru, the beautiful cobblestoned streets of Cusco and its rich history and architecture. The excitement and anticipation here is similar to that in Siem Reap where people embark on their journey to Angkor Wat. In Cusco, the prize for the intrepid travelers who sit in the many restaurants flanking all corners of the main square, sipping wine, is Machu Picchu.

The journey to Machu Picchu can be done in several ways. One way is via the ever-popular Inca Trail (which has never borne any personal interest to me), camping for four days and arriving at Machu Picchu exhausted, not to mention after the other hordes of travelers who have made it to the ruins for sunrise from the closest town of Aguas Calientes. When I went back to Machu Picchu some time later, I chose the simplest option of the panoramic train to Aguas Calientes. It's only a short hike back there from Machu Picchu. The first time I went, I, of course, took one of the more difficult options—by car.

As the crow flies, it's not that far, but in such a mountainous area, driving is a long and arduous task with such variations in altitude meaning the roads are long and painfully meandering to travel distances that appear short on a map. Of course, that car broke down, and of course the guy couldn't change the flat tire because we were on a part of the mountain that was entirely consumed inside a passing cloud, meaning visibility was zero, and of course the back pains from the dirt tracks with gargantuan craters lasted for weeks, but, being among the first people to arrive in Machu Picchu was almost worth it.

With my departure from Cusco came my biggest mistake on the continent, and the second of my major setbacks with bus travel. In 2009, there was a period where the people of Peru were unhappy with the government. As a form of protest, they blocked the roads, set tires alight, and generally brought the country to a halt. The intensity of these road blocks had stepped up in recent weeks, and despite the advice from many Peruvians who suggested I should fly, I insisted on taking the bus, mainly because it was cheaper.

As we were waiting at the bus station, we saw on the news that other buses were being ransacked and smashed to pieces. But my logic was that it was a huge country, it couldn't possibly happen to us specifically. Well, you guessed it, hours later, I was wakened by the bus being shook from side to side and witnessed the driver cowering for cover as stones pelted the front windscreen. The windows of the bus, from the windscreen to all down the sides were painted in white paint, and then this mob moved onto the next vehicle behind us.

Most of the bus was screaming and in tears, but we all stayed onboard. As hours passed, no one knew what the situation was like outside. More hours passed, and eventually daylight broke through the few untouched areas of glass that hadn't been so heavy-handedly sloshed over with white paint. I had only chosen the regular seat option on this bus, but if there was ever a time to book the beds downstairs this would have been it. But how was I to know that I would be spending three entire days on this godforsaken bus.

That's right, three long days.

There we were, the next morning, and we hear tapping on the windows, and women's voices who were attempting to sell us food. After a while, we began to emerge from the bus, and it appeared that the same people from the village who had cut down all their trees and gathered large rocks to block the roads, were now capitalizing on it by selling us food. Not a bad business model, I guess, creating cause and effect. And obviously we almost felt grateful to them for their food!

As the days passed, we congregated with other travelers from other buses, of which there must have been about 30. We sat on top of the hill, looking down at this small single lane dirt track perched on the side of the cliff. It was almost impossible to reverse out of. I was about as relaxed as I could be in a bad situation. I had nowhere particular to be except the beach in the north of Peru but, understandably, there were people who had missed flights, and it all felt a bit unnecessary.

Eventually, after three days, the road was cleared, and after windscreens were smashed out entirely to provide visibility for the onward journey, each bus was doused with a sendoff message across all sides reading some translation of "long live the road block." Car horns honked aplenty, and the locals who had caused us so much distress all waved us off in what felt like a fanfare procession. They were only trying to achieve an objective, and were completely harmless, and I suppose it did give me a story to tell. We continued all the way to Lima in this wrecked bus dripping with paint. But the amusing part was the amount of other buses and cars we passed along the way that had received the same treatment—this was nationwide, it seemed.

I don't remember much of my first visit to Lima, as it was a flying stop, but on my return, I fell in love with this city. A true melting pot of cultures, no more perfectly illustrated by the fact that they elected a Japanese-Peruvian president in the 1990s. This was the point at which Peru began to develop into the cosmopolitan center it has become today.

The gastronomy and fusion of different foods in Lima is really the heart and soul of the city. In the beachside districts of Barranca and Mirraflores, you can find some spectacular restaurants. From odd delicacies, such as pineapple juice with espresso, to finding pomegranates larger than my head in the local fruit market, black sweetcorn and hundreds of different varieties of potatoes, this city is a food lover's paradise. I tried my hand at creating the national drink, Pisco Sour and at making ceviche here. The only other place I have tried cooking classes was in New Orleans—another remarkable city for gastronomy.

Traveling north from Lima, it was finally time to stop, rest and regroup. I found a great hostel called The Point on the beach in Máncora. They were looking for an extra pair of hands when I arrived, so I worked in the beach bar and ended up staying for about a month, getting paid just a few dollars a day for expense money, but with accommodation, food and drinks being all but free. It was essentially a free holiday.

I'm told that, before I arrived, the parties here were wild as our hostel was in continual competition with another hostel in town to put on the best parties. But myself and the rest of the group—Sasha, Katie and Dan—preferred relaxing on the beach, chatting away, drinking all night. And we became a good group of friends.

It was also here where I temporarily, although initially unwillingly, adopted a semi-stray dog, called Mochi, who was a strange cross between a Labrador and a German shepherd. Although, I like to think that she chose me!

Mochi lived somewhere around this hostel with another semi-stray called Dingo, who used to like displaying his genitals, I vividly remember. Subsequently, Dingo ended up impregnating Mochi after I left, although I did my best to prevent this while there. I ended up sharing half my dinners with Mochi, and she slept under my bed every night. I couldn't go anywhere without her. She would sprint along the entire length of the beach after me each time I walked into town— probably because she knew we would stop for empanadas at the bakery she loved. I would then have to cradle her like a baby in a tuk-tuk on the way back to the hostel as she was scared of the cars after the initial rush from the food had worn off. I did make a serious attempt to bring Mochi back home with me, but unfortunately this never worked out. The people I met at the Point are still my friends today, and at this point in my South American adventure it felt as though the sun was setting on what had been a phenomenal journey. I had become more nostalgic of the continent and so certainly preferred procrastinating with some drinks and good company as opposed to wild parties, and that was exactly what I came away from Mancora with.

CHAPTER 15
Ecuador, Colombia and Venezuela

After my long stay in Peru, I ventured into Ecuador for a comparatively short visit on my way to Colombia.

Ecuador is a relatively small but eccentric and bright country on the South American continent, with plentiful rainforests and glaciers to trek located just hours from the capital, Quito. I found a week here passed very quickly. Quito is the only capital city in the world to be located on the equator, so there is an abundance of tourist equator-related fads to be found here. You will find yourself having to politely decline seemingly endless street demonstrations of people showing you water flushing down a sinkhole in different directions whether you are north or south of the equator (this, of course, is complete nonsense).

Ecuador has one of the largest concentrations of active volcanoes, and I coupled exploring these with a trek up Cayambe glacier, getting simply spectacular views. This enticed me to explore glacial climates further, when I later visited Alaska.

Colombia is definitely one of my favorite Latin American countries. It is a nation formed of some of the kindest, most intelligent people in the region. There are many common misconceptions about Colombia, particularly regarding personal safety. Narco activity is still a prominent feature of this country, but it is incredibly rare for tourists to witness anything unsavory. In my opinion, Colombia is one of the safest countries in South America, while neighboring Venezuela is the most dangerous. If you were to arrive in Bogotá directly from Europe or the U.S., it may initially come as a bit of a cultural shock as there can be parts of this city that seem dangerous and depraved. Of course, in a city of many million people, there will be big city problems, and with a gram of cocaine costing as little as $2 here, you may encounter many insane looking people who seem to be in their own world.

Bogotá is worth a stop for a day or two, with the historical center being relatively compact and easily walkable. Districts for food and drink are also conveniently concentrated into zones. Zona T, for example, is an intersection of streets (in the shape of a T) lined with great bars, including the famous Bogotá Beer Company, which is worth a visit. Beyond this, the stand out destination in the city is that of Monserrate, providing fabulous mountain views across the city. You can get to the top with the help of a teléferico. Once there, you can dine in some of the unbelievable restaurants while getting a real perspective of how big Bogotá is below.

There are of course many other great destinations in Colombia. The likes of Medellin and Cali are synonymous with this country but, by far, the place that encapsulated Colombia for me, and was my stand out destination across the continent, has to be Cartagena on the Caribbean coast. Many influential artists, writers and poets romanticized this city—Gabriel Garcia Marquez to name but one—and the instant you walk into the old town, it is easy to understand why. A multitude of open squares interrupt cobble-lined streets where beautifully crafted wooden balconies unassumingly protrude over the streets below. The colonial style architecture is encapsulated by a myriad of colors that dress the city up to look stunning both day and night. Many of the best restaurants and hotels in the San Diego district and the Old Town have been converted from old monasteries and convents, so maintain beautiful central courtyards.

With the hot weather and beautiful backdrop, it's easy to see why famous authors such as Marquez based themselves in this gorgeous Caribbean coastal city. Not only is Cartagena one of the most spectacular old colonial cities in the world, complete with horse-drawn carriages gently rolling through the streets; the adjacent coastline is home to some of the most spectacular beaches in South America.

While Cartagena attracts a lot of tourists, it is still a Colombian city; hence, being sat in an outdoor café or restaurant in any of the beautiful squares, you are more than likely to get pestered by street vendors who will try to sell you anything from cigarettes and Sombrero Vueltiaos to emeralds and cocaine. It is true that both alcohol and drugs are cheap and readily available here.

Those planning to continue their exploration of the Latin American continent overland from Cartagena have a choice to make; however travelling straight on to Panama is tricky, because of Darién Gap between the borders of Panama and Colombia, which makes crossing almost impossible. The Pacific Coast Highway that runs from California all the way down to

Chile has about a 40-mile gap through this dense rainforest that is considered lawless and subject to guerilla fighting due to its strategic location. The options are to continue to Venezuela or head to the port in Cartagena to find a yacht captain to take you to Panama via the San Blas Islands, which are simply spectacular, surrounded with crystal blue waters. There were certainly times on my travels where I loved a destination so much that I wished I could stay longer, and in fact not move onwards, as there was a very distinct feeling that my next location would not compete. This was how I felt when moving from Colombia to neighboring Venezuela, however by this point I had an objectified goal, but there were certainly times where it wasn't easy to pack my bags and head onwards.

From the biggest surprise of South America, Colombia, to stepping back into a former relic that misinformed travelers may wrongly compare with Colombia—welcome to neighboring Venezuela.

To me, modern day Venezuela seemed like what I imagine Colombia had been at the height of its socio-economic problems back in the 1980s. Crime and drug misuse are rife in urban centers like Caracas. There are regular fuel and food shortages, and foreign investment is lacking; foreign operated companies find it difficult to take their revenues, let alone profits, out of Venezuela, which has led to many quitting business in this country altogether.

I arrived in Caracas predictably late, at 1 A.M., due to a disheveled aviation sector which is subjected to daily and regular delays. Caracas, both in my own opinion (and statistically), is one of the most dangerous cities in the world. I entered the huge security gates of my hotel complex after getting scammed by the taxi driver. The hotel staff were all shocked at me wanting to walk outside to get food at this late hour and insisted that I hire a guard. After being strongly advised against walking outside at this time, I was still eager to explore, so I went anyway, only to find myself instantly accosted by a swarm of prostitutes the moment I walked outside the monstrous security gates. The overwhelming majority of these women were entirely naked, save for a pair of sky high heels and a purse. I was shocked—I had never seen anything like it. What is worse, these girls were also extremely aggressive—for example, they threatened to "cut my penis off" because I ignored their advances and kept my eyes on the road as I walked on. Later that night I was also stopped and aggressively patted down by "police" looking for drugs, but this was clearly an extortion exercise for the gringo on his own. I found that if you just laughed, were patient, and acted confidently, they would eventually find a new more naïve victim.

Sure, there are many and unsightly problems in Venezuela (the number of civilians I saw carrying guns and seemingly operating above and beyond what threads of law there were was slightly concerning). But, in general, the people of Venezuela were just as amazing as those in Colombia. There were also some simply magnificent natural sights in Venezuela. Although not easy to reach, Angel Falls is a spectacular wonder of nature. The highest waterfall in the world (popularized as the dream destination in the Pixar movie "Up"). The falls can vary drastically in appearance depending on what time of the year you visit and the recent rainfall. Being so high (over 800 meters!), you can find that sometimes the flow will actually fade out into a tame spray halfway down. Perhaps an even more remarkable sight for me than Angel Falls was Relampago del Catatumbo over Lake Maracaibo. This particular phenomenon was first written about in poems from the 16th Century, and on roughly half the nights of the year, you can witness a relentless lightning storm with strikes hitting the ground almost every second. Venezuela and Paraguay were the only mainstay countries on the continent where I felt the genuine absence of backpackers. I had vacated the tourist trail, and Venezuela particularly is a country that has so much to offer, and I would very much like to return to, as and when the situation on the ground improves. Venezuela felt lonely at times as a solo traveler, as its tourist sector seems to be in it's infancy, and although my stay here was brief, loneliness and solitude in my travels would however, be here to stay, as I would have to prepare myself for the upcoming and daunting prospect of traveling through over 50 countries in Africa, but not just quite yet...

CHAPTER 16
The Caribbean

Moving on from Venezuela, the least visited countries in South America beckoned next—the Guianas. My first stop would be one of the outliers of the Caribbean, Guyana. Although located on the South American continent and shrouded in dense rainforest, Guyana is widely considered to be part of the Caribbean. I didn't spend long in Guyana; apart from the bustling Stabroek Market in Georgetown, I found little to be of interest here, as was the case with neighboring Suriname. These countries certainly didn't even come close to rivaling Caribbean coastal settings in nearby countries like Colombia.

Suriname was a very strange country to visit. It is a former Dutch colony, and if you look closely, you can find definitive signs of Dutch influence in the capital, Paramaribo; yet the locals' proclivity towards decorating every bar, restaurant and hotel with bright and tacky neon lighting generally does an excellent job of concealing all the beauty of colonial architecture. On the whole, this city has little to offer apart from numerous casinos, which seem to be the most popular pastime in

Paramaribo. The inner city has been declared a UNESCO World Heritage Site, although, with the exception of a handful of buildings, I found it hard to see why.

Additionally, Suriname is one of the more annoyingly bureaucratic countries. During even my brief stay, it was necessary to go through the arduous process of notifying the authorities of where I was staying and of my presence in the country. The customs officer clearly reminded me that there were "strict penalties" for failure to do so. I would have thought this kind of unnecessary red-tape was a thing of the past, even here, but apparently not. Even the Dutch expats, who explained they had moved out there to pay less tax, were far from impressed with, shall we say, the "over-complications" in Suriname. Probably the one solitary highlight of Paramaribo was the luminously lit (of course) party bus that plied the streets at night.

So, relatively sour first impressions of the Caribbean aside, it was time to delve further into what would collectively become one of my favorite regions.

I was once told that to understand the Caribbean and its culture, I would have to understand the history behind the early colonialists and the slave trade in the West Indies, and that largely holds true. Centuries of hardship have produced a culture that is so distinctly varied, yet is one so widely recognized across the entire world. From Caribbean creole cuisine to steel drums, and drinking rum in a laid back setting while Bob Marley quietly resonates over the airwaves, these islands are not just a paradise visually but also have such an intoxicating depth to their people and culture.

With the exclusion of Cuba, which was a little less accessible, I found that island hopping in the Caribbean was made possible by the very reasonably priced airline hopper, LIAT. However, the ease of accessibility was extremely sporadic, and locals have a range of acronyms they use to describe the lackluster service this near-monopoly provides, including "Leave Island Any Time" and "Leave It At Terminal"; the latter refers to bags regularly not making it onto flights, which is something I experienced more than once. While digging deep for a sense of humor and that large dose of patience that is at times required while traveling, the hope that at some point, somehow, LIAT would always get me to my destination in the end, meant taking a laid back Caribbean approach to traveling around the islands.

The first island I went to in the Caribbean was Barbados. The gastronomy in Barbados has developed to incredibly high standards, and features restaurants in magical settings such as The Cliff, which as the name suggests, is built into a cliff face on the beach to cater for guests staying at the high range hotels, such as Sandy Lane, that now dominate this island. Water sports largely dictate the itinerary here, and not only was Barbados the first place I parasailed above the harbor but also where I first took a jet ski out for a spin.

After getting to know Barbados by day and taking multiple tours around rum distilleries, where "tasting" portions at the Malibu and Mount Gay distilleries became a quasi-drinking contest, the social scene after dark didn't disappoint either. I have seldom seen an establishment that mixes tourists and locals so harmoniously as Harbour Lights, where you pay an entry fee to drink copious amounts of rum punch in a great setting on the shore. This was certainly my favorite watering hole on this island.

After waking up with a raging headache and stinking of rum, it was on to the next island paradise of nearby St. Vincent and the Grenadines, which is actually visible from Barbados on a clear day. A very breezy 20-minute hop on a small turboprop aircraft and it seemed as though I had arrived in Barbados's less developed cousin nation. St Vincent is certainly in its infancy in terms of tourist development when compared to Barbados. I had a very relaxing few days on St. Vincent, staying in a tranquil guesthouse.

Barbados holds many similarities, in terms of culture and development, to nearby St. Lucia, with one major difference—The Piston Peaks in St Lucia. I dramatically underestimated the topography of this island, and must have proved quite the tourist attraction for relaxed onlookers as they watched me puff and pant up and down the incredibly steep inclines with a backpack while wearing flip-flops in an attempt to reach the beach and the beautiful postcard money-shot of the mountainous peaks in all their glory, separated by a pristine beach.

The most rugged landscape in the Caribbean must be that of Dominica, however, which, in my opinion, is also the most underdeveloped country in the Caribbean when it comes to tourist infrastructure. I traveled here with Elena and we underestimated the convoluted roads and travel times around this island. So, after LIAT decided to send our bags to a completely different island, we ended up staying at a less remote guesthouse owned by an incredibly nice couple who offered us spare clothes and toiletries.

Dominica is very rustic. There is, for example, a small waterfall and stream just meters away from the airport's arrival doors. You can imagine our delight at finding beautifully bright, red, carefully crafted log cabin rooms after our bags had gone missing. My fondest memory of Dominica was the community feeling here, and we stayed up most nights drinking wine with the owners of this guesthouse while their dogs pandered for attention. Several days later, our bags called an end to their rogue vacation and mysteriously turned up, and so we were off to Antigua.

As is possible on many Caribbean islands, we chose to stay at an all-inclusive resort in Antigua. I don't generally like to stay in all-inclusive hotels all that often because I feel it confines you largely to your resort. In many countries, the culinary and nightlife scenes are a huge part of culture, so I do like to venture out and explore these aspects. But in this case, we thought we would go for the zero stress, hassle-free option.

Aside from devouring the unlimited food and rum cocktails on offer, I managed to embarrass myself during what was designed to be a romantic horse ride down the Antiguan beach at sunset. The problem here was that I can't really ride a horse. Hell, I just about managed to unglamorously mount myself on top of one, so of course I could barely keep from sliding off during a leisurely trot down the beach. It was time to hang up my horse-riding boots and embarrass myself by belting out "Hey Jude" at the evening karaoke instead, much to the delight of my one and only fan it seemed, an elderly man who came on stage to belt out the chorus with me. Perhaps it was best for me to move on at this point, and although the familiar scenery of machete wielding farmers hacking down sugar cane, white sandy beaches and luxury resorts remained the same it was destination Grenada shortly followed by St. Kitts and Nevis.

Both of these countries were extremely pleasant and I felt they held a lot of similarities. Safe to say that Caribbean culture has become commercialized in St. Kitts, but as I traveled further south through the islands, from Grenada and on to Trinidad and Tobago, it became evident that its geographical positioning on the cusp of the South American continent dampened the tiny island vibes that can be found further north in the Caribbean.

The islands of Trinidad and Tobago really were like two separate countries. The divine beaches and tranquil environment of Tobago draw a stark contrast to the bustling capital of Port-of-Spain in Trinidad, where kidnappings and murders are reported in the local media all too often. Personally I have never heard of anything more than tourists falling victim to petty pickpocketing, usually at the hands of young children, but I did witness a woman taking a shit in broad daylight on the street in Port-of Spain, and then very calmly pulling her pants up and walking off. The locals also looked on in disbelief, but in a country where marijuana was offered to me more times than I care to remember, perhaps no one was too concerned after all.

From the slightly unsavory Port-of-Spain, I traveled to the west of the Caribbean, the home of Bob Marley—welcome to Kingston, Jamaica! This is a city that has had its fair share of recent social issues, but has become much safer in the last few years. Somehow the soundtrack of "Three Little Birds" in the background made watching a fight between two Rastafarian guys outside a bar much more, well, Jamaican. There are not many places I have visited in the world where no matter how bad things got, everyone still seemed inevitably relaxed with life. There was something about this place that I fell in love with, which included both the good and the bad aspects.

Although most tourists typically spend very little time in Kingston and the surrounding area, instead making their way to the northern shores of Montego Bay and Ocho Rios, I would highly recommend spending a little bit of time here, especially if you are a Bob Marley fan, just to have a taste of the real Jamaica.

My experience of Ocho Rios was slightly altered, shall we say, by an invasion of American spring breakers of the resort I was staying at. Predictably, the drinking and partying were endless until, of course, most of them passed out after a few cocktails. I guess spring breakers can't handle much alcohol after all. Good weather, great food and a rich culture ticks a great deal of boxes for any destination, but in the northern beach resorts, there are also some incredibly unique hidden gems. I took a trip out to Dunn's River Falls, which is a system of shallow waterfalls you essentially walk, swim and paddle through. Due to high footfall, the underlying rocks have become extremely eroded and very slippery, a feature that, as long as you don't mind slipping on your ass a few times, makes Dunn's Falls all the more fun. As night fell, I took a remarkable boat trip out on a lake from Falmouth to see a phenomenon on the lake—bioluminescence. Similar to seeing fireflies lighting up a clear night sky, the microscopic plankton illuminate the waters when you dip your hand or a stick in. The phenomena of bioluminescence brought out so much adolescent excitement that, before long, you find yourself splashing around the lake illuminating like a mythical underwater creature in a sight that photos simply can't fully capture.

From one cultural hotbed to another, a country that has truly stood still through the test of time. Previously forgotten to the Western world and isolated for decades, I traveled to the immensely popular destination of Cuba. It has become incredibly clichéd to say that, "You should travel to Cuba before it changes forever," however, I wholly disagree with this observation. Cuba has suffered regular food shortages and power cuts for decades due to the sanctions imposed on this country. Development of certain infrastructure is necessary, and of course there will be fewer 1930s Chevys on the streets as import restrictions are lifted, but as with many other World Heritage Sites and cities in particular, Havana will manage to keep its glorious legacy and fabulously crafted buildings, much like Cartagena. Is it fair for naïve tourists to deny Cuban people a path to greater development for their own selfish enjoyment of taking a few 'retro' vacation snaps? I certainly don't think so. Cubans know the beauty of old Havana is one of the country's greatest assets, so they would be insane to throw that away with clumsy development. However, the top of the priority list should be the quality of the food. Although I adore this country, the food is pretty mediocre even at the best of restaurants. On trying to find a romantic restaurant for dinner, Elena and I were essentially directed through someone's front living room and onto their coastal verandah. Although, this did rather rustically turn out to be strangely romantic with one of the family members strumming on a guitar, this is not a developed gastro scene, and the food itself left a lot to be desired.

What Cuba may lack in terms of food, it certainly overcompensates for in terms of alcohol and nightlife. Ernest Hemingway loved Havana, and there are plenty of watering holes that lay claim to being frequented by the man himself, from little bars in old Havana that can barely hold eight people to the ever-popular Floridita. I spent many a night here listening to live Cuban music and smoking Cuban cigars. After the sun goes down, this city continues to excel in simply feeling alive, with salsa dancing in a city where even the men know how to dance! Women outnumber men significantly in Havana, and there always seems to be an excuse to salsa. We even saw couples spontaneously dancing in the streets. How to tell a good bar in Cuba? The scruffier it looks, the greater time there is to be had. Scruffiness seemed to be a great barometer. If there were cracked peanut shells strewn across the floor and empty beer bottles camouflaging tables, then that was the place I would choose for my next drink!

As opposed to many other countries where the capital city might not be the jewel in the crown in terms of hotspots, Havana really is the heartbeat of Cuba, from Fidel Castro murals and Baroque architecture to the incredible experience of taking a tour around the city in the back of a 1930s pink Chevy convertible. This city did not disappoint. Of course, there are other fantastic ways to spend your days in Cuba, such as relaxing on the white sand beaches in Varadero, or watching men ride bulls near the spectacular Mural de la Prehistoria rock in Viñales, but Havana, with its abundance of Che Guevara monuments, mostly in the form of graffiti, is the heart of this truly fabulous country.

The Caribbean is bustling with culture and is synonymous with being a romantic getaway, and many of the Caribbean nations I visited were with Elena, however, some of the smaller nations in the region I did visit alone. Traveling to less touristy destinations by myself was actually quite easy to do, but I found it a little more emotionally difficult to enjoy beautiful holiday destinations alone whilst watching others revel in sharing memories with their friends and family. It's understandably a little more difficult to make friends and find like-minded travelers in the Bahamas, for example, as opposed to somewhere like Bangkok.

To go off on an apparent tangent here, the remote and chilly nation of Iceland was responsible for my impromptu extended stay in my next Caribbean destination—the Dominican Republic. I visited in 2010, the year of the infamous eruption of the ridiculously unpronounceable Eyjafjallajökull volcano in Iceland. The subsequent ash cloud grounded flights across the world, and as events unfolded, I was on one of the very last rushed through flights outbound before the European airspace was inoperable. This left me stranded in the Dominican Republic for almost a week longer than anticipated as overbooked and delayed return flights meant travel became chaotic globally. Yet this meant I had longer to enjoy a simply beautiful semi-island. I refer to the Dominican Republic as a "semi" island because the actual island it occupies is split in two by a fairly straight border with its westerly neighbor Haiti, which would be my next Caribbean destination.

However, back to the Dominican Republic for now, and the additional time I had on my hands meant exploring the jungles of the island around Punta Cana using 4x4 off-road buggies and venturing further out to visit the unspoilt beaches of La Choza. The rather unique halo around the scorching hot sun above, caused by the ash cloud, did little to dampen my enjoyment of the largely unpopulated endless spits of sand just moments from the mainland, or the continuous delight of local Dominican cuisine. I had what was probably my best meal, some delicious home cooked creole cuisine, at a school in a relatively underdeveloped local village, which I visited as part of a small group that brought learning materials to the kids. It was relatively simple home cooking of marinated chicken and rice with various spices and seasoning, but the local food made the trip here even more worthwhile. And besides, what else was I going to do? I was essentially stuck in the Dominican Republic.

The one big oddity I did notice in the poorer villages here was that, there were often expensive imported U.S. cars parked outside the rather simplistic dwellings. I cannot know if the explanation I was given is true, but I was told that local men would rather spend their money on an impressive car, to conduct extra-marital activities in, as opposed to investing it in the bettering of their homes.

Now, back to my incredibly poor timing of visiting countries. I arrived in neighboring Haiti about a year after the devastating earthquake that destroyed most of the capital, Port-au-Prince, and killed between 100,000 and 350,000 people. Estimates vary hugely, and there is no precise or agreed number on the awful loss of life. Both the loss of life and the physical destruction were strongly evident a year after this horrific event, and mass graves were pointed out to me at every turn. Almost every building in the capital had been destroyed, and all former landmarks, from the presidential palace to the Notre Dame cathedral, still lay in ruins.

While I observed Haitians attempting to salvage aspects of normal life, with makeshift markets and street parties being a frequent sight, ginormous U.N. tented camps still populated large swathes of land in a city that had very little remaining infrastructure. This is certainly not the side of Haiti that I want to write about in further detail as there are so many great things about this country. Above all, what I saw here was the unity of the people. With everyone knowing someone who had perished in the earthquake, I felt a great sense of community spirit. When talking to locals, their pain was evident, but so too was their determination to rebuild Port-au-Prince. I look forward to returning to Haiti.

My final stop in the Caribbean was a much less somber affair—the pretty, white beaches of the Bahamas. I had traveled to Freeport in the Bahamas before, but that was on a day trip from Miami, and hence I didn't have any proof of entry in my passport. So I returned to the capital, Nassau, for a brief swim (and clichéd kiss) with the dolphins at Atlantis in addition to my first time scuba diving. This was a truly remarkable experience, being immersed in the crystal clear waters and surrounded by colorful corals. What a way to celebrate visitng all the island nations of the Caribbean! This is not traditionally a backpacker circuit, due to the higher relative cost of nearly everything here when compared to nearby Central America. The beaches are pretty, but they are not the prettiest in the world, and the same can be said for the sea and corals, yet it is the immense culture of the Caribbean that makes this collective group of countries completely amazing.

CHAPTER 17
U.S.A. and Canada

I find that when travelers are asked about their favorite country, those who have traveled the most tend to opt for one of the more obscure destinations they have visited. Whether the deepest darkest swathes of Congo or Kyrgyzstan were actually their favorites or whether it's all a ploy which enables them to speak about a topic that is unattached and take the crown of the most off-the-beaten track traveler is often difficult to tell. I am regularly asked what my favorite country is, and although places like Iran and Europe as a continent are close to my heart, the one country that will always be close to the top of my list is the U.S.A., due to its sheer size and diversity. If Europe were, in fact, a country, it would likely be my number one.

The diversity across national parks, from Volcanoes National Park in Hawaii to Glacier National Park in Alaska, Yellowstone to Yosemite; spectacular cities such as Los Angeles and New York City; the adult playgrounds of New Orleans and Las Vegas; the US is a truly spectacular country.

I traveled to 29 states over the course of my travels. It began with family trips to Florida when I was a kid. Back then, I simply loved family vacations to Orlando, but as an adult, I also began to appreciate just how well everything is constructed and operates, in Disney World in particular. The attention to detail is spectacular and both young kids and grown-up kids who are keen travelers can revel in the excitement of the World Showcase at Epcot theme park. Mini versions of countries are so authentically constructed you can even get a piece of home away from home. Maybe when I visited these miniature versions of countries as a child I caught the travel bug without even realizing it at the time. During the evening fireworks, you're able to enjoy the range of countries by "drinking around the world"—participating in wine flights in mini Germany, Italy and France and moving on to sake in Japan and tequila in Mexico. Just don't get so drunk that you are escorted out of the final pavilion in Mexico, like I did, just before my victory tequila—that's always slightly awkward and embarrassing at Disney World! To top off this truly magical destination, you have world class waterparks, Universal Studios and an unforgettable trip to NASA.

Further south in Florida lays the sun drenched city of Miami. Aside from locals tanning themselves on the pristine sands of South Beach and in the flamboyant beach clubs (Nikki Beach to name but one), this city is famous for its neon lit art deco style architecture that lines Ocean Drive. There are hundreds of colorful buildings that date back to the 1920s, and in among this tourist sight in itself, I found some hidden gems, such as the Versace mansion. Dinner here was pricey but certainly an experience dressing up in white and beige Miami-esque colors to dine with the well-tanned and impossibly high heeled elite of the town.

There is rarely a dull moment in Miami at nighttime, and I didn't find myself short of options, particularly along South Beach. However, when I found myself craving more from my days of sunbathing, even out on the pristine waters of Biscayne Bay, a trip to the Everglades National Park was the highlight. Taking airboats out on the swamps allowed for lots of alligator sightings. These animals grow to be massive, and it was in the Everglades that I saw the true size and powerful nature of these beasts. I don't think one would last long in the water around here. I was actually due to skydive over the Everglades shortly after, but as we got kitted up with parachutes and boarded the light aircraft, we frustratingly had to turn back around due to the volatile summer weather in Florida as thunderstorms encroached. Next time I visit, I will be alligator bait as I parachute over the Everglades!

It wasn't until 2010 when I took a four-month trip to North America that I truly discovered the U.S.A. Even now, ever so distantly, the American Dream flickers, having been greatly doused after the financial crisis. There is still a plethora of clichéd activities from the East to the West Coast that are symbolic of living that dream: from driving a Mustang convertible from San Francisco to San Diego down the Pacific Coast Highway with the wind in your hair to gambling big in the casinos of Las Vegas.

Boston was where my four-month North American adventure began. A great city that has been living in New York's shadow for over a century, but it holds its own charm. While you can escape the New York summer heat in the Hamptons, Boston has Provincetown with a resident dancing policeman and a coastline populated with great seafood and endless ice cream trucks. Summer on the East Coast of the U.S. is fantastic.

The clothes get skimpier, the tans darker, and in Massachusetts, it is possible to soak up some of the most fascinating history of the country by day, and then go on a neon lit party tram and play beer pong by night. And why not also throw in some whale watching for good measure?

Post Boston, I ended up in Washington D.C. for the Fourth of July celebrations, and better still, I somehow ended up on a super-yacht for the evening fireworks display, wearing an American flag t-shirt, complete with an American flag top-hat. I managed to blag my way onto this yacht with someone at the hotel bar I had met the previous night, which again goes to prove, you never know who you might meet in the right place at the right time. Understandably, when the British accent was heard, there was a lot of friendly "banter" directed my way, but a warm summer night in D.C., watching fireworks over Washington Monument in fantastically high spirits was an experience I'll never forget.

Similarly, I'll never forget my tour around D.C., where I decided to take a Segway trip (those electric 2-wheeled buggy-type vehicles that move depending on your weight distribution and are mostly used by mall cops). After whizzing by the Jefferson Memorial and the White House, our group stopped outside the Capitol Building as we waited for someone who had fallen off their Segway. Struggling to believe that someone could be so incompetent as to actually fall off, I took this opportunity to test out the capabilities of my Segway to the maximum, turning sharply at high speeds on the gravel tracks outside this heavily guarded building—until I too flew off my Segway at high speed, over the handlebars, ripping my leg open as I went crashing into the gravel stones. The security officials ran over as it looked like I had probably been shot as I rolled around on the ground, screaming in pain. This whole situation can only be explained as arising out of my idiocy, but in a country where you are legally allowed to own a tank in every state or legally own a brown bear as a pet in nine states, I'm sure that stranger things have happened.

So onto the Big Apple it was, my leg strapped up and me hobbling along. I have been to New York several times, and every time there is always that "wow" moment when you first see the concrete jungle of New York City. Manhattan, an island where girls seem to always outnumber guys in bars, and where you can pop into wild house parties on the East Side in mansions where playboy bunnies serve alcohol and little people stripping, this city always outdoes itself in debauchery.

Two of my good friends, Zach and Tom, live in New York, and they are very "American"—the kind of guys that chant, "U.S.A.! U.S.A.!" in bars, and like to "make me American" whenever I visit. So, from eating hot dogs and drinking Budweiser while watching the Yankees, to enjoying basketball at Madison Square Gardens, a visit here always felt authentically American. There is simply so much to do in this city, beyond the tourist check offs such at the Empire State Building (where I have now seen multiple people proposing), and the neon jungle in Times Square, there are many free tickets to TV shows available, like Good Morning America where queuing early will get you up close and personal on national television and it was here that I bizarrely got pushed aside by Dolly Parton.

In a city that has been used as the setting of countless movies and TV series, there are seemingly infinite famous spots to recognize. Between shopping trips on Fifth Avenue and catching a show on Broadway, head out to Brooklyn and Greenwich Village to see many of the famous listed locations.

Amongst taking helicopter rides over the metropolis of Manhattan and visiting world class museums and art galleries, you can venture out above the city and drink on some fantastic rooftops, in bars where New Yorkers let their hair down. I was taken 27 stories above the streets below (relatively low for N.Y.C.) to the top of the New York Athletic club, by my mate Zach, my wife Elena and her friend Steph, for a surreal experience. We had the whole rooftop to ourselves above the buzzing city.

The fun rarely stops in the city that never sleeps, with bottomless boozy brunches at every corner and a young population that wants to party and have fun, but eventually it had to end. Therefore, a trip on to Philadelphia for some famous Philly cheese steaks and seeing the birthplace of the U.S.A. was next, after a brief stop through the very strange and bizarre Amish country. People in Amish country have almost entirely rejected the use of modern technology and ride around in traditional horse-drawn carriages. Despite being told stories of incest and forced ideology, they actually seemed quite content and peaceful to me after I spent some time there.

Between my travels through the U.S.A., I intermittently hopped back and forth through Canada, and visited Toronto, Montreal and Vancouver. Having recently visited New York, Toronto seemed a very quiet city by comparison. I enjoyed the gastro scene here, including several return trips to The Supper Club, and after ticking off the tourist attractions of the CN tower, and a leisurely bike ride around Toronto Island for a fantastic view of the city, I more or less used Toronto as a base to explore the nearby thundering Niagara Falls. Unlike other great waterfalls of the world, Niagara Falls is instantly recognizable due to the standard issue of blue ponchos you see hordes of tourists walking around in. Look, you're going to get wet either way, just embrace it. Bring a change of clothes, and enjoy the unique boat ride that takes you under the falls. Make up smearing alert: this is also inevitable here.

On to my favorite place in Canada: a short journey took me to Montreal. Montreal is a must-visit destination for food lovers; from smoked meat sandwiches to poutine, the mix of cultures and heritages in this mostly French speaking cultural melting pot has created a fairly unique take on fusion. To wash all this fabulous food down, ice wine is popular here, and this was my first time drinking it. Apart from the Notre Dame cathedral and a ride around the Jacques Villeneuve Formula 1 circuit, I found fairly little to actually see in Montreal, but the music and the food were enough to keep me more than satisfied during my visit.

Although it was later in my trip that I went to Vancouver, in general I found the city very similar to Toronto. It was certainly a nice city, but I discovered the real gems lay outside the city in the surrounding areas, such as the Capilano Suspension Bridge, which is breathtaking, perched over treetops and swaying from side to side, and the spectacular Rocky Mountaineer train, taking you up to the mountain ski resort of Whistler through the beautiful British Colombia scenery. The glass domed roof of this train allows for spectacular views, and I was almost disappointed when I arrived at my worst nightmare—a ski resort! As my wife can vouch, I am potentially one of the worst skiers in the world—cue the hot sweats as soon as I get near a pair of skis—but we will get to that later. Luckily, I traveled to Whistler in Summer, but despite being utterly incompetent on skis, I do love everything that comes with ski resorts, particularly Whistler. Beautiful lodges, great food, and magnificent après ski drinking. So summer in Whistler for me was more about eating, drinking, quad biking and mountain cycling. What better way was there to finish my trip to Canada than with a late night BBQ atop a mountain, which was spectacular!

After delving into Canadian territory, I returned to the U.S.A., and it was time for a change of scene, so I headed to the Deep South: the Big Easy, New Orleans. I have visited New Orleans several times, the first time being very soon after Hurricane Katrina, where I saw a depraved city that seemed to be crumbling at the seams. Houses were largely abandoned across whole neighborhoods, with signs of vandalism evident, and graffiti-covered shacks peppering every street. This was a time when Louisiana was in deep need of funds from tourism to rebuild. On returning to NOLA (as the locals call it) several years later with my wife, there can be no doubt that it became one of my favorite destinations in the U.S.A. This amazing city was heavy on my stomach, liver and ears, with amazing food—from gumbo to seafood and po'boys—accompanied by fantastic jazz and blues providing the true soundtrack of the South, plus plenty of alcohol in the ever-lively French Quarter. This city is bursting with its very unique culture.

The raucous Bourbon Street is the heart of the French Quarter, and became the scene of many stumbling nights, caused by the infamous "4 for 1 Big Ass beers" and intoxicating Hand Grenades, which have a top secret recipe, that could only, I assume, be of interest to the consumer if ever revealed, because, let me tell you: these things are lethal.

Among the beautiful squares, evening trips on the steamboat Natchez and taking trips out to the old slavery plantations toward Baton Rouge, I ended up riding mechanical bulls in a rowdy bar, going to a strip club with my wife where there was unlimited sushi that you could pick off naked women, and watching a crazy riot taking place in the French Quarter when spirits boiled over. In a city with many ghost stories, there are many voodoo queens, which quite frankly give you goose-bumps with their ability to make you think there is something spooky about this city. The bottom line is that New Orleans never fails to surprise. Mardi Gras takes things to a whole new level here, but fully expect to see naked women with perhaps simply a slither of neon paint covering their nipples happily strolling down Bourbon Street, just because they can. It's New Orleans—so why not, I guess. From the Big Easy it was on to the Lone Star State, Texas, where everything is Bigger!

Gas guzzling S.U.V.s, that make your average car look rather inferior, roll past the seemingly endless shopping malls. The Texas "novelty" dress of cowboy boots and hats are actually very much commonplace. Sure, I visited a classic honky tonk, where patrons ride on automated bulls and shots go down like water. Then, from the big and bold in Texas, it was onto the outrageous in Las Vegas.

This city truly is the Disney World for adults. Super-clubs like Drai's and immense pool parties at the Mirage hit you hard in the wallet, but somehow it seems utterly worth it for the opulence of individual tables around swimming pools while world famous D.J.s, like Calvin Harris, allow a well-heeled crowd to party the night away, in true Sin City style.

I found that Vegas was not just about the gambling, despite Elena and I meeting a very fun local couple to gamble and drink with until daybreak. We walked out of the casino slightly poorer and very bleary eyed into a brand new day. This city had so much more to offer. The shows; where to start with the shows? There are so many to choose from. Sure, they come and go, but in a city that has as many as eight separate Cirque de Soleil performances on any given night, it is not just the strip shows that garner attention. I have had the pleasure of watching renowned performers, such as Aerosmith and the magician David Copperfield in Vegas. There is always something new to do here, from petting baby lion cubs at the MGM Grand hotel to watching the mainstay attraction of the magnificent Bellagio fountains. Vegas is an incredible place to come for a few days and let your inhibitions go, but after your liver can't take it anymore, what better way to escape than going to the nearby Grand Canyon?

I took a helicopter out to the Grand Canyon and had a brilliant visual perspective of nature's destruction and erosion over millions of years, creating this immensely deep valley. I had previously taken a helicopter all the way to the valley floor and rafted down the trickling Colorado River, but it really does illustrate just how small we are as a species as you attempt to fathom the size of this place. A stop by the Hoover Dam contrasts the canyon with a man-made wonder, and I even went inside the dam, which was an incredibly unique experience.

From an abundance of water in Lake Mead that is enclosed by the Hoover Dam itself, I travelled to where there is almost no water at all, one of the driest places on Earth—Death Valley. Despite scorchingly hot temperatures in the day here, across a vast landscape of rugged mountains and sand dunes, where it is hot enough to cook an egg on the ground, the weather can also become bitterly cold in Death Valley as the sun goes down. Wearing shorts and a t-shirt can leave you shivering. Make no mistake about it, Death Valley is a great national park to visit, but people do die here every year due to the expanse of this incredibly harsh environment. We made it out without issue, and it was back to the debauchery of the Las Vegas strip and, after a quick ride on a rollercoaster through the New York-New York hotel lobby, we decided to explore the old town, so we headed to the Freemont street experience. Old hotels still line this neon lit parade where revellers drink extra strong drinks out of plastic cups while watching the more daring partygoers zip-lining down the street right above their heads. The Golden Nugget casino is a reminder of a bygone era, where older patrons of Vegas still seem to gamble away their wages on anything upwards of the one cent slot machines.

After Las Vegas, it was time to head back to reality, but that reality came in the form of swapping desert scenery for that of glaciers in Alaska. Such is the extreme diversity I love about the U.S.A., where you can move from the desert to glaciers, and then on to see volcanoes in Hawaii.

After a short stop in Seattle, I got on a cruise ship for a one-way trip to the rather depressing and cumbersome town of Anchorage, but not before seeing some of the most spectacular scenery I have ever witnessed. The novel "Into the Wild" by Jon Krakauer was a fantastic read, and a great inspiration to me, so I was itching with anticipation to get to Alaska after having read so much about it. As the ship rolled through Glacier National Park, right up to the foot of the incredibly monstrous moving sheet of ice, I was in awe. The scenery only continued to impress, and a helicopter ride to the Mendenhall Glacier in Juneau was breathtaking. The incredible crevices of ice below were completely untouched and, on reaching the top of the glacier, we were told to pour out our bottles of water and refill them with the melting glacial ice—bacteria do not survive in these conditions and this was some of the freshest water I had ever tasted. Our daring trek across the glaciers was intense as this environment is so volatile (particularly with the summer sun melting the ice rapidly), and large canyons of ice descending into an unforeseen abyss appeared all too regularly. Nowhere was the intense melting of the glaciers more evident than during a canoe trip through the still perilously cold waters around Skagway, where thundering waterfalls of freezing cold water and ice thunder off the face of the glacier. I had to navigate around large iceberg chunks that had become dislodged, but oh my, what a sight this was!

Although an incredibly harsh environment during winter, summer in Alaska is not solely about icebergs and glaciers. A trip to Ketchikan meant participating in some traditional Alaskan entertainment, such as wood chopping competitions (which I thought I was fairly good at, but popular opinion was that I was adequately useless) and participating in a salmon bake. Salmon is so abundant here that at times the entire town smells of it, with half-eaten salmon strewn across the roads after larger birds of prey have gorged on their lunch.

On that note, it must be said that Alaska has a fairly impressive array of wildlife, particularly in terms of its black and brown bear populations. I walked across many a rope bridge seeing entire families of bears frolicking just below. This was the closest I had come to seeing these large powerful creatures in their natural habitat.

After sheer glaciers creaking through ginormous mountains, it was on to see other mountains covered in vegetation—destination Hawaii.

I love everything about this state, from the Polynesian culture to lu'aus in beautiful settings where you feast on an entire

hog cooked in leaves in the ground while Polynesian performers entice with anything from traditional dancing to fire eating.
Everything here is relaxed: the outdoor shopping malls and the
laid back vibe around Waikiki beach. I tried to surf on the mini
boards, but failed spectacularly, so before embarrassing myself
further, I headed to Pearl Harbor, the sobering sight of the
sunken U.S.S. Arizona. Still visible above water with oil pouring
from the hull, this is a much more mellow part of any trip to
Hawaii than the many black sand beaches and Jurassic Park
type mountain scenery.

The main island of Oahu, with the capital Honolulu, pre-
sents Hawaii's introductory vibe, but a trip to the islands was a
must-do here. I chose to travel to "The Big Island" of Hawaii to
see the barren landscape of more recent volcanic activity. Welcome to Volcanoes National Park. Kilauea volcano is constantly
pumping out red hot lava and, as the sun went down, it made
for quite an amazing sight, as did the steam plumes in daylight. Roads on this island are intermittently cut off by solidi-
fied lava flows from constant eruptions and, trust me, this stuff
is sharp and unforgiving when you walk on it. Holes get torn
through the bottom of shoes and feet get cut. But for geogra-
phy geeks like myself, this place is paradise. You can even take
a walk and boat ride through the extinct Thurston Lava Tube,
imagining the molten hot lava flowing here hundreds of years
ago. Because of the developed nature of Oahu and the vast
nearby natural beauty to the built up areas, Honolulu is somewhere I could envisage myself settling someday in the future.

From the beauty of nature, to the man-made beauty of
California. First stop: San Francisco.

Quite simply, San Fran is cool, super cool. The home of so
many pioneering tech firms in nearby Silicon Valley, this city

has a lot to offer. All you can eat oyster deals pepper the shores, and these establishments provide glorious views of the infamous Golden Gate Bridge. After I had taken a trip out to Alcatraz Prison and walked down the truly uniquely crooked Lombard Street, where cars weave down a steep but manicured hill with so many bends, it was time to explore the surrounding area.

A short ride out of San Francisco took me to Muir Woods where giant redwood and sequoia trees grow to insanely large sizes. These trees grow so large that there are actually instances where a road has been cut through the excessively large trunks so that cars can pass through. If natural selection was illustrated in terms of trees, these beasts would be the uncontested survivors.

If you are a wine lover like Elena and me, you have to head out to the world renowned vineyards of Napa and Sonoma. The setting is picturesque and the pace of life around Sonoma Plaza is incredibly laid back. Try not to drink too much wine during your day trip here, otherwise your drunk ass may be embarrassingly and forcibly asked to leave the Cheesecake Factory in Union Square on returning to the city.

If life in nearby Los Angeles is dominated by how people look, then San Francisco is dominated by how 'cool' things can become. This place rarely stays the same upon each visit. You can do wine flights in the ever-popular fisherman's wharf while watching continually varying street performances, stuff yourself on some of the best ice cream I have ever tried at Ghirardelli Square, and end the evening by trying out one of the super-chic prohibition-era bars peppered throughout the city. The Wilson and Wilson Private Detective Agency proved a hugely fun evening at a prohibition bar that likes to put on a show. There you get interrogated on arrival and have a specific story about who you are sent to when you make a reservation here. You have to get yourself into whatever characters you have been given on arrival and pass the test to be allowed in, but it really does amalgamate in the feeling that you have stepped back in time into a bygone era.

After San Fran's hip nightlife, and quirky wave organs on the coastline aside, it was time to pay a visit to the rich and famous of Beverly Hills.

Los Angeles, the City of Angels. You really do spot celebrities on a daily basis here, most likely due to their high concentration in this city, and the rather touristy must-do homes tour around Beverly Hills is as fun as strolling down the infamous Hollywood Walk of Fame, which is speckled with celebrities' handprints. We were lucky enough to witness the premiere of Fast and Furious in full swing at the nearby Kodak Theatre, and Hollywood is certainly the main draw of this city. I would highly recommend doing a movie backlot tour here. Elena and I chose the Warner Brothers Studio tour, which is a must-do for all movie buffs out there.

Shopping on Rodeo drive and drinking at famous joints such as Johnny Depp's Viper Room on Sunset Boulevard aside, this city is a true urban sprawl that has so much to offer just a short drive away. Gaze at the stars from the Griffith Observatory to get a true indication of the sheer size of Los Angeles, but then get out of the city to the surrounding areas. Los Angeles is a collection of smaller cities, and beyond the downtown area, lay some of my favorite locations along the US Pacific Coast.

Santa Monica pier was a beautiful escape. After we'd made our way out there, watching incredibly tanned locals plying by the pier on rollerblades while stuffing our faces with the delicious infamous Pink's hot dogs (must try!), there was no turning back from the coastal road, better known as Pacific Coast Highway.

Nearby Venice Beach is awash with people offering "medical marijuana," and has attained the nickname of 'muscle beach', due to some incredibly stacked people exercising along the waterfront.

If the early morning mist clears in time, a trip up to Malibu allows you to paraglide off a cliff with a motor strapped to your back. Unfortunately, there was too much haze when I had this booked, but running off a cliff with a parachute strapped to your back looked pretty incredible, if not an infamous Los Angeles law suit waiting to happen!

From here it was a Ford Mustang convertible ride down to Orange County and onward to San Diego. Roof down, radio on, and the open road of the Pacific Coast Highway ahead. After stopping through Long Beach, Huntington Beach and Newport Beach, it was non-stop to San Diego, and boy, did this city positively surprise!

San Diego is well known for the controversial Sea World where, as I witnessed, the animals are kept in very confined spaces. So, despite the orca show being impressive, visiting here poses a moral dilemma to many, and I believe this situation will soon change through protest. We stayed in the vibrant Gaslamp Quarter in San Diego, at the Marriott, which had a fantastic rooftop bar to watch over the nearby baseball stadium during a game. What an experience! As nighttime drew in and our "duck tour" on a hybrid road and water vehicle was over, it was time to get our drinking boots on in the Gaslamp.

This place is awash with bars offering numerous drinks promotions, and although it cannot rival the debauchery of Bourbon Street and the French Quarter in New Orleans, it did serve up one of our favorite restaurants in the U.S.—The Gaslamp Strip Club. As the name and logo may loosely suggest, this used to be an old strip joint. The restaurant came with an interesting quirk: we had to cook the steaks ourselves. Because of the assumed human margin for error, the meat cuts have to be of extremely high quality here, and they certainly didn't disappoint. Standing around a large smoking grill with a pair of tongs, we put our chefs' hats on and seasoned away. I found the food in this city to be pretty spectacular in general, and there is also quite the appetite for boozy all-you-can-drink brunches, particularly in the quaint nearby town of La Jolla. What better way to spend a Californian summer day than sinking a boat load of mimosas at brunch and then heading out on canoes around the La Jolla caves to see the large local population of lazy sea lions? San Diego is located right on the border with Mexico, and I traveled southward through the congested crossing to Tijuana, Mexico. This border is one of the world's most heavily guarded, and after hours of edging closer to the comprehensive checks I finally made it to Mexico.

CHAPTER 18
Central America

Tijuana is something of a tourist fad, and despite huge improvements in safety in the city in recent years, the area around the Zona Norte (the red light district) still clearly shows the sinister underbelly of this town, with prostitutes and their pimps roaming freely and groups of unsavory looking gangs hanging around almost every corner as night falls. It seemed like every tourist passing through here was interested in having novelty photographs with "zebras" (white donkeys painted with black stripes!) while wearing a sombrero in front of the colorful Mexican background. Aside from visiting one of the world's tallest flagpoles, I was only interested in sampling tacos and tequila in Tijuana, in preparation for Mexico City.

The capital of Mexico is a cultural dream, with beautiful architecture flanking open squares where munching on empanadas while people watching became a part of my daily routine. Mexico City is a fantastic place to base yourself when visiting this country. Just a short drive away lie some of the country's best preserved Mayan and Aztec ruins. I traveled to the

Teotihuacan pyramids, where intricate carvings and other-worldly architecture awaited, and there are few sights that rival observing Teotihuacan at sunrise from a hot air balloon. Apart from the back tingling painful landing, whereby I had to huddle into a little ball inside the basket, bracing for what would be a firm approach to say the least, the experience of flying in the hot air balloon was a true spectacle. The rising sun glistened off the ruins below and the only sound was the intermittent combustion of the balloon's gas. The tranquility of this experience contrasted to my exploration of the ruins on the ground,, where I had a pack of incredibly friendly dogs following me around, jumping up on me any time they could. I likely spent almost as much time taking photos with the dogs as I did of the pyramids. This was one of those occasions where I experienced something magical but in solitude, and despite having enjoyed Mexico, I always had an ever present anticipation about returning to share this place with someone in the future.

I didn't continue to journey further through Central America on this particular trip to Mexico in 2010, and instead explored Central America from south to north, with Panama being my first destination directly after my previous trip to South America in 2009.

The Panama Canal: one of humankind's greatest engineering accomplishments. A sight that is on many people's bucket lists, with some willing to pay relatively hefty prices to take cruise ships down the canal. What can I say about the Panama Canal? It was incredibly dull to see. Unless you have a time lapse video and are willing to sit and observe the intricate canal system in progress (it is an excruciatingly slow process to fill and drain each chamber in order to bring ships to different water levels within the canal) you will struggle to ascertain the true feat of engineering here, so visiting the Panama Canal was hardly an exhilarating experience.

Panama City itself is referred to as the Miami of the South, and it was easy to see why. Glitzy bars populate palm tree-lined boulevards that flank pristine beaches, and the beauty of the Casco Viejo, the old Spanish city, is a nice contrast to the modern day Panama of high rise skyscrapers. I met an American guy called Chris here under some rather strange circumstances. Chris called out my name while drinking a beer at the bar of the hostel we both happened to be staying at. Before I first traveled to South America I was keen to find like-minded travelers to share this experience with. Chris and I linked up on a travel forum, and we had planned to meet in Brazil to travel together. Unfortunately, he had to cut his trip short due to family reasons and he only traveled through Colombia and Central America. But here we both were, thousands of miles from home, in a place on a date neither of us knew the other would be present. I guess that illustrates just how small the world can be at times.

Days later it was time to visit the ever-popular Costa Rica. For the first time in quite a while, I started to encounter tourists on vacation, rather than traveling backpackers, and it was easy to see why. The capital, San Jose, is a city that felt intoxicatingly alive. A pulsating mix of Latin American food, Spanish colonial architecture and beautiful women made San Jose my favorite capital city in Central America.

Moments away from the city, my eyes were awash with a spectrum of greens as the dense Costa Rican jungle surrounded the human-made cities in this country. A trip to the jungle from the luscious beaches of both the east coast and west coast is viable in one day, given the geographical nature of this relatively petite slither of a country. Rain in the rainforest you say? Oh yes, Costa Rica doesn't mind having itself a sudden and torrential downpour without notice, as I found out rather inconveniently during this particular trip while trekking toward the Arenal Volcano.

My footsteps on the tourist trail continued into Nicaragua where more volcano gazing awaited, but with a difference, and a slight upgrade. If you would like to become the proud owner of a very touristy t-shirt that says, "I went v-boarding," then head toward the Cerro Negro volcano near the old town of León, an architect's dream. This town is full of travelers walking around in cheesy tshirts boasting their achievements of volcano boarding down the black sand cones that have been formed by volcanic ash from previous eruptions. After trying sandboarding in Dubai and having a quite shocking track record when it comes to balance, I simply had to give this a try. Volcano boarding was something I had never heard of before, but the cheesy tshirt with my name on it firmly remained in Nicaragua.

As I traveled northwards, rainforests and volcanoes became an increasingly common sight, and to a large extent, Honduras, El Salvador and Guatemala have a lot in common, both visually and culturally. However, the most undesirable similarities lie in their incredibly high murder rates, which have spiraled yet higher in recent years. Honduras has one of the highest murder rates in the world, fueled by gang and drug violence, as a result of its strategic position for cocaine smuggling from the South American source to the consumer markets in North America. I witnessed heavily armed military patrols at almost every turn in the capital, Tegucigalpa. An elderly man in a bar educated me about the drugs issues as he described how he used to run drugs through remote landing strips buried deep in the rainforest, cutting out makeshift runways, which made for compelling sensory storytelling if nothing else.

Bus travel through Central America was the simplest method of transportation, with limited border checks complementing multi-country visas. I would sometimes awaken on the bus in a different country without even realizing; this clearly illustrates how contraband can be easily transported across the borders of these relatively small nations.

Similar to Honduras, there are many reports that claim El Salvador to be the most dangerous country in the Western Hemisphere, where homicide levels are now described as pandemic. Again, I found that talking to locals to be the best way of obtaining an indication of what life in San Salvador is like. I was told that, the recent attempts to crack down on violence had only led to gangs fragmenting into smaller groups. Despite never having posed any danger to me on my travels, gang members do visibly loiter on almost every street corner in San Salvador after dark.

Notwithstanding the threats in these countries, and an ever visual presence of gangs and violence that can be intimidating at times, the majority of travelers pass through without incident in a country where there is so much to see. After visiting the magnificent Tazumal ruins, I continued on the so-called floral route west of San Salvador, passing through petite villages and multiple Mayan ruins, such as Joya de Cerén, which are all well preserved but covered in volcanic ash, similar to the ruins in the Roman town of Pompeii.

There were regular stark reminders of the dangers in this country, however, and on passing a bar in San Salvador, its walls peppered with bullet holes, I was told that a shootout had occurred here several nights before. When innocent by-standers are caught in gangland violence here, there is little protection or sympathy, and even the public buses are regular targets for gang ambushes. So, on my continuing journey to Guatemala, we were told very strictly by the driver that there would be no stops under any circumstance, even at check-points.

I made it to Guatemala City incident free and, as you might expect if traveling around the world, not every single country is going to have an exciting story to tell. Guatemala was just that for me. A brief look around the national palace and a land-scape that was not too dissimilar to what I had experienced in neighboring countries, and I travelled on to Belize.

There is one incredible standout and unique attraction in Belize—the Great Blue Circular Hole. For divers, this is the place to get your flippers in a twist, but the breathtaking per-spective of this deep water ocean trench is best seen aerially. While flying over this circular trench, the color contrasts are truly spectacular, with light turquoise blues surrounding what is a very prominent deep royal blue where the Great Blue Hole submerges deep below the surface, which illustrates just how far this ginormous trench ploughs.

Back in the city after spectacular sightseeing, I had some time to kill. I parked myself in a scruffy local bar on the water-front. It looked like this might have been a bad idea when I found my table suddenly surrounded by some rather unruly looking guys. I was used to this sort of mild intimidation, regu-larly looking the odd one out, and the majority of the time it was all very jovial, but in this particular case something rather strange happened. Their aggression toward me was abruptly abated when one of them noticed the mark on my wrist. Rather amusingly, (although I didn't reveal this at the time), the 'mark', a black cross in a circle, was simply the entry stamp from the bar I had been to the previous evening. I rather coyly declined to comment on it, saying it was, "Nothing, really." At this point these guys spawned an idea that it was a type of gang marking, saying, "That's definitely something, you're someone, man!" Moments later, their friend arrived and, to my utter bewilderment, showed me a tattoo on his arm, similar to my club stamp, saying he had got it in prison! I wasn't going to dispel their utterly preposterous notions about me, but almost for my own safety, I had to play along, acting coy and ignoring their questions. I just had to try incredibly hard not to burst out laughing—it was all so absurd. I continued to drink with them all day, and it almost felt like I had been accepted into their seemingly low level gang, hearing stories of their every-day lives in Belize as we sank the beers. This was a strangely amusing end to the trip, but with my departing from Belize, I had traveled to every country in north and South America. Two continents complete, which put me well on my way to visiting every country in the world.

CHAPTER 19
West Africa

After months of future planning back in London and god-awful trips to embassies waiting days upon days for visas, it was on to what some call The Dark Continent—Africa. This would be my biggest challenge to date and, unlike previously mentioned areas of the Middle East where my safety may have been disguised to a certain extent because of my Mediterranean genes (my father's father was Spanish and my mother's mother was Greek), Africa was a continent where there would be nowhere to hide for the boy from England, particularly in West Africa where tourist numbers hover close to zero.

There are many parts of this continent that were simply about survival. It would be four months of getting stared at continuously and called racist names, most of which I can't even remember, but were certainly imaginative. Additionally, breaking up with an ex-girlfriend the day before this trip, traveling to an area where English would be of little use to me, getting by with pigeon French at best, proved to be self-reflective in many respects.

Make no mistake about it, this continent is absolutely huge, and much larger than the representation you see on most maps. Overland journeys seem to last forever, and there is simply no way to calculate how long things will take here—almost non-existent dirt track roads, minibus crashes, multiple breakdowns and even one instance where the bus driver was dragged out the bus kicking and screaming. My journey was represented by overland border crossings boasting machine-gun wielding extortion experts, and guerrilla groups roaming streets that have so recently and often been plagued by civil wars that these tragedies are still visible in the older generations' eyes.

This is Africa.

Except, this is only a part of Africa. As the months rolled on and I slowly became accustomed to the smell of my own body odor, I can genuinely say that, despite almost breaking me, when it actually came to being in the one place I had longed for through all the testing times on the continent—with my ticket in hand, boarding the flight home—Africa became the hardest continent to say goodbye to.

I had once read in a guidebook that Ghana was Africa for beginners, and to a large extent, I could see why: very friendly people and, statistically speaking, one of the safest countries on the continent. However, I began my journey in Sierra Leone—a country that has had a very troubled recent past with civil war ripping the country apart for 11 years and displacing one-third of the population.

A lot of Sierra Leone's problems (as with many other African countries, such as the Democratic Republic of Congo) is that it has an abundance of natural resources, and so the distribution of wealth is highly distorted. This was shown in Sierra

Leone's case with the Leonardo DiCaprio movie "Blood Dia-mond."

My flight going there was delayed, so my first foot into West Africa with nothing but one small backpack was at the rather unhelpful time of 1 A.M. Stepping off the plane, I already noticed I looked very different, and the very first solicitation I received on walking out of the airport was to buy diamonds. Upon refusing this, the next option was gold. I thought I was prepared for hustling after trips to Southeast Asia, but this was on a whole new level. I would be surrounded by a group of five or six men, who would grab my arms, feeling my pockets right outside the airport, where the few uniformed police officers didn't seem to care. "Hey, come on, man, we have best diamonds." The only way to counteract this scenario was to essentially fight fire with fire, so a few aggressive shoves back and eventually the contentious welcome seemed to abate. After taking a few minutes to myself to judge a book by its cover and find which "unofficial" guy with a car would drive me to the hotel, I hopped in with a guy who offered to drive me to Guinea a couple of days later. Safe to say, I gave out my email address and phone number to many new "friends" on this continent. Much time was spent engaging in conversation with just about anyone who wanted to chat, and many people seemed excited by the prospect of exchanging contact details.

The first thing that struck me about West Africa was the amount of white U.N. jeeps rolling around everywhere, mostly parked in front of international hotels. These U.N. workers know how to drink, and largely, that is their main pastime here, within the safe confines of gated properties. As I walked into the hotel bar at 2 A.M. in Freetown, it was like the end of a student party. Beer bottles strewn across the floor coupled with smashed glasses and the calamitous whiff of a good party in the air. Spontaneously, a grotesque baldheaded Irish guy stumbled over to me, slurring the few words he could manage: "Hey, you. Yeah, you, newbie. What you doing here?" he spurted out. This rather beefy looking fella proceeded to explain how he had fought in many wars, but the situation outside the hotel gates was the worst he had ever seen (apparently), and then proceeded to invite his wrecked mates over to back up his story.

I tried to rationally explain I had obviously already been outside by myself, but the conclusion of this quasi-lecture (from their perspective at least), was that I was going to, and I quote, "die tomorrow." This obviously turned out to be utter nonsense, as Sierra Leone was probably one of my most hassle-free countries I visited in Africa, but it was really quite illustrative of a particular group of macho-travelers. You know, the type that have been to a handful of places, had a bad experience or two, and then attempt to intimidate and scare others away, whether this is to demonstrate they survived a less savory area, or simply to prove something else. We have all met travelers like this. For example, when you're with a group of travelers and someone asks the question, "What's your favorite country?" You always get that one person who might reply (without a second to think), "Well, definitely my time in deepest Somalia, when there happened to be a war going on." Essentially most people can't comprehend with this far-fetched scenario. This then becomes a great self-centered opportunity for that "wild" individual to lecture everyone about their forthcoming travel experiences rather than share and learn. Sound familiar? Now, who am I to judge if that hypothetical obscurity is in fact someone's favorite destination. Good on them if it is, I just remain skeptical of the obscure intrepid traveler who attempts to intimidate others through unassociated stories.

So, random scaremongers in bars aside and despite continuous and blatant Foreign Office warnings against all but essential travel to many of the countries on this trip, not least Côte d'Ivoire which was in the middle of a civil war at this point, and similarly Mali and Chad which were highly unstable, it was time to begin a largely overland journey across West and Central Africa.

I guess attempting to visit every country in the world seemed essential to me at this point, and so I refused to heed the various warnings. I believed I was quite an experienced traveler by this time, particularly as I had the confidence to travel Africa alone. Despite this, nothing really prepares you for this continent.

I was struck at first by the almost complete lack of roads outside the urbanized centers in some parts of the region. Many cities, such as those in the Central African Republic and Chad, had mostly dirt tracks, even in the capitals. There were often just a handful of fixed structures with markets, houses and schools that amalgamated to tented and makeshift structures in many of the villages. There was certainly not a lack of home brewed bootleg alcohol in villages particularly. Tastes varied from OK to bad and then to toxic (quite literally). Africa was never lacking in AK-47 wielding military police and, as a white man, I was the subject of regular attention, and often extortion. By the time I had driven out of Sierra Leone and into neighboring Guinea, this had become so commonplace that I simply shrugged my shoulders and laughed. This would work on most occasions, and became time I had to factor into most journeys. Usually, sitting at a border crossing being asked by the guard for his "little bit" passed uneventfully if I had more patience than them, demonstrating I was in no rush, lighting up a cigarette, smiling, waiting, waiting, and digging deep for that patience and sense of humor you need on this continent.

The initial drive from Sierra Leone into Guinea not only produced an insight on how overland Africa looked but also how things worked, or didn't. There were five or six pick-ups and drop-offs along the way, seemingly the driver's various friends. Eventually there were then three of them in the jeep. Unsurprisingly, they started to joke around with me about how the price of the journey had gone up. I took this jovially, and rightly so in this instance, but the more time I spent here, it seemed that jovial "giving it a try" to see who would fall for the attempt to garner more money became almost a way of life. Anyway, they somehow convinced themselves (after an irksome argument among them and with little actual input from me) that they didn't want to damage potential business relationships with the U.K., incorrectly believing they would be able to export diamonds through me, but the journey to Guinea continued.

From there began a common theme through West and Central Africa: large presidential palaces surrounded by some form of idolized monument in honor of the current president, but no real display of former presidents. Surrounding this mainstay government façade was poverty and crumbling buildings beyond the more developed capital cities of Dakar in Senegal and Accra in Ghana. This is a passionate continent where the people have so often demanded more, illustrated by so many civil wars over the last few decades since independence from European colonizers. There were, however, many times where I visibly saw the "passionate side" broil over into something more. This ranged from seeing a bystander stabbed in the arm during what seemed to be no more than a heated discussion at a market in Senegal (it happened very quickly, and the victim seemed in utter shock as he was shouting, "Who has stabbed me in the arm," rather than removing the knife and getting help), to having a gun pulled on me while riding a motorbike from Lagos to Port Harcourt in Nigeria. Again, with so many hair-raising moments in Africa, this incident passed before I really had time to digest and deal with the situation. I was alert to all the possible dangers basically all the time in Africa, and so when I was actually in harm's way, the adrenaline began to circulate before my brain really dealt with the scenario.

In this particular instance, I (rather stupidly, perhaps) decided it was a good (and cocksure) idea to drive a motorbike along the coast of Nigeria from Lagos. I bought this bike for $150, and it was a disheveled piece of shit wreck to be honest, although I know one level above zero about motorbikes (see aforementioned story with Chris in Vietnam). So my one rule was no driving at night as I was obviously alone. In Nigeria, I may as well have put a big flashing light on my head asking to be robbed. Nonetheless, contingency measures didn't prevent the continuous vocal abuse I received from bystanders over the days it took me to drive the distance to Cameroon. This accumulated in (what seemed completely out of the blue at the time), having a handgun pulled out on me and put to my temple while stopped at a junction. I still don't know to this day just how close I was to getting myself into serious trouble here. But, as I said, I tended to find that a smile and sense of humor got me a long way on this continent. Similarly, reading the other person's smile was vital (whether it was one of those insincere "I'm about to shoot you in the head" type smiles, or in fact an overly zealous humorous smirk that was difficult to read). In this case, after another bout of "Hey, white boy" shouts, a guy walked up to me with a couple of his friends laughing, being boisterous. This was nothing new, or particularly intimidating to me by this time but, as he got closer, he put a gun to my head and said something along the lines of, "What are you doing here, white boy?"

As the traffic moved forward, I began to edge forward as well, as they were laughing. Whether I misread this as banter I will never know, but the way the guy was showing off and laughing made me think I would get out of this situation unscathed. I drove away without incident to, "Hey, where you going?" billowing behind me, and I will never know just how close to danger I was there.

Whilst I made my way through this continent, overland border crossings never became any less tiresome. It was almost disappointing and too easy if I didn't have a soldier waving an AK-47 at me, demanding money because my papers weren't correct (apparently). It seemed like your papers could never be "correct" here. Time after time, there would always be a "problem," and you guessed it, I would have to negotiate my way out of it. There were certainly times where my patience and sense of humor prevailed, yet others where I would be at a remote jungle border crossing at midnight, which supposedly "unofficially" closed at 11 P.M., and my options were limited.

I had some pretty awful overland crossings in Africa, probably none worse than that into Somalia, which I will get to later, but surprisingly, the worst experience while entering a country was when arriving by plane into Nouakchott in Mauritania. This, quite frankly, is a country I don't want to return to. I was arriving from Mali, which is another country I have mixed feelings about. Mali has had its fair share of troubles in recent years, with key historical sites in Timbuktu being the main attraction during my visit to this huge country that mostly occupies a giant slab of the Sahara and is fairly barren otherwise as well.

All travel outside of the capital, Bamako, was strongly advised against as rebel factions were making huge advances to the west, particularly around Timbuktu, claiming hundreds of kilometers of land a week, committing atrocities as they pillaged through village after village. However, Timbuktu was what I had come to Mali to see, and I nervously made the three-day journey on back-breaking dirt tracks out to Timbuktu to see it for precisely an exasperating half day. My jeep driver had already told me he was not sure which roads we would be able to take to get there and, after arriving at the ruins in the early morning, we were greeted by the crackling sound of gunfire from over the horizon. A quick panicked phone call later, to who I can only assume was his better-informed local friend, and the doors to the offroader were slammed shut, sand kicked up from the tires and we were pelting back toward Bamako. Worth it? Marginally, but I'm alive at least. This was illustrative of so many scenarios in Africa, where at times, it was actually best not to overthink a situation and just go along with whatever scenario you had found yourself in.

So after this rather bittersweet trip to Mali, I landed into Nouakchott airport in Mauritania 1 A.M. on an incredibly old plane. There were only three or so flights a week with this airline on the Bamako-Nouakchott route when, of course, they weren't canceled, which was all too regularly, but we made it after a lengthy delay.

Mauritania seemed imminently different in nature to the West African countries I had already journeyed through, including Gambia, Senegal and the Guineas. It was not as welcoming and didn't seem to evoke the carnival spirit that I had begun to fall in love with. I was slightly nervous as I landed because, in the particular case of Mauritania, I didn't have a pre-arranged visa, as I had been told in Mali that a visa on arrival was possible, despite seeming like vague information. This rarely meant a quick or simple outcome here, with possible conclusions ranging from bad—in the form of a hefty visa "fee"—to very bad—locked up in prison. It was almost impossible to obtain all the visas (particularly at home in London) for some of the more obscure countries in Africa, with embassies spontaneously deciding to close down, civil war in the case of Côte d'Ivoire, or quite simply no embassy existing. This was the case with Mauritania, unless I did a visa-run to what would have likely been Paris, or spent longer in neighboring countries waiting for a visa, both of which seemed like a waste of time and money. I decided to try my luck upon landing.

There were a handful of instances where I would attempt to obtain a visa on arrival, only to be told it was impossible (regardless of how rare, it was worth a go right?). Was it worth the gamble in the case of Mauritania? Probably not. I was misguidedly optimistic as I hopped off the plane first and balled up to the immigration counter, wrongly believing that I may get through. But, after one brief flick through my passport, a stern face looked up at me and simply asked, "Visa?". My explanation was in vain, and I was sent to sit in what appeared to be the naughty corner until the entire plane had disembarked. It was just me left. In those situations, I had on occasion taken comfort from at least one other person being in a quandary with me, but it began to feel very lonely as I awaited a condescending lecture from the "head" of immigration. As I knew full well, I was in what is referred to as "no man's land," at least until I passed through immigration, and so the rules here are often blurred. Regardless, I was told that I would be placed on the next flight back to where I had come from—which turned out to be the following evening! Air travel is certainly an irregularity on certain routes in this part of the world, and this was a double-edged sword for me on this occasion. My passport was confiscated, and I was ordered to follow the guards to spend what would be an evening in a boorish and dowdy police cell until my return flight. At this point, I had to dig deep for that sense of humor and patience as this was a fairly uncompromising situation. The strange thing was that I wasn't locked in a police jail per se. Yes, I was in a "cell," but it was apparently decommissioned, and after all I hadn't done anything wrong. The door was wide open and it was utilized as a rest area for the guards. So there I was, on what can only be described as a shit-stained mattress that was no more than a couple of centimeters thick, on the ground in a room with four or five guards. The minuscule TV in the corner constantly played various adaptations of seemingly popular African soap operas, and the food I was provided never improved beyond minuscule and borderline inedible to say the least. We have all heard the stereotypical stories about spending a night in an African jail, but this would pass without incident or any physical harm, thankfully. I was determined to try and make the best out of the situation, and so I tried to befriend the guards who, strangely enough, mostly ignored me, but likely out of strict instructions not to interact.

The day turned into night, and I made attempts to befriend the younger guards by going outside with them for cigarettes, which, as the hours passed, turned into offers of some form of bootleg alcohol (alcohol is hard to come by in Mauritania). So the elephant in the room was eventually discussed, and I explained why I was in Mauritania. This was received well, with some of the guards taking to my story of traveling to every country in the world and saying they would help. The next day, I went with two of them into the city to get food, which also turned into a very bizarre tour of Nouakchott and, I must admit, being "escorted" around with two soldiers brandishing guns was a pretty unique experience.

By the evening, it was time to be removed from the country, but on having my passport returned with a boarding pass, I was told by one of the younger guards whom I had spent time with to get in line in the regular immigration exit line. He opened my passport with a beaming smile, and presto, a full visa with entry stamp was in my passport. Somehow, through a few days of tough living conditions and sinister thoughts for my safety and well-being, this had turned into an official visit, and despite seeing virtually none of this huge country, I could say I had been here, unlikely to ever return!

The drama wasn't over yet though. On disembarking from the return flight and arriving at Moroccan immigration, I was immediately escorted off the plane and taken to the police station, where they ordered me to pay around $1000. For anyone that's unaware, if you are sent back from a country to your original destination, whatever the situation, the majority of the time it will be you picking up the tab, and it won't be the kind of prices you get on a travel comparison website, they will charge you as much as they like. So this next part is where I believe I achieved a moral victory. On their demands for payment, I pulled out a piece of paper from my bag, illustrating that I was in fact already booked on the flight they had put me on! It was always going to be a long shot, but I thought there would be a fairly high probability that things would end up the way they did, and so this was my back up plan, on the next flight out of there via Morocco. Reluctantly, from the police chief's perspective, I was free to go, and so I strolled out with my freedom back, but more on Morocco later.

My regained freedom took me on a long route via Morocco to what is potentially Africa's greatest success story, Ghana. This is a great place to start for anyone looking to garner a "taster" of West Africa. The people are friendly, the country is relatively safe and the economy is booming. This is an innovative nation where the norm is seldom accepted. I frequented fantastic bars around swimming pools where the waiters were zooming around, delivering drinks on rollerblades. The social scene was cosmopolitan enough here to even have established private members' clubs and such food variety stretching as far as sushi. And this is a nation that rewards you for venturing outside the main cities. I took trips from the Black Coast, which was a sobering sight of slavery in Africa, all the way to inland rural areas to witness the Kundum harvest festival. This festival showed the true Ghanaian spirit and demonstrated a plethora of colors and sounds, with dancing until no one could dance anymore! I genuinely felt like a tourist again in Ghana, and not just a traveler fighting for survival. However, the contrast to neighboring Côte d'Ivoire was fairly spectacular.

Côte d'Ivoire was right in the middle of a civil war when I took the short journey to Abidjan from Accra in Ghana. Côte d'Ivoire has strong links to France, as Ghana does to the U.K., and foreign investment here had been rife before the civil uprising. I could tell when I arrived that there was a booming economy in Côte d'Ivoire, but considering visas weren't being issued when I visited, and all travel was strictly advised against, I had made few plans beyond a quick visit. After begging to be granted a visa on arrival, the immigration official abruptly gave up and, after a stern warning about my safety in Côte d'Ivoire, allowed me enter.

I spent very little time exploring Abidjan alone on foot, as my initial attempt at this was futile, being told to turn back to the hotel by gun wielding kids who could not have been any older than 16. Fires burnt from oil barrels and tire stacks across the city, and almost all businesses were shuttered. Despite hearing intermittent crackling gunfire and screams on the few streets I walked in this city, it didn't actually feel entirely lawless. Sure, there were signs of looting and extreme vandalism but, in general, there appeared to be an objective here, despite the ever present fear that the situation could broil over in something far more dangerous without warning. I will certainly return to Côte d'Ivoire to experience the country in better times. However, being here at this tense and historical time was certainly an incredible, if somewhat brief experience.

Traveling through Burkina Faso and Niger was also not without incident. Firstly, I found myself caught up in a political protest during a brief stop in Burkina Faso. Another one of those incidents where the situation develops so quickly that you barely know what is happening. From a quiet stroll down the street one minute, to the next where I was blockaded by police on both sides—similar to the situation in Lima, Peru, as mentioned earlier. In the instance in Burkina Faso, the apparently peaceful protest in Ouagadougou rapidly turned sour, and I was soon at the epicenter of a group of demonstrators who were surrounded by heavily armed police with shields. Tensions boiled over when, what I could only assume by the shouting and screaming of "tear gas," was in fact tear gas, and as I already looked hugely out of place, I had to get myself out of there immediately. It's important to remember that everyone has a lot of adrenaline and panic running through them in these kinds of scenarios, even the police. This is hardly an everyday situation for them either. I ran over to a gap in the police line, pointed and said something that was likely inaudible and passed through. A tense and scary moment, but illustrative of how volatile situations and scenarios can be in Africa.

Similarly, in my next destination of Niamey, the capital of Niger, the one standalone "international" hotel that I was indeed staying at (largely for security purposes) had been stormed by guerrilla terrorists just weeks before I had been told, going room to room looking for Westerners. At this point, as anyone who has traveled to the more remote and dangerous parts of the world would vouch for, it was simply too late to adapt plans now. I had to cross my fingers and hope for the best. Niger was largely without incident, but, particularly in the poorer Saharan countries where poverty is rife as natural resources are relatively minimal and barely accessible, my guard was well and truly high. However, the main annoyance for me here was the plethora of bugs and mosquitos, particularly at night. Never have I seen so many. Thousands buzzed around any light source. Eating and drinking outside was diabolical as the food would be covered in insects. But, as with so many other places, I adapted, and it quickly became the norm. Therefore, picture me walking around with a self-made tool to swat the swathe of bugs away as I looked over the plains with my home brewed Niger beer, watching giraffes strolling by the river. A truly memorable experience.

CHAPTER 20
Central Africa

Onwards I traveled to the Central African Republic, statistically one of the poorest nations in the world. I spent three days here, eating very little and being a tourist attraction of my own as this is certainly off the beaten track. I guess there is a much more widespread itinerary to discover this country in which I only scratched the surface, but food was scarce and basic, and C.A.R wouldn't be anywhere near my list of favorite countries, so my time here felt aplenty.

My guide, Patrick, had organized the logistics of the trip, and somehow there had been a miscommunication where he believed my visit "in three weeks' time," meant I would be visiting for a total of three weeks. The disappointment was visible when I explained this to Patrick as he read through an itinerary the length of my arm. The disgust and anger he demonstrated toward me for the next few days was visible too. Although I paid him more, as I felt bad, this guy was simply not willing to let me leave unless I paid him for three weeks, following me right to the plane door on departure (security is severely lacking here) and demanding more money, despite me already paying him about twice more than I should have. Eventually, as the situation was explained to the eavesdropping police officer (a regular occurrence once voices are raised here), the officer actually took my side. This was surprising, not least because I was used to feeling the outcast on this continent, and he gave me a form of police escort onto the plane!

This was the not last time I witnessed tensions and passive aggression in Central Africa. From C.A.R I flew onwards to Chad—visa-less again—and predictably I had a half-day delay in the airport. The withering metal wreck of a plane had been duct taped up (I kid you not, there was duct tape around the wing), and we were ready to go. But, where were the rest of the passengers? I was alone on this Chad Airlines plane, doors about to close, then in the last minutes, around 20 huge Chadian soldiers dressed in army greens boarded. In this type of situation, I had found through experience it was usually best just to keep myself to myself. I was not sure of their situation, but they dispersed themselves around the plane and we departed.

Chad is a Muslim country, and alcohol was fairly non-existent here, so the soldiers appeared to use this flight as some sort of fun-flight. They were grabbing the stewardesses' asses and sinking beer upon beer until, inevitably, they were so rowdy that a couple of them came and sat next to me. So much for my plan of staying quiet sitting in the corner. An arm was placed around me and I was asked, "Why are you going to Chad?"

I thought I would use this situation to my advantage and, several beers later, I explained that I had no visa. Without hesitation, the so-called chief offered to help when we arrived. He kept saying there would be no problem as everyone knew him. But here's where my catch-22 situation arose: he began touching my leg in a very forward and odd way. He knew that he was my only option on landing, now that I had admitted my precarious situation, and he continued to invade my personal space throughout the flight. My only option was to keep drinking, smiling and removing his hands. This was a very grotesque situation, being semi-violated by a 6'5" Chadian army chief!

When we landed in the capital, N'Djamena, he kept his word, obtaining a visa on arrival for me. And, despite my skepticism that he may not have been who he claimed he was, all worked out well. The risk had paid off, for my first and likely last visit to Chad.

This place was scary though. Leaving the capital, which was dangerous in itself, seemed borderline suicide. N'Djamena was fairly rustic, with street upon street having no electricity. Instead, roadside fires raged from old oil barrels. There were makeshift bars where, I can only presume, bootleg alcohol was served. It may not sound hugely intimidating, and my visit here passed by without incident, but you can picture how egregious the situation was visually, with fire upon fire across the city accompanied by billowing screams wherever I went, particularly at night. It was, in short, a very intense place.

My onwards travel took me to Sudan, and the most recently created country, South Sudan—which was not even officially a country when I began this adventure. South Sudan had voted to split off and become what would be one of the poorest nations in the world. There was next to no infrastructure in Juba, the newly named capital, with virtually no paved roads, but it did have a very friendly population. The message was clear: South Sudan was trying to distance itself from the poor human rights record of the north, and it was open for business, despite being a very infantile nation in its early stages of existence.

I hadn't slept for two nights as I passed through Juba, which was largely due to poor planning on my part as I was transiting through the evenings. As you can imagine, it was certainly no easy task planning a visit to a newly formed country that was only beginning to establish links itself. It is a relatively safe country, but my guard still remained high. I remember barely being able to stay awake, constantly falling asleep, hugging my backpack at bus stops, in cafés and generally anywhere I sat down for five minutes. Juba really didn't feel like any more than a small and basic town. And, because of the attacks over the highly disputed oil fields on the border with Sudan, which were a regular occurrence at the time, there was limited scope to travel further round South Sudan. After a brief taster of a country I felt I would like to revisit to see how it would develop in a few years' time, it was off to the larger and dominant northern neighbor (a day late obviously, because the flight was canceled, naturally).

Sudan. A country that is famously difficult to enter. My research told me about the difficulties of obtaining a visa (which took several days of begging at the embassy in London), but I hadn't realized it was equally, if not more difficult to get out of Sudan. I thought I would indulge in a little much needed luxury in Khartoum, so I stayed at the Corinthia Hotel, which is also probably the best known landmark in this city. A large wave shaped white hotel that even features on Sudanese bank notes.

However, trouble began when I was told on checking in that international credit cards weren't accepted at the hotel, or anywhere in Sudan for that matter. This I wasn't aware of, and I clearly hadn't done my research thoroughly enough. Any mishaps and I would certainly have problems here, but what could possibly go wrong in Central Africa? After handing over my last chunk of USD to pay for the hotel, I was left with only around $100 to my name. However, this didn't seem a problem to me as I was making my way to Ethiopia where I knew I would have no trouble taking out cash. That was until my attempt to leave Sudan was met with a stern, "Where's your exit visa?" I knew nothing about this, and with just a few hours until my flight, I had to race back to the city to obtain an exit visa—which took almost all my last remaining cash. I made it back to the airport just in time for my flight, but alas, no one had bothered to explain at immigration, or indeed from where I had obtained my exit visa, that this needed to be validated by some obscure government agency, which was also back in the city. Were they just mocking me? I wasn't sure, but what was certain was this plane had departed. Except it hadn't. On rushing back to get the necessary validation, and being given a free ride back to the airport by my very kind driver who took pity on me (as I had completely run out of money at this point), I was told that the very airline I was booked on, had canceled every flight for the last two weeks, and no one knew when they would be flying again; indefinitely suspended.

The airport was carnage, with people aimlessly walking around, and the airline still checking people in every day, in the hope that, I don't know, the pilots would suddenly turn up? It was absolutely mindless, but the pressing issue for me was that I didn't even have enough money for a taxi back to the city, let alone a place to stay for the night. The airline ticket desks only took cash. Of course they did. So my long shot hope was to call home and see if my mum and dad could book

150

me an e-ticket on the next Ethiopian Airlines flight out of there that evening. My parents were always there for me when, as the expression goes, "the shit hit the fan," and I will be eternally grateful for that. A lot of wasted money later, and I was on my way to one of the hidden gems of Africa; Ethiopia.

CHAPTER 21
Horn of Africa

I quickly found that Ethiopia has strong Indian routes, particularly in the booming industrial sector. I spent the majority of my time being shown the best Indian restaurants by a guy called Sanjay that was in Ethiopia on business from Mumbai. Addis Ababa is one of the more vibrant cities on this continent, with good restaurants and lively nightlife, if you know where to look. There are also well-preserved examples of Ethiopia's colonial roots such as the Sheraton Hotel in beautiful grounds in the city; the place to be seen in Addis (as the locals refer to their city).

I had some interesting experiences in Ethiopia, not least being invited to the house of the self-proclaimed "Prince of Ethiopia." I believe this referred more to his financial status than an actual line of royal blood. But we ate and drank like kings there anyway. The highlight of Ethiopia was my encounter with the so-called hyena men in Harar. A trip out here, especially at night, is highly recommended. It was fairly spectacular to see the obedience these creatures have to their owners, who live and sleep with the hyenas, which yes, you can feed as well!

Another country in this region, and another canceled flight. However, this time, with Ethiopian Airlines actually being a half-decent carrier, a bunch of us destined for Djibouti were put up in a hotel near the airport. A special mention here to a very kind American guy called Phil with whom I shared many whiskeys and laughs that evening. He not only insisted on picking up the bar tab, saying, "You can do the same for someone when you're older," but also had a very chunky satellite phone. He urged I use this to make a call to my family at an extortionate cost of $25/minute to him! Even when "the chips are down" so to speak, I discovered that there was always good to come out of bad situations when travelling, and this evening almost felt like more fun than I would have had alone in Djibouti.

Travel was not simple around these parts of the Horn of Africa, and neighboring Eritrea was fairly complex to reach, as it had apparently made enemies with many of its neighbors. There were no flights or border crossings, so a flight through Aden in Yemen and back was the very limited accessibility I had to this slither of land, despite bordering Ethiopia. You can really begin to get a basic understanding of the troubles in this part of the world with a visit to the tank graveyard in Eritrea. For me, this was an eerie visual representation of the devastation the years of war have had in the region, which have led to extreme famine and unnecessary loss of life.

Neighboring Somalia is possibly one of the most dangerous countries in the world. It was certainly a challenge making my way to Somalia, as the roads were peppered with large red crosses and warning signs about unexploded land mines.

There were stark reminders of the dangers illustrated by pieces of shrapnel littered along the sides of the roads when stopping for toilet breaks, and my driver wasted no time in warning me that straying just a meter or two off the path could very well lead to losing a leg... or worse.

I took the easier option and traveled overland to the "much" safer northern self-proclaimed Somaliland, which I attempted when I did finally make it to neighboring Djibouti. Compared to the immensely unstable Somali capital of Mogadishu, this seemed like the only viable option at the time. It was never going to be a simple process entering Somaliland and, despite having the correct visa, the stoned border guards wielding machine guns still insisted on "extra payments." My patience prevailed this time, but my brief trip here was far from uneventful.

Later that afternoon, I had finally made what can only be described as an unforeseen bad judgement call when I got in the wrong person's car to take me across town. As we drove farther and farther from civilization, and the buildings and people diminished to none, I realized something was wrong. I continually asked and was reassured everything was fine, we were driving the correct route. I had been in similar situations many times, and they had never ended badly for me, so you kind of have to warily accept the scenario. Except, in this situation, as we began to slow, the driver accosted me to hand over my belongings. We were in the middle of nowhere, with just a handful of huts every so often. I didn't feel particularly threatened and there was no weapon involved so, as the car slowed down close to walking pace, I inelegantly hopped out of the car with my rucksack that had been by my feet, only to have the car door slam shut on my trailing index finger—ouch! The pain was excruciating, and I was convinced my finger was broken. This was later confirmed when I visited a hospital back in Djibouti where the sympathetic doctors kindly contributed to pay the hospital fee to patch up the broken finger. Again, I was truly lucky with some of the people that helped me on my journey around the world, and this instance I don't remember their names, but I certainly won't forget the kindness that was selflessly shown towards me.

But, there I was, broken finger, unrelenting pain, remote location, in one of the world's most dangerous countries, as the driver sped off (I have found that, at any sign of potential conflict, petty thieves usually disappear as there are plenty of other unassuming victims). I had little choice but to wait for a passing car to give me a ride, and that came in the form of a very kind Somalian man with three female passengers. He drove me as close as he could get to the border—it was certainly time for me to leave Somalia. I did not have any appetite to have my finger treated in a country with a near non-existent healthcare system.

The ride back to the border was incident free, except for a very bizarre situation in one of the towns as we passed a group of women walking. The driver rolled down the window and started shouting "sluts" at almost every woman we drove past in this village. The ladies squeezed into the back of our car were in hysterics at this. I smiled out of confusion more than anything. Was he doing this to show off? A very bizarre moment that I won't really understand, but will certainly remember.

CHAPTER 22
North Africa, Gabon and Angola

My onward travels took me to North Africa, of which I have bittersweet memories. There was an element of escapism from the harsh conditions of West and Central Africa here, with the ability to relax and recuperate on some stunning beach resorts in Tunisia and Algeria and change pace around the souks of Morocco. The people here are generally friendly, and the culture is very different to other parts of Africa, with a strong Middle Eastern vibe. These countries have some beautiful mosques, particularly in Casablanca, which has also been the infamous backdrop in so much literature. My downtime in some of the luxury coastal resorts was all too brief, but it was time to visit the outlier of the region at the time—Libya.

As seemed to be the case with so many of my travel itineraries, my timing was less than impeccable, and my visit to Libya came just two weeks after Colonel Gaddafi and his government were toppled. In other words, the country was highly unstable and travel was not recommended. In the instability and power vacuum, it was actually fairly simple for me to obtain a visa (which was strangely handed out as a business visa). But, in the months that followed, the country was closed off from the outside world, and certainly tourism, so I was actually lucky to visit when I did.

I arrived in the ravaged city of Tripoli, with plumes of smoke billowing from all angles and bullet holes peppering almost every building. If I had to count on one hand the amount of buildings I saw with the entire side façade blown off revealing the exposed stories, I would have run out of fingers within five minutes of leaving the airport.

The majority of the population here were against Gaddafi's undemocratic and eccentric rule, which had produced years of questionable foreign deal making. His seemingly limited popularity was illustrated by my guide taking every opportunity to point out as many burnt out formerly opulent presidential buildings as possible. This was a country in a deep transition, where no one seemed to grasp what the rules were at this point. For example, my guide met me on the plane (yes, we got to the gate and he just strolled up to my seat and picked me out, no questions asked). Walking though immigration, the officer was casually smoking in his little glass box, as were passengers while they walked through the metal detectors.

In the city, it seemed to be the done thing to deface any statue or former tribute to Gaddafi. The amount of graffiti I saw with the message, "Down with Gaddafi," seemed endless. Tripoli was truly a city on the brink when I visited, but it looked like the young population were intent on making Libya work. My experience there was incredible, and the solidarity of the people made me feel relatively safe, despite smoldering wrecked buildings across the city. But it is rare to witness the rebirth of a country after the toppling of such a longstanding ruler.

During this particular trip, my doses of island paradise and "downtime" came in the brief form of hopping off the mainland continent to Cape Verde, São Tome and Principe and Equatorial Guinea: all stunning island paradises. The untouched beaches in São Tome particularly, seemed endless, and the majority of the time, you might not see another person all day on some of the more secluded beaches. This former Portuguese colony was just a quick plane ride from the ginormous coastal land mass of Angola and to Gabon to the North.

After sunning myself on these island escapes, it was, forgive the clichéd term; "back to Africa." Overland distances are much larger than they appear on any regular Western designed maps here, and my attempt to travel from Gabon to Luanda in Angola was futile. Progress over the dirt tracks was less than insignificant. I took a regular local minibus as far as I could toward Angola in a back wrenching drive where I had to sit on a child's plastic chair at the back of the bus. The chair kept flying into the air and smashing back onto the bus floor every time the suspension-absent bus dropped into another crevice in the road. My misery was compounded as we broke down, not once, but three times. These guys that had put on this basic bus service seemed to be some super mechanics. With calm regularity, they hopped out, unloaded the tool kit, and we would be on our way after some makeshift modifications. However, it seems they may have been more than just mechanics and bus drivers. They wore bandanas and vests and had faces with more scars than a botched plastic surgery job.

As we passed through a town to make yet another cargo pick-up/drop-off, an argument ensued between one of the drivers and a group of men banging on the side of the bus. The driver was pulled from the bus by a group of locals who proceeded to beat him on the ground with their shoes. The entire bus was screaming, peering out of the windows, yet no one attempted to help. As I had learnt by this time, as the odd one out in any unfamiliar place, you do as the locals do. And that was nothing in this particular instance. What had this driver done? Was it to do with carrying what was likely some form of contraband as his cargo? The regularity of "cargo stops" would certainly suggest that this was more than possible. But, after witnessing him scramble away from the bus and ensuing aggressive mob through an alley, the other driver simply strapped himself into the driver's seat and off we sped. Quickly. Like absolutely nothing had happened. Everything about this situation seemed wrong. At that point, I made a decision to get off the bus at the next town and find my way back to civilization in Gabon, choosing to fly to Angola instead. I will never know what happened with that bus or the guys that ran the route, but what I can vouch for is you certainly get what you pay for. At remote bus stations, you will generally have a bunch of cowboys offering a slightly cheaper fare or a quicker departure. If you can, stick to the main bus company. As you will remember, this isn't the first time I made this mistake. Remember Cambodia? It seemed as though a few years on, as despite my own advice to myself, sometimes in the heat of the moment, I rarely learnt.

After purchasing a flight ticket, my first impression on flying into Luanda, Angola, was one of extreme inequality. This was different to many other cities in this region. An oil rich country that housed large corporations in glitzy skyscrapers in a very confined central area, surrounded on all sides by slums, for as far as the eye could see. My time in Angola largely served to recuperate for the finale of this particular trip, and what was a fairly intense finale at that—the Congos.

CHAPTER 23
The Congos

Two separate countries, Republic of Congo and the Democratic Republic of Congo (D.R.C.) that house the two closest capital cities in Africa, Kinshasa and Brazzaville. It's just a short boat hop between the two. These countries, particularly the D.R.C., are absolutely huge, and rich in largely inaccessible natural resources buried deep in swathes of jungle. This inaccessibility has led to extreme inequality and years upon years of violent civil wars. Was my safety questionable here? Absolutely. You hear some horror stories about kidnappings and guerrillas, particularly toward the eastern jungles of the D.R.C.

However, the worst experience I had in Congo was having a group of locals throw bottles and bread rolls at me when I refused their quite blunt requests (or demands) for one dollar. Many of the children here would just randomly come up to me and say, "Give me one dollar, mister." Despite the striking poverty, I felt handing out money was counterproductive as it would then be expected as an easy option for these kids in the future. If any kind of hard working service was provided, I was always willing to hand over money. The sad truth is that child labor here is a way of life, and education is lacking.

By the time I got to Brazzaville, I had spent months alone speaking next to no English, and a bizarre situation arose when at a bar in the city one night. I had a strange encounter with a lady who kept following me, asking me to "make love" to her, and to be honest, the attention and ability to have a conversation in English was incredibly refreshing, but conversation was all that I was looking for. As I mentioned earlier, I had broken up with my girlfriend just before departing on this trip and, despite the loneliness, there was no dilemma in this situation for me. A rather public breakdown ensued as this lady wailed loudly at the bar, "He doesn't want to make love to me." At that point, I thought this may be some kind of elaborate set-up as this all seemed very farfetched and over the top considering we had been speaking for only a matter of minutes, so I was quick to remove myself from the situation.

We parted ways, and I headed almost immediately onto a cargo barge that traveled between the two capital cities. This contraption seemed indescribably unsafe, with literally hundreds of people hanging off the sides as we ambled our way across the river. I had made friends with the chief of police while leaving Brazzaville, and he assured me that he had contacted his equivalent on the other side, in Kinshasa, meaning that my transfer between countries would be relatively painless. Now, I tended to take these types of exaggerated claims with a pinch of salt, but alas, as the floating so-called boat neared the muddy embankment, where passengers scrambled off and waded through the waters, there was a small entourage of machine gun wielding troops with a Land Rover that plucked me off the boat, and whisked me into the city, no demands, no more questions asked. This was fantastic!

I had a desire to explore the eastern beauty of the D.R.C., just a plane hop away. We landed on nothing more than a grass landing strip in the middle of the jungle. The absolute must-do highlights are the lava lake at the Mount Nyiragongo volcano, which was truly spectacular, and trekking through the mountain gorilla habitats to get as close as possible to these wild primates. Safety was, and still remains an issue in the Congo, but this is a spectacular country full of incredible nature. What an end to my time in Africa, but not for long. The rarely trodden paths of West and Central Africa were now firmly behind me, and what an adventure it had been. I felt as though I was now able to travel anywhere after overcoming some incredibly adverse situations and this section of the trip had certainly been one of the most challenging. I met almost no travelers excluding a group of backpackers in Ghana and the odd handful of people on some form of business trips, so planning my return to East and Southern Africa almost felt like a walk in the park so to speak. There would be like minded travelers and a greater abundance of "on the path" tourist attractions to see. So a few weeks of planning and I would return to the well-trodden part of this mammoth continent.

CHAPTER 24
East Africa

It is safe to say that I had fallen in love with Africa. Sure, not in the same way that I fell in love with South America for example, but there was just something so indescribable about this continent. When I returned home, it was already time to plan my return trip to explore East and Southern Africa.

Nairobi, Kenya was my new starting point. A fairly cosmopolitan city that has wooed travelers for decades for the lure of the Maasai Mara and the so-called big five animals on safari. Safaris are not cheap here, so doing several in one trip seemed slightly excessive. Instead, I chose to get my main fix of wildlife in the Serengeti, Tanzania. Not, however, until exploring some fantastic activities in Kenya such as having breakfast with giraffes just north of Nairobi in the Ngong Hills. As with everything around here, this was mighty expensive, but where else can you say greedy giraffes popped their head through the windows to munch on your morning meal?!

This proved to be a taster of what was to come in terms of wildlife, and my trip through the Serengeti was filled with phenomenal sightings of lions, elephants, giraffes and rhinos, to mention just a few. When it came to viewing elephants and hippopotamus in particular, I would actually say that my visit to Chobe National Park in Botswana provided an incredible and marginally better safari as this was mostly conducted as a water safari, on a little inflatable dingy. We were able to quietly creep through the marshes, giving an uninterrupted view, getting up close to these beasts in the wild, but allowing them peace in their habitat.

Don't be fooled into thinking that Kenya and Tanzania are the only places to do safaris in Africa. Despite being probably the best places to see all the famous wildlife in one place, and allowing a plethora of options like camping in deluxe tents under the midnight sky while sipping on whiskey, there were certainly other options.

After a couple of days of looking on in awe at some amazing wild creatures and hearing unusual Tanzanian rap music (called bongo flava) blaring out at night, it was time to explore more of this beautiful country. From Arusha to Mount Kilimanjaro, the options seem almost endless. I opted to travel to Dar es Salaam, and take the ferry to the island paradise of Zanzibar.

What a mistake that was.

Not Zanzibar, that was fantastic, I mean the ferry. These boats regularly capsize, sometimes killing not dozens but hundreds at a time on this stretch of rough sea. The ride was turbulent, to say the least. I'm certainly no shipping expert, but that boat should not have been sailing in those conditions. I didn't make the same mistake on the return journey. Despite being slightly more expensive, a tiny six-seat propeller airplane was the best way back to the mainland it seemed, and also provided some fantastic aerial views.

I am unlikely to be the biggest fan of Zanzibar. Overcrowding and certain obvious dangers diminished its island paradise status, but Zanzibar can really be anything you want it to be. Aside from relaxing on the pristine beaches, I explored as much of the Arab heritage as possible in Stone Town, when the sun was absent behind the clouds. Prison Island, which, as you might guess, houses old prison ruins, was a great trip to make on a little boat. The island has been taken over by giant tortoises mooching around, so many that you have to be diligent to not step on them around every corner. And the spices. Oh, the spices. Some of the markets are so pungent, it feels like you have been teleported to the Middle East.

This is certainly a must-see destination, but I was eager to get back to the mainland, and Rwanda was next on the agenda. What a sobering feeling this was. Staying at the real life "Hotel Rwanda," popularized in the Hollywood blockbuster depicting the mass genocide in this tiny nation. The contrast between the friendly citizens of this nation and the pain that was so visible in many peoples' eyes from such a recent tragedy was truly hard to fathom. Sitting poolside, sipping a coffee at the Hôtel des Mille Collines (as it is actually known), compounded a compelling image of what this place was like and the events that unfolded here. It seemed tasteless to bring this up with locals, to get their story of the exploits, as it was so recent and came between so many friends and family. This picturesque hotel seemed like the perfect place to base myself to explore the neighboring nations of Burundi and Uganda, while transiting on top of the roof of a bus no less.

Uganda is the largest country, both economically and physically, of the three landlocked nations that were dwarfed by neighboring behemoths, the D.R.C. and Kenya. Uganda has been highly publicized, not only positively for the ability to trek with mountain gorillas (which I found was much cheaper in neighboring Congo), but also in a negative light for its unforgiving laws on homosexuality. Uganda had a strange dynamic that was hard for me to pinpoint. Apart from spending some time around Lake Victoria, I was mostly in the capital city, Kampala, and boy can they drink a lot there. Uganda is a fairly underdeveloped country, and alcohol consumption is quite simply off the charts. Worst part of my stop through there— being fed deep fried grasshoppers.

From one of the great lakes of Africa, to another—Lake Malawi.

CHAPTER 25
Southern Africa

I had a school friend, Richard, who grew up in Malawi, so it was somewhere I had heard a lot about. It is a relatively simple nation, where agriculture plays an important role. I distinctly remember being able to purchase Carlsberg beer here for almost nothing, as there is a Carlsberg brewery in Malawi. I believe when I visited, this was the first Carlsberg brewery to be built outside of Denmark, but the important piece of information was that the beer was flowing, freely, cheaply and almost everywhere!

Taking a bus through Malawi meant being squeezed in with goats and squawking chickens, for me at least, and I finally made it to Zambia on my second attempt, after some random mystery illness struck me and left me bed bound for a few days on my first attempt. I was lucky it had taken this long to be affected by illness in Africa. Despite having some fantastic national parks in Zambia, after a quick stop through the capital Lusaka, I had one place I wanted to get to—Livingstone.

I used Livingstone as a base to explore Victoria Falls and to venture into Zimbabwe. This town was named after the legendary explorer and, with strong colonial routes, one of the highlights in town was to have a traditional British afternoon tea at the incredibly well kept Royal Livingstone Hotel. As I sat there sipping tea and eating scones with a couple of German friends I had made while traveling, giraffes would stroll right by the terrace that was perched above the Zambezi River. Watching the sunset here was an incredibly mellow and reflective experience after an action packed day of witnessing the thundering Victoria Falls from as many photogenic angles as possible. Rules and regulations are, as you might imagine, not as strict as they may be in, say, Niagara Falls. If you exercise common sense, it can reward you with a more up-close experience. The most enthralling activity that I did here was Devil's Pool—possibly the world's ultimate infinity pool! The Zambezi River thunders over the lip of the falls just meters away, and you can sit there and get possibly the most daring pictures of your life. After exploring the falls on the Zambian side, I hopped over into Zimbabwe.

This once wealthy nation has had its fair share of socio-economic problems in recent decades, most notably the hyper-inflation of 200 million per cent in 2008. The souvenirs that I certainly cherish most from here are the bank notes that are no longer used as official currency, but that you can buy almost everywhere as a historical reminder of the economic plight that continual printing of money caused. Notes reached denominations as high as 100 trillion dollars, when the billion dollar notes were worthless. That is a bank note with 14 zeros on, imagine that many zeros was still barely enough to buy a meal! I managed to get my hands on some of these, and was told a story by the woman who sold them, that she had a basket full of money stolen during hyper-inflation. "There were stacks of it," she said. "Hundreds and hundreds of individual notes, and the thieves left them all, all the notes they chucked out, and just stole the basket, the money was that worthless at the time."

Novelties and waterfalls aside, Zimbabwe is a country with huge potential, illustrated by having one of the highest literacy rates in Africa, yet plagued with such a low life expectancy due to AIDs. My travel took me swiftly through Zimbabwe and on to South Africa, but I will certainly return.

South Africa, what to say. Catch this country at the best of times, it will blow you away, but see the wrong side of it, and it will leave a sour taste. This divergence can perhaps best be summarized both between and within Johannesburg and Cape Town. Two incredibly different cities with grotesque amounts of inequality in both.

Cape Town is a stunningly picturesque city, which, quite rightly, lays its claim to one of the most beautiful cities in the world, under the shadow of the famous Table Mountain. Similar to the heavyweights of Sugar Loaf Mountain bearing down on Copacabana Beach and Venice's setting around the canals, Cape Town challenges these cities with its unique location. However, as I quickly discovered, Cape Town has a dark history. Similar to other cities in South Africa, Cape Town's human demographics were altered irrevocably in the 1970s during apartheid and, although the physical setting of the old city center may not have changed drastically since, the story on the ground is distinctly different, and that is clearly visible today. District Six was particularly telling. Here, I witnessed vast swathes of unoccupied land that more than 60,000 people had been forced to vacate due to the color of their skin. There are still many starker illustrations of "non-white areas" across the city, a sobering reminder of the apartheid policies that damaged this country. So, while I was enjoying a brew (as the local phrase goes), on one of the many rooftop and balcony bars on Long Street, it was worth remembering that there is more to this city than the palm tree-lined Victoria Road, which is dubbed the St. Tropez of the south.

Before leaving Cape Town, I had to take a trip to the stunning Cape Winelands. Similar to Napa and Sonoma in California, the landscape changes drastically as you leave the nearby city, and enter a day of wine tasting in a beautiful setting. The wine was great, and the visit seemed all too brief as I hopped over to neighboring Namibia.

The distances in Namibia are incredibly vast, and I greatly underestimated the travel times, particularly by road, when looking at a regular map. This country is huge, make no mistake about it. This former German colony still maintains much of its German architecture and heritage, although that's less so in the sleepy capital of Windhoek, where I briefly passed through. Much of the bygone German occupation can be absorbed in the very popular tourist town of Swakopmund. Granted, eating bratwurst in a German-looking town in Africa seemed fairly bizarre, but the novelty of this town and its prime location along the Skeleton Coast makes it a must-see destination.

The coastline of northern Namibia is referred to as the Skeleton Coast because of a book by John Henry Marsh who wrote about the shipwreck of the Dunedin Star here. Some of the world's largest sand dunes roll all the way to the ocean here, where little vegetation grows, emphasizing how barren the environment is, and shipwrecks are still visible near the coastline today. I would say the Skeleton Coast is a perfect nickname for this stretch of coast.

A short drive from Swakopmund put me in the similarly difficult to pronounce Sossusvlei and its sand dunes. These are best seen by kicking up an unnecessary amount of sand and going wild in a dune buggy. Soon after the ringing in my ears of dune buggy engines had abated and gas fumes had cleared, I made a quick stop by Walvis Bay to see the thousands of pink flamingos that have inundated the bay, and then I headed back to South Africa.

I flew into Bloemfontein for the sole reason of catching a minibus to the country of Lesotho. It was all going so well, crammed into the back of this vehicle, while pungent thick black smoke filled our lungs from the incessant burning of something unknown in the fields for miles upon miles. Unfortunately, this cut price budget minibus with its reckless driver had windows that could not be closed, so as we traveled, I longingly stared out of the window watching the spectacle of orange flames lighting up the dark sky wondering when it would end. The answer was: abruptly. Or should I say, it became less relevant when our completely incompetent driver crashed the bus. But, of course, he carried on. It was only into a metal barrier, and the bumper was just hanging off and scraping the ground, but we were late, so why stop right? If this sounds sarcastic, it's because it's meant to be. Cue that sense of humor in Africa. Cue that patience you have to dig deep for too.

We eventually rolled up to the capital of Lesotho late at night in a banged up wreck, and things weren't about to get any better for me. Stupidly, I had done very little research about Maseru as I hadn't expected to be arriving so late at night. As a result, I was forced to do something I hate. I had to ask for advice on where to stay from the taxi driver at the bus station.

More often than not you're going to be ripped off and sent to low quality, overpriced accommodation, yet, on this occasion, although it was low quality it was not overpriced –

it was free! He took me to a church. This was not some type of modern hipster converted church, this was an actual church that played gospel songs on repeat throughout the night from TVs spread throughout the attached Christian center. I was given candles as the only light to navigate the rather eerie complex. Although I was extremely grateful for a roof over my head, this wouldn't have been my chosen place to rest, in barracks style accommodation that housed row after row of empty bunk beds. Lesotho is one of a handful of countries that is landlocked and entirely surrounded by a single nation, and the similarly unique country of Swaziland was my next stop, wedged between South Africa and Mozambique.

I must admit, I found very little to do in Lesotho, and although the very welcoming Swaziland provided more pastimes for the intrepid traveler, this was still only a stop worthy of a few days. My journey to Swaziland took me through the urban sprawl of Johannesburg, often touted as one of the most dangerous cities in the world. Although I got used to looking behind my back constantly, I wasn't the victim of any nasty incidents here, in a city that seems to have improved its safety drastically over the last few years. There are, of course, still visible signs of the everyday dangers in Johannesburg, illustrated by my taxi drivers rarely stopping at red lights in a city where carjacking is all too common, and the constant sight of electric fences and armed response teams throughout the city.

But, as most travelers will attest, this is a city which occupies little time on the majority of peoples' travel itineraries.

I made a quick stop at the sobering Apartheid Museum, but remember this city especially for the abundance of mega casinos, such as the spectacular Montecasino, which wouldn't look out of place in Las Vegas. Nonetheless, a brisk trip through Joburg took me to Mbabane, the capital of the small nation of Swaziland. In a country that holds such proximity to the well-known Kruger National Park, you would expect similar wildlife across the plains of Swaziland, and alas this country was full of smaller private game reserves. I had game reserve fatigue at this point on my Africa excursion and didn't explore the reserves in Swaziland. I was, however, impressed by the amount of trips on offer. Instead, I visited what was touted as a local version of Australia's Uluru

Sibebe Rock is an exposed dome shaped rock that was a good day's trip outside of Mbabane. I topped this off with a visit to the Mantenga Cultural Village, where you can watch traditional dances and explore what life is like in a Swazi hut. This felt like the closest I had come to witnessing traditional African tribes like you might imagine them historically or if you had never been to Africa before, and the friendly, welcoming people of Swaziland were certainly this tiny nation's greatest asset.

A short drive from Swaziland took me to Maputo, the capital of neighboring Mozambique. Similar to the strikingly unique architecture and culture of Namibia, which still retains much of its original German heritage, Maputo felt immensely like stepping into a former relic of its old Portuguese colonizer. There were occasions in these types of well-preserved cities where I had to pinch myself (metaphorically, of course) to remind myself I was still in Africa. The Portuguese heritage was most notable in the old fort where much of the original architecture remains.

Mozambique is a huge country, occupying vast amounts of the East African coast, and there are simply too many idyllic beaches to explore in one lifetime, let alone one visit. So, I only traveled to Inhaca Island, but goodness the white beaches were pristine here; a far cry from the hustle and bustle of the markets in Maputo.

From one expansive country to another, and my very last country in Africa—Madagascar. The only feasible entry point remains the highly unpronounceable capital, Antananarivo, referred to by locals as just Tana.

For such a huge country that has so much to offer to anyone that even vaguely appreciates wildlife and nature, this must be one of the most relatively unappealing and soulless capital cities in Africa. Mud track roads filled huge parts of the outskirts, and the atmosphere upon arriving at the bus station in Tana, seemed detached from the rather pleasant nations of East and Southern Africa. It was as though I had stepped back to some of the more undesirable locations on the continent. I was mobbed by aggressive touts trying to force anything and everything they could on me. There was dog shit all over the streets here, the same streets that house the many street children in Tana.

Poverty is rife in a nation that has become so well known for its natural beauty throughout, yet the issue of poverty has clearly been largely sidestepped by the authorities in Madagascar. Getting even basic tasks done here is a chore. The car that took me outside the city to visit the crocodile farm (they are ginormous in this part of the world) was also peculiar in that it had a hole on the floor where my legs were meant to be. For anyone who has ever seen The Flintstones, you can imagine why this is amusing, but it certainly wasn't at the time as I had to ride along with my legs hoisted on the dashboard. However, this did little to distract me from the stripy tailed lemurs that are unique to Madagascar at lemur park. Then, I discovered that Madagascan ariary is not a convertible currency, so imagine my annoyance when walking out of Madagascar with some of this currency that was essentially completely worthless once off the island, money that could have better been used buying food and water for Tana's many street kids.

With my visit to Madagascar, I had completed the mighty African continent. All 54 nations visited and what an adventure it had been. I had come out of this profound continent in one piece and with the complex feeling of loving and hating the many aspects of this land mass that make it so unique. I can't help but have a special place in my heart for Africa. It was incredibly difficult at times, both mentally and physically draining. There were times when I wanted to turn back and throw in the towel, and I think if you can travel around Africa for months at a time, then you can travel anywhere. Unlike other continents such as South America or South East Asia, my stories from Africa were certainly much less entertaining, and I have many fewer shared memories with people that I still keep in touch with today, but it was more of a journey. Lonely at times, yes. Self-reflective, absolutely. But I felt as though I had achieved a personal feat. Africa is often the most ill-conceived continent, with Western media portraying a barren and almost forgotten landscape at times. Granted, there were certainly areas that remain hugely underdeveloped and where there needs to be significant assistance in providing basic means, but this is a fully functioning and working continent where the people laugh, cry and interact just as many other diverse destinations around the world. If you ever have the chance to go to Africa, I would highly recommend it. There are dangers for sure, but then that can be said of anywhere and everywhere to a certain extent. Africa can be everything you want it to be, and couple that with some beautiful landscapes and exuberant people, you will almost certainly want to return.

CHAPTER 26
Turkey and South Asia

By this time, I was starting to think that traveling to every country in the world would be attainable. I even began to research the possibility of becoming the youngest person to do so. Now I never wanted to let the achievement of a record get in the way of actually seeing and experiencing countries, but there were always going to be some smaller and potentially more dangerous countries that were visited to simply "tick a box", yet these remained just a handful of the 196 countries in the world. It was never something I envisaged or originally set out to do when I first backpacked around Southeast Asia with Jack and Chris. But now, this very realistic possibility would mean "filling in the gaps," visiting countries I had missed. Some countries would be very remote, such as those in the South Pacific, but my journey there would take me through Asia, with the first stop on my agenda being Istanbul, Turkey.

I have very fond memories of Istanbul, from the infamous and stunningly beautiful Hagia Sophia and Blue Mosque opposite, which provided me some fantastic photo opportunities, to the contrasting life and smells of the Grand Bazaar. I found Turkish people to be incredibly passionate, and they will not let their opinion be unheard. Always willing to engage in conversation too, I found.

Istanbul is an inconceivable mix of cultures, religions and people, most notably in Beyoglu. After roaming the intricate streets of the city, and stripping off at a hammam (traditional Turkish bath), it was time to descend on the raving heartbeat of nightlife. The streets here are lined with bars as far as the eye can see, and thumping music plays from watering holes offering numerous drinks deals to the unsuspecting passerby, but trust me, in Turkey you will be clearly notified about and types of goods and services that are being offered for sale, in varying forms of forwardness.

Anyway, one drink here turned into five and, as a plume of sheesha smoke encompassed the table I was at with a bunch of Australian backpackers, the rather unintelligent (but humorous idea) of blowing condoms up over our heads was proposed by our Turkish drinking peers. This adolescent activity appears ridiculous to onlookers, but it was jovial fun, until one condom burst when one of the guys blew up it over his own head, making an incredibly loud bang. Not only was he seemingly dealing with the pain of this, but several police officers told us to leave immediately. They had been watching this immature condom balloon competition develop for a while and had had enough.

After Turkey, it was from the liberal to the well, not so liberal, and a visit to Pakistan dawned.

My trip through Karachi was brief, as Pakistan was. It remained a dangerous country at the time, especially for pale Westerners. On landing in Karachi at midnight, I was already told I "would be kidnapped" as I left the airport by a group of rather sketchy looking gentlemen. What a welcome this was! Petty crime is arguably more limited here than other cities, but what makes Karachi so incredibly dangerous is the high number of attempted kidnappings, if media reports are to be believed. As I spent more time here, the amount of suspicious stares directed toward me only seemed to increase.

Another danger I encountered was the traffic. Twice I had someone smash into the back and side of the taxi I was in, and both parties continued as if nothing had occurred. To try and take my mind off what seemed like imminent annihilation from a truck or the car flipping over in Karachi traffic, I tried to engage in various conversations while driving around. Just don't mention the disputed ownership of Kashmir here. This is a topic of much controversy, as I found out the hard way. It's not a subject that Pakistanis like to discuss with foreigners. My options were limited as a solo traveler in Pakistan, but this is a country I certainly want to return to in the future, however it seems that this is a nation where you need to know a local to really gain a full insight to the underbelly of Pakistan.

Nearby Bangladesh, my next destination, posed little improvement in terms of being stared at. There are next to no flights between the regional neighboring powerhouses of Pakistan and India, so I took a convoluted route. I have fond memories of a very rustic horse and cart trip around Dhaka to tour the capital of Bangladesh. Granted, there are limited tourist sights here, but the best experience I had was watching a cricket match in the capital. Cricket is a beloved sport in Bangladesh, and the incredible and passionate atmosphere was truly an episode to cherish. I found that Bangladeshis rarely showed their emotions, but if you want to see that side come out, then go and watch the home crowd erupt when a six is hit during a cricket match! I was mobbed by the surrounding Bangladeshi fans as soon as wickets fell, and this felt like being at a rock concert at times. As long as I was supporting their team, I was welcomed as their friend, which was a pretty cool way to integrate with the locals.

It was time to escape the madness of the large populaces of South Asia, and my next destination Bhutan would provide perhaps the greatest contrast between nearby countries I had experienced to date. But a trip through Nepal beckoned beforehand.

Kathmandu had an amazing vibe, with so many travelers using the city as a base to scale the Himalayas and the mighty Mount Everest. The excitement was electric as evenings passed in the capital where you would hear stories from climbers and Porters alike while sharing a whiskey about adventures to Everest Base Camp. I, unfortunately, had to settle for watching beautiful sunrises over the towering distant Himalayas on the horizon, but Base Camp is at the top of my remaining travel wish list. Away from the Himalayas, the culture of this country was a fantastic appetizer for Bhutan, with intricate temples and fantastically colorful squares. An entire spectrum of colors blew regularly from sheets in the wind wherever you walked, which are referred to as prayer flags to bless the surrounding landscape in Nepal, and similarly in Bhutan, which defined colorful from a multi-faceted perspective. Nepal was an incredibly friendly country and as I sat on my final night enjoying a beer with a guy called John, we both seemed envious of each other in different ways. The following morning he would head to Everest Base camp, and I would head to one of the most peaceful countries on Earth.

Welcome to "the happiest nation on Earth"—Bhutan. This tiny landlocked Himalayan nation, also called "the land of the thunder dragon" due the incredible thunderstorms that occur here, particularly at night as the winds whip off the mountains and through the valley. This country adopted a gross national happiness index, as opposed to the traditional gross domestic product index. This incredibly peaceful Buddhist nation was closed to tourists until the 1970s, and only recently has the quota on tourists per annum been lifted. That was still in place when I visited. There was also a complete ban on TV and internet until the early 2000s. It really did feel like stepping back in time to another era.

After arranging my visa through the government, and a breathtaking flight weaving through the mountains, I was met at the airport by a beaming monk who would be my guide. I can honestly say that this place had truly found national peace, and I have rarely felt as relaxed as I did here. Bed times were early, with little life after 8 P.M., even in the capital Thimphu. I woke up on a Sunday to find that, in yet another quirky twist, this was pedestrian day in the city, with not a car in sight.

Smoking is banned in Bhutan, yet, bringing cigarettes into the country largely goes unchecked. My experience was that my guide and his friends were more than willing to ask for cigarettes, which made quite a sight—huddling behind buildings with everyone dressed in bright orange sneaking a cigarette. It felt like being back at school and hiding from the teachers. The scenery here was incredible, with the absolute highlight being a trek up to the Tiger's Nest Monastery. The weather in Bhutan is volatile and, with little notice, biting winds made the two-hour trek up a pathway strewn with dislodged rocks ever more difficult. However, passing ever brightening and colorful prayer flags and rattling wheels made the hike fairly special, and reaching the summit of the monastery felt like an achievement, rewarding me with fantastic views of the valley below. What a phenomenal way to watch a final sunset on my time in Bhutan.

The mellow pace came and went, as one of the most populous and hectic countries beckoned. Namaste, India.

I had traveled through Mumbai before, and I have taken several trips back to Delhi and the surrounding area of Agra since I first stepped foot in India in 2008. India has an incredible pulse that rarely abates. On my first visit to India, I was instantly struck by both the pace and the hurried nature of people here. There are very few rules when it comes to getting everyday stuff done, and usually a bit of extra money can expedite almost any process. But when it comes to personal space—well, this is something that you can't buy in India. I found that everyone here pushes and shoves to get where they need to be, and forming lines is literally a foreign concept. From the very young to the very old, everyone ensures they achieve their objective regardless of you being there or not. This was something that I found both infuriating and invigorating, and I actually missed this after I left India to a certain extent. If there is a 20-person bus, you can sure expect they will try to fit 30 people in there. And if you don't fight for your space and move up to make more room, that room will be filled by someone else.

However, what wouldn't I miss? The smog and the excruciating summer heat. Boy can it get hot here in summer, and the air quality is so heavy that you almost feel the pollution in every breath. But hey, where else can you see a Bentley Continental rolling past a man riding atop an elephant in the street?

Several times I have traveled to Agra, seeing the beautiful red fort and the main tourist attraction of the magnificent Taj Mahal. That never seems to get any less spectacular.

There are, as with many things in India, two ways of getting to the Taj Mahal—the easy way and the hard way. If you find a guide who is looking to save on even the smallest of costs, the toll road will be avoided and you'll find yourself meandering through mud and pot holes for four hours on the long way round, as I found out the hard way. The very real back pain dissipates as soon as you enter the magnificent grounds of the Taj Mahal, and you are never short of a fantastic photo opportunity here. I could not stop taking photos all day, except for when I entered the hot, sticky and, quite frankly, pungently sweaty mausoleum. I was desperate to get outside and breathe the smog of Agra again! Especially around the tourist sights, people rarely just want to engage in casual conversation with you, most of the time to sell you something. Products you never thought you needed. Attempts to sell a lighter as you light a cigarette or to offer a shoe shine service for flip-flops. The possibilities seemed endless, and the hard working spirit cannot be knocked. I observed a similar mentality when I visited India's pearl-drop shaped island neighbor, Sri Lanka.

Sri Lanka is becoming an increasingly popular vacation destination and, although I enjoyed my visit here, I wasn't blown away by the country. There are some stunningly beautiful beaches and beautifully tranquil rice fields rolling up mountains for as far as the eye can see, but I failed to fall in love with Sri Lanka quite like so many do. I wanted to get out of the capital Colombo to experience more of Sri Lanka. Despite having some great restaurants and trendy bars in Colombo, like the much-enjoyed pub at the Galle Face Hotel (where I made a complete fool of myself during karaoke night), I made my way to Kandy and Galle as well as some remote but worthwhile national parks. Galle Fort is steeped in history and is picturesque at sunset, as is a trek up to Sigiriya.

The trek was relatively simple, and this stands out as the highlight in Sri Lanka. A standalone rock protruding from flat ground gave me a feeling of accomplishment on reaching the summit. You will sweat a lot as you reach the top of this mammoth rock when the weather is hot and dry, so this called for a dip with the elephants afterward at Pinnawala elephant orphanage. This place is great, and they really seemed to take care of their elephants, allowing a decent amount of human interaction. After hiking and playing with baby elephants, it was time to take myself "off the grid," and a short flight took me to the Maldives with my wife.

This country is unique. The resorts are situated on their own spits of sand and coral and are pure unadulterated luxury. It has to be enjoyed for what it is. Are you going to indulge in excessive amounts of culture here? Unlikely, unless you explore the very congested capital, Male, which doesn't seem to have a spec of sand undeveloped. You have to accept the Maldives for it is and what it has become to really enjoy it. We opted for an all-inclusive package at a hotel called Kurumba, which not only saved on the extortionate seaplane flight to farther and more peaceful hotels, as it only required a speedboat ride to get there, but has since become one of my favorite hotels in the world. Lying on hammocks with your own stretch of beach right outside individual beach huts, outdoor bathtubs and an all-inclusive package that allowed for drinks out of coconuts day after day. The food here is varied and spectacular, with diverse options that even allow you to sit out on a dock around a teppanyaki grill while the chef prepares your food.

I can genuinely say I have never felt so relaxed as I was on this little island, which meant the other Indian Ocean paradise islands of Mauritius and the Seychelles had an awful lot to live up to. Granted, there were more activities and island tours in Mauritius and the Seychelles, and the ocean remained a dazzling turquoise spectrum, but the prices are also extortionate, and I found that money did not go very far, although obviously, that largely depends on the accommodation. As for food options, there is some delicious local creole cuisine to try in the Seychelles and Mauritius but the Indian Ocean paradise island that stole my passion (for being as lazy as possible) was undoubtedly the Maldives.

Before long, a return to the mainland continent dawned, and my next stop was Myanmar (or Burma to some). I wouldn't claim to be an expert on politics in Myanmar, but there have certainly been well publicized disagreements hindering the country's political progress on the global stage in recent years, with civil unrest being a common occurrence. However, the overwhelming feeling I got on my travels through Myanmar was that of a country rapidly on the rise again, with the incredibly popular Aung San Suu Kyi, one of the world's most famous ex-political prisoners, having a hugely positive influence over the development of the country.

Probably the greatest danger tourists now face in Myanmar is that of temple exhaustion. There are so many temples to see, but the jackpot for me by far was the Shwedagon Pagoda. I had to take my shoes off, as all visitors do, and explore this stunning complex barefoot on incredible intricately crafted marble floors. This posed a fairly amusing sight for onlooking monks as they witnessed me hotfooting it around the pagodas running to find the next piece of marble that was covered in shadow on a day that was close to 40 degrees Celsius—and there weren't very many places of shadow. However, somehow the incredible centerpiece of the gold leaf covered pagoda was such a luminous sight in the bright sunshine above Yangon that I regularly forgot about the impending foot pain. My eclectic travel routes seemed to yo-yo between manic metropolises and peaceful serenity, and my onwards travel to the huge, vast and barren country of Mongolia did not break that pattern.

Mongolia is huge, and unforgiving. To explore Mongolia and the remote Gobi Desert, would arguably be best done by applying for the Mongol Rally, but even during my visit to Ulaanbaatar, the incredibly harsh environment became visibly evident. Summers are hot and winters are bitterly cold, but the howling wind that rarely appeared to abate through the streets of Ulaanbaatar seemed to aggressively combine with the other harsh elements to crack roads and buildings. I found that power cuts were excessively regular in Mongolia. I experienced no less than eight power cuts on a single day (maybe this was just a particularly troublesome day). And there really didn't seem like an awful lot to do here.

However, what was evident as I had traveled northwards from Myanmar, was that there were increasing Chinese influences as I edged ever closer to China. Soon, it was time to explore the Far East, and what better place to start than China.

CHAPTER 27
East Asia

My first visit to mainland China was to Beijing during a bitterly cold winter. This was a huge mistake. I was very badly prepared for just how much the temperature drops here, and this made for fairly unhappy trekking of the Great Wall of China in nothing more than a sweater. I visited the Great Wall with the blasé attitude that "it's just a wall," but what a breathtaking surprise the views were. The wall winds through the hills for as far as the eye can see, and I thought it was incredibly preserved in the areas I visited. I even went on a slide down the Great Wall, which was unique if not a little tame.

China was quite simply incredible. I saw things there that both dazzled and confused me at the same time. Some aspects were so detached from how I have lived my life in the West that they were so mind-boggling. Japan had that too, where you simply have to observe and respect it. For example, getting picked up by a makeshift taxi in Beijing; it was a minuscule fridge on the back of a scooter that lead to more questions than answers. I had to actually sit inside the fridge which I could barely squeeze myself inside. What an introduction this was to the oddities of Beijing, but I found that embracing this perceived strangeness led to a much more rewarding experience.

Away from the must-see tourist sights of the Forbidden City and Tiananmen Square, a trip to a street market will certainly need that "why not?" attitude. Live scorpions on a stick you say? Sure, I'll try a bite. Fried cockroaches? Yeah, I'll try that one too, reluctantly. However, donkey penis? That's where I drew the line. No thank you. Then came the awkward moment where the old lady selling these delicacies started shouting: "Hey, mister." (Everyone, everywhere here referred to me as "Hey, mister.") "Hey, mister, try some, try it." She waddled after me through the market with a donkey penis in her hand. This was slightly awkward. Beyond this, and the masochistic chopping off of chickens heads off right in front of me as I walked through the market (as if this was meant to appeal to me), the food in China was incredible, and the Peking duck was abundant and mouth-watering.

China may not be the ideal destination for animal lovers, but it certainly is for tea lovers. In among the few cons, such as being told the hotel opposite the Birds Nest, the spectacularly lit Olympic park, was a seven-star hotel "like in Dubai" (It was nothing more than a good five-star hotel in my opinion), you really can get to see the everyday side of China and its hardworking people. A trip through the traditional hutongs on a bicycle seemed very authentic to me; stopping off for traditional tea as soon as you can no longer feel your fingers from the biting January cold or maybe need a toilet break. Ah yes, the toilets. Mostly fine in China, but there are certainly some strange ones, where there are no doors or partitions at all, and occasionally large signs on the walls saying "no pooping" that have ironically been smeared in feces.

As I traveled on through China, the strange and bizarre scenes I witnessed could actually be commercialized. I'm referring to Taiwan and its strange obsession for themed restaurants, not least the toilet themed restaurant where patrons eat out of actual recycled toilet bowls, but you know where to go if you're looking for a shit restaurant (pun intended).

However, themed restaurants don't stop there. Cue a visit to a sex themed restaurant in Taipei where they serve rice in the shapes of penises and breasts (for example). Sitting eating my meal was, to me at least, awkward, yet both men and women sat there munching away like this was perfectly normal. The oddities continued. Imagine my surprise at discovering animated news. Yes, that's right, there is actually animated news in Taiwan, and if you want a good introduction I would suggest finding the clip of the animated events of what could have happened after Tiger Woods's extra-marital affair allegations were revealed (it was so damn ridiculous, they actually had his wife chasing him with a golf club).

Aside from the borderline insane, I found that Taiwanese people are seemingly terrified of the rain. Once the rain starts they will find anything to cover themselves and run around to point of almost getting run over by a car to find any type of shelter. That aside, Taipei is a modern, innovative and pulsating city, home to Taipei 101, once the world's tallest skyscrapers. This building was built to withstand even the strongest typhoons that regularly hit Taiwan, and a visit to the enormous pendulum that allows the building to sway from side to side during extreme winds made me feel like a child again, it was incredible. The last thing I will say about Taiwan is don't go to the hot springs unless you're willing to get naked. There is a certain stigma to not stripping naked in the hot springs. Everyone does it, young and old, so be prepared to be naked (I was instructed through hand signals to strip naked by a lady who must have been at least 80, which was embarrassing).

Next up was the tiny former Portuguese colony of Macau, just a short ferry ride from Hong Kong. The Ruins of St. Paul's is a far cry from the towering modern casinos in this Chinese gambling mecca. Visually, I would call it a mini Las Vegas, as there are certainly a lot of similar casinos here, such as The Venetian, but actually Macau now pulls in six times more gambling revenue than Las Vegas, which would have been inconceivable 20 years ago. Gambling aside, this city is a ghost town in the morning, until about midday. Most people come here purely to gamble, and are generally uninterested in other activities. That means they miss out on the world's highest bungee jump from A.J. Hackett at the Macau Tower. A gut wrenching 233 meter drop awaited me as I got to the top, and I am not ashamed to say I had second thoughts about even my second thoughts up here. The weather was pretty dire when I did my bungee jump. As my feet neared the edge, I could barely see the ground below. For anyone who has bungee jumped or skydived, you'll know it is such an unnatural human reaction to want to throw yourself off a building the first time, so, without warning, the Australian instructor pushed me, which was probably hilarious for his colleagues especially as I was screaming, "No, no, no" on the way down. That was a terrifying seven second free-fall where I thought I would die, but, as some of you may also know, after you have done it once, you want to race back to the top to jump again.

Away from the gambling mecca and to a mega-city, where night markets are more popular than day markets and double story trolley cars ply the streets in an effort to carry the transport some of this city's dense population—welcome to Hong Kong.

My mum had talked fondly of Hong Kong ever since I was a kid, as she grew up there with my grandmother and grandfather. She always talked about how she lived in Kowloon and was able to "almost touch the wheels of the planes landing" at the now redundant Kai Tak Airport, which would have been quite an experience.

I was very fond of Hong Kong during the couple of times I visited the city. Where else can you take an old junk boat on the harbor while drinking yourself drunk watching fireworks over the skyscraper-infested Hong Kong Island, take a cable car up to one of the largest Buddha statues in the world, visit a beautiful beach in Repulse Bay, and finish the day by drinking beer at Happy Valley Racecourse with expats? The diversity in this city is incredible

And it seems rooftop bars are the done thing here. Whether it is internationally acclaimed bars or a more makeshift drinking spot, so often I witnessed people drinking after work on office roofs 50 stories high. Although Hong Kong was not categorized as one of the 196 sovereign nations, as a major city and part of China, it was always going to be somewhere I longed to visit.

I later returned to Beijing to catch my flight on the world's only one-star airline, Air Koryo, into the incredibly closed off nation of North Korea.

North Korea is especially unforgiving of political traitors, and there are unconfirmed reports of Kim Jong-Un's uncle being killed by anti-aircraft artillery guns and eaten by a pack of dogs and of his political opponents being executed by flame-throwers. One thing was for sure, from boarding the plane to the capital, Pyongyang (where we were made to watch propaganda videos of the great leaders of North Korea on repeat) to the moment I left North Korea, the whole escapade felt like a show, put on by the government. After having a guy in China sort my visa and entry to North Korea, I was forcibly placed in the Yanggakdo International Hotel, as all other tourists were, and given two tour guides who stayed with me at all times. There were two guides not just to watch me, but to watch each other, to prevent any kinds of unwanted reactions or potential free speech, for which they could potentially be punished. My initial thoughts were that the hotel was fairly full, but all the tourists seemed to be crammed onto one floor to give the impression of occupancy.

I spent lonely nights gazing out of the window at the near pitch black city below yet, unsurprisingly, the power never went out in the hotel, as the North Korean regime kept up the pretense of wealth and happiness. Yanggakdo Hotel is on its own island in the city, and getting off the island is impossible, mainly because at least one of my tour guides was always on lookout duty in the lobby. However, on one occasion, when I meandered down to the lobby, I was able to stroll outside the hotel uncontested. However, as I approached the bridge, I was forcefully warned by guards to return. So much for my self-exploration of Pyongyang.

Day broke, and the propaganda show must go on. I was provided large, tasteless meals in grandiose restaurants that had music blaring, and I was the only customer. In a nation of food shortages, I could not turn my nose up at the food on offer, but it was truly revolting. If you're looking to lose weight, going to North Korea is probably the best diet program anyone could do.

Because of the severity of the regime here, it was difficult to refuse anything that was offered or to practice free speech. Cue a rather demeaning experience where I was made to get down on my knees and drink what was essentially muddy puddle water from a well at King Jong-Il's childhood home. Now, supposedly he came from a very poor background, but this didn't prevent the authorities from installing a full service Robert Bosch cooker as an illustration in his childhood home, which was also surrounded by acres of parkland as a tribute to the great leader. You would be forgiven for thinking that the façade of North Korea is not questioned by its people, but in a country where women seem to adore their supreme leader, and men want to be him, even as far as getting the same haircut as Kim Jong-Un, I wanted to ask whether this is simply popular opinion. However, I quickly found that although the guides were willing to engage in "off-piste conversations," if you ask the wrong question, they will simply change the subject or avoid the question altogether. This was not just a nation solely dedicated to the adoration of the leader's family, despite ginormous pictures and statues of the Kim Jong family dotted all across the capital. North Korea has mass games too, which is quite an immense display, with over 200,000 people crammed into one stadium for one of the greatest spectacles on Earth. There are over 100,000 performers and the ceremony is a great demonstration of teamwork on a grandiose scale varying from ballet to gymnastics presentations.

The subway in Pyongyang is also spectacular, comparable to the Moscow subway, with beautifully crafted stations. This was a tourist attraction in itself. The people of North Korea are very similar to those of the south, they have just been instructed what to believe in for so many years. Outrageous stories, such as their great leader inventing the hamburger, or making a round of golf almost entirely of holes in one.

The South was never far away and, after a quick stop through the university where outdated boombox stereos blasted to absolutely no one in the music department, it was off to the demilitarized zone. The D.M.Z. is one of the most troop-heavy locations in the world, and the sense is that if war was to ever break out, this area would see the bulk of the initial fighting. After several days of barely edible food and condescending lectures on the "American pigs," I was having insane thoughts about running across the 10-meter open border at the D.M.Z., where troops from North and South face each other 24 hours a day. I even briefly attained a phone signal at the D.M.Z., and the prospect of essential freedom in the South (despite the 100% probability of being shot on the spot) sent my mind into a tailspin.

I had already visited South Korea, and this technology and whiskey-obsessed nation was extremely suave. There is still aggressive propaganda in the South, but this is certainly a free country, with fantastically friendly people. South Korea also had its fair share of quirky activities, similar to Taiwan, such as when I took part in a silent disco near Gyeongbok, which actually turned out to be no more than walking with headphones through parks, but it was a unique experience nonetheless.

My dreams of returning to the South aside, it was time to be lectured (again) on the reunification of the North and the South. I don't claim to be an expert on this subject, but on repeated questioning of the matter, I had had enough and said to a certain soldier who was interrogating me that I didn't think reunification would happen, purely because the economies and social practices of the two countries had become so diverse. This was the wrong answer it seemed. This guy was accompanied by another guard, and as I attempted to leave the D.M.Z. with my guides, they were forced to hand over my passport details. When I asked my chaperons why they were giving the troops my passport number, they claimed they didn't, as denial is so often the default reaction here. But on pressing the issue, my guides claimed that sometimes, when foreigners make a good impression with the authorities, they want to know their details. This, I knew was utter bullshit. It compounded the web of lies that seems to be the foundation of information in this country. I had, of course, heard stories about likely false accusations of spying and journalism and of tourists attempting to leave North Korea, and by this point I was eager to get out of the country. Alas, when it rains, flights rarely depart from here for some bizarre reason. And it was raining. Of course.

After spending hours waiting at the airport, showing my guides pictures on my laptop from around the world, I managed to make it out of the most enclosed nation in the world, and I felt a huge sense of relief. This was certainly a once in a lifetime experience, but I can safely say that unless the situation here changes dramatically, I will be in no rush to return. After writing this, I would probably be arrested on return, anyway.

From one very unique country to another—Japan. Not too dissimilar to Taiwan, in that things can get slightly weird here. Fantastic food (if you like sushi), and green tea kit-kats aside, this is a country obsessed with the unusual, from "love hotels," which have a vast array of themed rooms, as I found out when curiously asking to look at one (I was shown the S&M room) to vending machines that sell just about anything from underwear to sex toys.

Tokyo is quite simply electric and after getting over the oddities of seeing people quite literally stick their fingers up people's assholes in a jovial game supposedly called "kancho", the bustling nightlife around the famous Shibuya crossing was the perfect welcome to this gigantic city. If you want to get taxis around, beware of how expensive they are! A trip from Narita airport will set you back $250, but you could always save money by exchanging a hotel room for one of the many simple sleeping pods they have in this country.

My wife was brave enough to try more daring foods here, like horse-meat sashimi, which I just couldn't fathom. But if you're feeling hungry after visiting the sights of the Tokyo Tower or taking a day trip on the world famous bullet train to see the perfectly snowcapped peak of Mount Fuji, then stop at the robot restaurant. Contrary to what you might think, this restaurant does not have robots serving you food, but in fact bikini-clad women having battles with robots, which was rather strange to witness. But in a country where people slide around bathtubs naked as a competition, and rather oddly gigantic blow up dolls straddle the train tracks for the train to go through its legs, all in the name of art, very little surprised me in Japan. I love the Far East, and despite the great diversities between countries here, I was always going to have a very warm place in my heart for this region after my very first adventure with Chris and Jack. I am certainly not finished with exploring this part of the world, and countries like Japan and China have such an array of regions to explore, that despite having visited every country, I have only just scratched the surface in some of these cultural behemoths in Asia.

CHAPTER 28
Southeast Asia

A flight south took me to a much more conservative nation—Singapore. But this place still has a wild side. Clarke Quay is a raving bar scene where I hopped around some fantastic places. My favorites here were varied, from the shot bar, with hundreds of different mixed shots, the hot wing roulette bar (cue me sipping milk like a baby after eating the super-hot wings), to the hospital themed bar. The Hospital Bar was unique, but morbidly designed, with wheelchairs and old hospital beds and a drinks menu with shots from syringes complementing longer drinks served via a drip. With such a large expat scene, drinking and socializing are big in Singapore, with rooftop bars, such as that at the top of the Marina Bay Sands hotel, with its infinity pool perched over the Singapore skyline being the highlight for me. However, once the boozy brunches at the Fairmont were out of the way, Elena and I explored Singapore, and we were rarely sober there. We had drunken trips to Universal Studios followed by afternoon tea at the Raffles

Hotel and then a very unique night safari at the zoo, making up the agenda for a fantastically small city.

However, drinking is expensive in Singapore and, after significantly overspending at the stock market bar where, in my drunken state, I kept excessively buying the same drink that sent the price up (which was the objective, yet in a sober state I would have realized that this was only negatively affecting myself), we attempted to find slightly cheaper drinking spots in the city, with little luck. We thought watching cricket in some local bars by the canal would provide more economical drinking opportunities but, to our surprise, it just seemed as though everything, everywhere, is fairly expensive here. So topping off the trip with a visit to the luminously lit sky gardens, we made our way to Singapore's more reasonably priced neighbor, Malaysia.

Kuala Lumpur also has a popular rooftop pool bar scene, and there were many to choose from that provide gorgeous views of the Petronas Twin Towers that are so symbolic of this city's skyline. But, after some great food and shopping in Petaling Street, I found the real gems in Malaysia to be outside of the city. Petaling Street is one of my favorite markets in the world, and the imitation brands here are of such high quality it makes you wonder if they may in fact be real. Upon asking the stall owners to see the higher quality goods, I got taken to a back room, and when I asked for the best quality goods, a secret door behind a shelf was opened up and I was taken upstairs. This didn't seem legitimate, but the market on the whole was like nothing I have seen.

We then, once I had filled my stomach with caramelized BBQ pork, left the city, and an initial stop at the magnificent Batu Caves beckoned. There are a lot of steps to get into the cave, but this is a must-do, especially for those who like aggressive monkeys! We found friendlier monkeys at the aptly named Monkey Mountain, although Elena won't say that after getting bitten by one. Warning: they love the mini bananas here and will do anything, including biting through your finger, to get to them. After stopping at the wildlife park where clumsy deer jump on you for parsnips, elephants eat whole melons from your hand, and a massive sun bear licks honey off you, nightfall descended, and in Selangor, that means the fireflies come out to play. We took a little wooden boat down the river after sunset to see entire banks of the river flashing with fireflies in a dazzling array of nature at its finest. This remained my favorite sight in this country.

Nearby Malaysia lie the tiny nations of Brunei and East Timor. What to do in Brunei? Not very much. Aside from seeing the pristine Sultan of Brunei Mosque, this tiny nation offered little, as did East Timor, despite having parts of the country untouched by humankind and some gorgeous beaches.

I quickly made my way to nearby Indonesia. After a brief stop through the heaving heavyweight city of Jakarta, it was a complete contrast to visit the Gili Islands, where there are no cars. None at all. Riding bicycles around in the tropical rain became a nostalgic memory I now look back on with great fondness, but the destination that really enticed me was Bali. Quite simply paradise, and it was understandable why this has become a top destination for travelers. Bali is another hugely contrasting Island with rice fields and hills in the center of the island flanked by world class beaches with some fantastic bars and restaurants. Many a great night was spent at Ku De Ta with my wife, and even some failed attempts to clamor through the wire fence at nearby Potato Head Beach Club during a private party.

Bali has something to cater to all budgets, from the backpacker booming party town of Kuta to the independent boutique stores of upmarket Seminyak. To be honest, I found the atmosphere slightly strange in Kuta, as huge amounts of drinks deals were washed down with thumping music in the background of a structurally questionable six-story bar that overlooked the Bali bombing memorial below. Quite sobering.

Bali did not let the terrorist attacks dampen the tourist industry, and has continued to develop and pioneer. You used to be able to bungee jump into a swimming pool when I last visited, and we had lots of fun at this bar. Tanah Lot temple is possibly the greatest cultural sticking point, with visitors coming from far and wide to walk across the shallow water to reach this incredible temple built on a tiny rock in the sea. Sunsets here are truly fantastic.

Bali is great, and I would go back there in a heartbeat, although Seminyak was the one and only place I was mugged while on my travels. I was walking down the street with Elena and some bastard grabbed one of my arms and, simultaneously, a guy with a hook on motorbike scooped and grabbed our bag from my other arm, speeding off with it. To be honest, the police were less than helpful, and despite this incident leaving a sour taste on departing Indonesia, looking back, this did little to dampen my love of this country.

Indonesia's nearby scattered island neighbor, the Philippines, was my next destination.

Similar to Indonesia, the Philippines has a huge population and, combined with technological developments, it is on an exceptionally strong growth path. There is so much to see in this vast country, and despite the noticeable presence of security guards with guns almost everywhere, particularly in the capital, Manila, I seldom felt threatened here. After spending a couple of days in Manila, seeing the San Agustin Church (where it seemed entire packs of stray cats wanted us to adopt them) and watching magnificent sunsets from the popular Sofitel on the coast (which by the way, does one of the best dinner buffets I have ever enjoyed—lobsters, caviar, foie gras—all on offer and delivered to your table), it was time to see more of the Philippines.

The one constant while traveling through this country was the incredibly colorful jeepneys. These are small buses that serve the country and every single one seems to be custom designed and ever more colorful (or brighter and louder, even). Luckily, jeepneys can't get onto the beautiful beaches of Boracay, or through the unique Chocolate Hills of Bohol. These hills were quite some sight: perfect cone shapes with a hint of chocolate color for as far as the eye can see. Also, the best thing about coming to see the hills is the abundance of marmosets. These adorable little things look slightly evil at first, but their cute and massive eyes make them one of the more unique and lovable creatures I have had the pleasure of getting up close to.

By this time, I had traveled to the majority of countries in Asia, I only had Russia and the former Soviet republics to visit on this continent. Despite being geographically located on the same continent, this brought an end to the distinct culture across the Far East. There is rarely a shortage of tourists here, but there is also rarely a shortage of new and incredible places to discover. I have travelled this region with friends, family and my wife, not to mention being a fantastic place to converse with the many expats and travelers crisscrossing around the Far East. No matter how many times I return, even whether briefly stopping through, I always get a certain amount of excitement travelling to Asia. Unique, friendly people, great food, and a region steeped in cultural and religious history. What more could you want?

CHAPTER 29
Russia and the Former Soviet Republics

I had traveled to Russia a few years before, but I began to see a very different side of the country when I stopped seeing it as a tourist and rather as a part of my wife Elena's heritage. Elena was born in Moscow, and I began to make increasingly regular trips there to see my now extended family.

The Russian Orthodox calendar is slightly different from the Christian calendar. Their Christmas is over what is traditionally my New Year, which meant I traveled to Moscow every New Year to celebrate. I have grown incredibly fond of celebrating the New Year in Moscow, gathered around a big family table with frequent vodka toasts to the old year, the New Year, and just about anything that will allow for another dose of vodka. The atmosphere is electric as crowds gather in Red Square, beside the red bricked Kremlin, to drink and watch fireworks no matter how hard the snow is pouring. This is a great time of year to visit. The winter sky allows for the city to be lit up beautifully from the iconic Saint Basil's Cathedral to the incredibly dazzling GUM department store that flanks Red

Square. I much prefer the warmer temperatures of summer, however, when there is Moscow Day and the parade of tanks and missiles through the streets in a demonstration of military might that is quite the spectacle.

Summer also allows for better exploration of the city by foot, very different from winter when I ran for shelter into the quite magnificently beautiful Metro or in the warmth of the Moscow State Circus. If you want to see the original circus with boxing kangaroos and brown bears doing tricks while flanked by spinning witches, then head here.

This is a true 24-hour city and, after spending a fortune at some of the city's vantage point bars, like the 02 Lounge or White Rabbit, where a beer may require remortgaging your house, you can still grab some of the best and reasonably priced sushi and caviar at all hours in Moscow. The grandiose and brightly lit Stalin towers that surround the city are one of the many symbols of Moscow, and are a mere part of the multitude of buildings that adorn this huge city.

In neighboring Turkmenistan, the story was much the same with regard to flamboyant architecture, but with one major difference. Where are the people? Huge government buildings populate the capital of Ashgabat in what is described as a showpiece capital. Pristine white marble megastructures inhabit a city that was seemingly designed to show off but don't actually provide any sense of a living population. The wide boulevards give little to no shade on scorching summer days, but that didn't seem a problem as it appeared anyone in a car driving past would have happily given me a ride if I'd stuck my arm out. The countless police officers were quick to tell me which buildings I wasn't allowed to photograph, and indeed the police seem to greatly outnumber citizens in this part of the former Soviet republic that is still so reminiscent of the Soviet era. Turkmenbashi declared himself president for life, and there is still a plethora of monuments across the city that pay homage to him.

This is a far cry from Turkmenistan's northerly neighbor, Kazakhstan. Kazakhstan's oil rich and young population seems to have become one of the nations that is more detached from the former U.S.S.R., attempting to carve out its own destiny. An extensive range of incredibly expensive cars ply the streets of Almaty where the stifling summer heat brings out waves of young Kazakhs to frolic in the parks and eat fruit cups along the pedestrianized streets filled with musicians. The brightly painted yellow Zenkov Cathedral is the iconic symbol of this city, but it is unquestionably the outgoing people who convey the best image of Kazakhstan.

Contrastingly, nearby Tajikistan remains a relic of the U.S.S.R., and many of the people that I spoke to there wanted to see a return to communism as they used to be heavily supported and subsidized by Moscow. The food in Tajikistan was a mix between Turkish and Persian. But, in a country still prone to food shortages, the quality of meat was not great. There was not an awful lot to see in Tajikistan beyond the spectacular mountain scenery on the border posts with Uzbekistan.

As I mentioned earlier, I had previously rushed out of Uzbekistan after essentially being robbed of my money when I left Afghanistan, so I was certainly in no mood to enjoy the mountain scenery at the Uzbek-Tajik border, where further attempts of extortion were made by border police. The funny thing about this situation was that I had nothing left to give. I remember very sarcastically waving my bank card at them saying unless they had an A.T.M. in the hills, I had nothing. I was almost beaten at this point and, after hours of painful and pointless discussion, I was allowed to pass into Tajikistan, where I made my way to Dushanbe.

Exhausted and completely fed up, I found a place to stay, but this wasn't your usual hostel. After leaving my bag to take a stroll around the city and get some food, I returned to find a topless and rather large hairy man banging his head against the wall continuously, shouting to himself in Russian. Great. Absolutely fantastic. Exhausted, robbed, fairly demoralized, and now I was sharing a room with a maniac. I had almost reached the end of my tether, so put use to my emergency budget and went to stay at the Grand Hyatt in what felt like the best bed I had ever laid my head. It was just a shame that it was only for around six hours and came at a cost of mostly eating rice during my next trip to Kyrgyzstan.

I flew into the capital of Kyrgyzstan, Bishkek, to find yet another city embedded with Soviet architecture. Wide open boulevards, such as Chuy Prospekti, that have parades and demonstrations of exuberant nationalism give this country a distinctly Soviet feel. It seemed like Kazakhstan was the only outlier in the group of C.I.S. countries that had carved a different path away from the past. Capitalism was rife in Kazakhstan, whereas the other groups of countries seemed to long for a return to communism, as I discovered from conversations with as many locals as possible. Despite feeling like one of the safer cities in the region there was a distinct Soviet feel in Kyrgyzstan, which was most prominent in Ala-Too Square where Kyrgyz music blared from crackling speakers that felt like brainwashing propaganda.

Despite this, I tried to embrace it, and what better place to people watch than in the Kvartira café, which seemed a unique

Soviet relic to me, yet probably no different to any other café to the locals. I also took a trip out to the old city airport. To no great surprise, especially in this part of the world, the old terminal complex had been converted into yet another government building. However, the remainder of the overgrown and decaying airport was open to explore; an incredible experience. With the vegetation-infested tarmac and graffiti-covered buildings in front of me, I stopped to think for a second, and it dawned on me that I had now traveled to every country in Asia. A simply formidable continent with such a diversity of people, from Turkey all the way to Japan. Where do the borders of Asia start and end? This is a topic of much debate but, however you dissect this continent, I absolutely love so many things about it.

But now it was time to explore the remaining parts of the continent I call home—Europe.

CHAPTER 30
U.K., Ireland, Nordics and the Baltics

I had traveled to different parts of Europe while growing up. Other than the large amounts of time I've been traveling, I have spent my whole life living in the United Kingdom. London is home to me and it is a fantastic location to explore cities and destinations in Europe, both at short notice and over shorter periods of time. The massive expansion of low-cost airlines, in Europe particularly, has made traveling relatively inexpensive and opened up significantly more destinations for viable weekend excursions.

Unfortunately, I will never see London as a tourist. Friends from all over the world fall in love with this city, with its profound cosmopolitan nature and its incredibly rich history and deep rooted British cultural element that seems central to the thematic approach of the main tourist sites. I have, in fact, never been inside some of the main attractions in London, such as the Tower of London, and I have never watched the changing of the guard at Buckingham Palace. Sometimes the tourist sites in the place you call home escape you.

Away from the bustling metropolis, is another city in the U.K. that features regularly on any tour of the British Isles— Edinburgh in Scotland. This part of the U.K., that also seems to be intent on becoming the 197th country, is also very special to me. My grandfather is from Scotland, and I have family in and around Edinburgh who I used to visit as a child.

When I started university, I made many more regular trips up to Scotland as some of my best friends went to university there. I went to see my good friend, Mike, in Edinburgh, and I remember ending up in the casino at an ungodly hour and spending several hundred pounds of winnings at the Hard Rock Café on Princes Street the following day, through buying lunch for everyone. I also regularly visited another friend, Gij, in the beautiful university town of St. Andrews, which holds claim to being the birthplace of golf. Yes, deep fried mars bars exist here, and, yes, they do get eaten all too regularly too, but they are delicious.

Just off the coast of my home nation, lies the Emerald Isle, better known as Ireland. The Guinness factory in Dublin is a must-see destination, and usually there are plenty of free samples lying around as some tourists can't handle their first sips of stout, I certainly wasn't a fan of my first sip when I was younger at the Guinness Factory. The atmosphere in this city is electric in the evenings, particularly around Temple Bar, where live music disperses down the lively streets from almost every watering hole. Guinness, whiskey, you name it, the Irish can certainly drink, and I'm sure any Irish person would agree. These guys know how to have a great time, a good craic as the Irish say. I was actually in Temple bar on valentines night, and despite the prices seeming to double, the fun I had singing songs on the top of the bar with strangers was symbolic of the friendly atmosphere here.

One of my very first trips to Europe as a young boy was to visit the opening of the original Legoland in Denmark. I remember taking the night ferry to Copenhagen. It must have taken close to 20 hours at the time, and the conditions were extremely choppy. To be honest, that actually put me off traveling when I was younger, and under no circumstances did I want to take night boats in rough conditions. Little did I know how my mind would change as I grew up, when I wanted to explore the world and ended up on questionable boats in much more severe conditions much farther from home.

I returned to Copenhagen a few years later, and it was my gateway to Scandinavia. There were of course the main sights, such as the Royal Palace, the beautiful Tivoli Gardens and the iconic little mermaid statue (that I did well to see among the swathes of tourists crowding around for photos). However, the unique side to Denmark doesn't just come in the form of a strange penchant for pickled herring (which I despise), and electric-techno basement nightclubs which are unusually popular across Scandinavia, but in the form of the autonomous self-declared Freetown Christiania.

Let's be clear, this small patch of land in Copenhagen is strange. The area looks largely run down, with disused car seats and whatever scraps have been salvaged being bunched together to create makeshift "whatevers" in an area that probably has more graffiti than anywhere else (although some of the graffiti was very creative). The inhabitants will interact with almost anyone here in an autonomous region that has created its own currency and flag, and where weed is readily available. The constant smell of weed and the fact that the majority of residents seemed to be stoned slightly detracted from Christiania's credibility to become its own country, in my opinion. I personally do not see this autonomous area breaking away from Denmark anytime soon.

Close to Denmark is Norway, and I took a trip to Oslo with my sister. What was funny (in a masochistic sense) was that, when we visited Oslo, there were some low-cost airlines involved in a price war on the route from London, and so we got our tickets for just one euro each. It was the cheapest flight I have ever and likely will ever take. Those types of super discount fares seem to be fading away. However, the irony was that this was the cheapest flight to likely one of the most expensive cities I have visited. We heard a naïve group of guys behind us boarding the flight, who had apparently also picked up the super cheap tickets, joking about how they had very little money on them but would figure out a cheap place to stay when they arrived in Oslo. Considering that even the bus from the airport costed about 25 times more than the flight, they would have got a nasty surprise, and may well have found that place to stay on the airport floor.

Not dissimilar to Denmark, there are unique aspects of Norway relative to mainland Europe, as there are in all Scandinavian countries. Norway obviously has a Viking heritage, but the double horned hats and grandiose ponytails that are somewhat of a novelty to us now, are still an unusual cultural aspect for a country that is now so detached from that way of life. Don't be surprised if you see groups of locals wearing these as fancy dress for a night out on the town, but I guess this wouldn't be out of place as fancy dress anywhere, they can just pull it off better in Norway.

Mind the gap with the Norwegian krone! Once we started to run low on the prized and mightily expensive currency, we put our last few notes to use by visiting a movie theater in Oslo. This seemed to be where most teenagers would hang out on cool autumn days, but this place was an experience in itself. Not only can it lay claim to being my most costly movie theater visit ever but it was an incredible waste of money. The volume was turned down to such low levels that even the most audibly capable animals would struggle to hear the movie, yet this seemed to be part of the "experience" where giggling, laughing and non-stop talking was the main soundtrack. Therefore, the movie theaters in Oslo have these security guards at the front who intermittently and all too regularly let out loud "ssssshhh" noises. Very bizarre.

Among my traveling around Scandinavia, I visited the Northerly island of Iceland. There is so much to do in this country that is awash with natural beauty and, despite its name, it's generally more green than it is covered in large swathes of ice. Although I never explored the geysers and volcanoes of Iceland in great depth, I did have time to see the number one attraction, which was the quite unique and magnificent Blue Lagoon. This geothermal spa was beautifully lit, demonstrating the gorgeous sparkling blue waters with steam arising. It made for a great photo shoot!

Nearby is the capital, Reykjavik, where it's possible to take a tour of the Icelandic landmark church, Hallgrímskirkja with its unique spike shape that is also claimed to be the tallest building in the city. Although it doesn't get fully dark here over the long summers, the flip side of that coin means that there is barely any sunlight during the long and cold winters, which supposedly statistically leads to increased depression here.

Next stop was Sweden, which is similar to Norway in many ways, yet seems to have developed into a trendier destination with the advent of hugely popular, pioneering global brands such as Ikea and Volvo. The famous Swedish meatball is abundant here, in a country that still adores one of its most famous exports, ABBA. The women are attractive, with many having the stereotypical Swedish feature of long blonde hair.

The capital Stockholm is a trendy city with a gorgeous setting on the waterfront. Why wouldn't it be for a country where 9% of its surface area is covered by lakes? I traveled to Stockholm with my Australian friend, Zach, who I met in London. Similarly to the tourists I called naïve in Oslo, we landed in Stockholm with no place to stay. After spending the day roaming the well-preserved medieval streets of Gamla stan, we spent the night hopping around the many city bars, from the quirky multi-level Spy Bar to the even quirkier Tradgarden party, which was an immense outdoor party under a bridge that had no closing time. Eventually, the night had to end, although it was pretty late, and we remembered that we had no place to stay. Luckily we met some people who said there was a spare bunkbed at their hostel, so they let us in, only to be awoken by a raging angry Swedish woman hours later who was furious at the sight of us huddled in the bunk bed without checking in. If she was there when we arrived, we would have happily paid, but unfortunately she refused to let us stay there, even though we paid. After finding new accommodation, night fell on Stockholm again, and there were too many trendy bars to check out in such a short space of time, but the Ice Bar is definitely worth a visit. This bar is constructed differently and from scratch every year, using just ice. You get given big Eskimo type coats to drink out of glasses that, you guessed it, are made from ice. There are now more ice bars popping up around the world, but there's nothing like visiting the original concept in Sweden. Prices here are also leaning toward extortionate, and even in places like McDonalds, where you might expect relatively reasonable pricing, as night falls, you see the staff changing around the boards to the "late menu" which is, predictably, about double the day prices in another wallet shattering event.

Sweden's eastern neighbor, Finland poses the most similarities to Sweden, in my opinion, although Finland is not technically part of Scandinavia, contrary to popular belief. Many people here seem to constantly chew on Snus powdered tobacco during cold winters. Combine this with long nights and I saw many people sitting in bars at all hours of the day and night (it can be hard to tell the difference in deep winter so far north). Finns are a much more introvert population. People tend to drink at bars not to socialize, but in fact to drink, which I witnessed many times during my stop through Helsinki. Souvenir shops like to play on words with their capital city, and so there is a lot of tacky merchandise such as "Welcome to Hell" and "I survived HELsinki." I could go on, but I'm sure you get the drift.

Helsinki itself has a very strange mix of architecture, and the best way to get a view across the city of Senate Square and the famous Helsinki Cathedral must surely be from the Torni toilet. This unique toilet allows you to sit down in peace in your own cubicle with large paneled glass all around the toilet, that facilitates taking a number two with a view. I'm not sure if that phrase has been used or trademarked, and I actually didn't intend for it to rhyme, but maybe there is a marketing angle there. Despite enjoying Helsinki, I didn't visit Finland to spend time only in the capital but to head up to the Arctic Circle to see Santa Claus in Finnish Lapland during a bitterly cold December.

I arrived at Kittilä Airport to an airfield that was likely 10 feet deep in snow in some places. I had never experienced temperatures anywhere close to this, and by the time I reached Levi, which is 170 km north of the Arctic Circle, the temperature had dropped to as low as minus 34 degrees Celsius in the morning. It is difficult to describe just how bitterly cold it was, but walking outside first thing felt like someone had punched me hard in the lungs. It completely takes your breath away and, to be honest, although being too cold to notice the difference between minus 25 and minus 34 degrees Celsius, everything still seems to freeze over. I spent five minutes outside and my eyelashes had stuck together with ice. It looked like my hair and eyebrows had turned white and, to help you visualize, the sky was clear and there was no snowfall. The temperature was so bitterly cold that the water particles we cannot see in the air were actually freezing on objects.

Some of the activities that in the Arctic Circle were simply amazing, such as taking a husky dog sled through the woods, ice karting where the track was so slippery I slid most of the way around and riding a horse through the deep snow. As a throwback to Antigua, you know by now that I am not the most eloquent on a horse, and so I was fairly apprehensive. Luckily, this horse couldn't go very fast because of the depth of the snow, and also I didn't have very far to fall, as every step the horse took through the snow came up to my knees—while still on the horse!

The most difficult part about walking outside each morning was the fact that Finns love their saunas. Almost every house and hotel has a sauna, so the extreme differences in the temperatures I felt were quite the experience. This culminated in the most painful part of the trip, which was where I was somehow encouraged by a Finn to jump into an ice lake. Everyone strips off naked, and then, for a matter of seconds, you jump in a tiny carved out hole through the ice into the lake. Any more than a matter of seconds and you would quickly develop frostbite and pneumonia in those temperatures, but the Finns love this pastime as it's meant to be good for blood circulation.

Enough of getting into the ice covered lakes, and more of staying on top of them. A group of Sami people dressed in reindeer fur offered me reindeer meatballs (which were disgusting) then took me cross-country skiing over a lake. Let's just say, with my poor balance, lack of skiing ability, and a very sore and cold ass from continually hitting the ice, this was not the most enjoyable part of my trip.

I headed off to the Ice Hotel to warm up (ironic isn't it?), which, similar to the Ice Bar in Stockholm, is reconstructed from scratch every year and never has the same design. A few snowmobile rides later, where I was having a lot of fun jumping over barriers of snow, it was time to take an evening trek through the eerily snow drenched trees of the forest to witness the Northern Lights. The night sky was lit in greens and yellows, illuminating the forest where trees looked like giant snowflakes. For a few brief moments, I forgot about the cold and the fact that I couldn't feel my fingers or toes anymore, and enjoyed the stunning view.

Shortly after Lapland I headed back toward civilization and, from Finland, the unofficially named "booze cruise" to Estonia awaited. This ferry is full of Finns making the duty free trip to Estonia to pick up cheap alcohol, much of which has ironically come from Finland to begin with. By 8 A.M., before the ferry leaves, there was already a significant line at the bar, and by the time the boat returned to Helsinki that evening, these Finns were tumbling down staircases on the rocking boat and catastrophically populating the dance floors. This was like a party boat but, after a full day of drinking, the boat now looked more like a scene from a particularly messy party. Additionally, half the boat indulging in cocaine shots during the stop in Tallinn probably only compounded the situation we found ourselves in. Right, so these cocaine shots, let's be crystal clear to start. There is no cocaine in them, but whatever is inside these shots certainly does some strange stuff to people. It's safe to say that I saw a large proportion of the younger crowd from the boat queuing for these shots but, after quickly drinking one (or three) myself, I wanted to explore some more of this medieval city.

Tallinn is incredibly picturesque, and the medieval turrets that populate the town wall are very well preserved, as is the town hall square, which has a market most days. The medieval heritage can also be seen from the high numbers of petite restaurants that are medieval themed and some, including the one I stopped at for dinner, solely being lit by candlelight for a equanimous experience.

Estonia lies in the Baltic's, which is perhaps one of the least visited parts of Europe, but actually contains some hidden gems.

Like Estonia, Latvia has its own unusual drink called Black Balsam. This you have to try if you're here—it would be like visiting Jamaica and not drinking rum. Not only is traveling to Latvia relatively cheap compared to Western Europe, but the city itself is incredibly idyllic. Beautiful cafés line old cobbled streets in the old town which is a UNESCO World Heritage Site, where old wooden buildings blend with stone and brick for that medieval charm that is so evident in Estonia. The House of the Blackheads is the most famous building here and is a masterpiece of architecture and art. Without a doubt this is the most recognizable symbol of Latvia. I had actually traveled to the Baltics when I was about 10 years old on a trip with my school to Lithuania. Although my memories of the city of Vilnius are vague, in addition to the landscape of the city likely changing drastically since, I do distinctly remember the Museum of Genocide Victims. The sights I saw during a visit to this quite grizzly museum became engrained on me, and at quite a young age it was difficult to forget the tour there. We visited the nearby prison cells, which had padded wall chambers, and a trip to the execution room was graphic in its education to say the least. However, my most prominent memory was that of the torture chambers where we received a demonstration of a form of water torture where victims would be made to stand one footed on a small outlet over freezing cold water, until physically they would be unable.

With the Baltics being one of the least visited parts of Europe, you have the added benefit of fewer tourists, which is the unfortunate problem in my favorite country in Europe, Italy.

CHAPTER 31
Italy, Vatican City and San Marino

Overcrowding around Italy's seemingly infinite sites and attractions is nothing new, and is unlikely to ever change, such is the popularity of this famously boot-shaped Mediterranean destination. Why do I love Italy so much? I find it incomprehensible to not like this country with its rich, ancient history, incredible art, passionate people and delectable food. All this while occupying an enviable location in the Mediterranean with long hot summer days, and ski slopes in the Alps to the north during winter. I have spent extensive time traveling around Italy, yet there are still so many undiscovered places for me here.

Where better to start than in Rome? I don't need to compile a list of sights in a city bursting on every corner with things to do, see and admire. The Colosseum and the Spanish Steps with their Baroque architecture were the highlights for me along with the Trevi Fountain. It is always incredibly crowded around the Trevi Fountain, and it is almost impossible to avoid a stampede of tourists during the day there. I returned in the middle of the night to see the fountain spectacularly lit up, and virtually no one in sight. I walked up to the fountain with no crowds in my way, and flicked my coin into the trickling waters.

The nation within a city can be found in Rome. Welcome to the world's smallest country, Vatican City. If I thought crowds at the Trevi Fountain were bad, I was in for a nasty surprise when joining the line for the Sistine Chapel. It wound so far that it was going out of one country into another, such was the popularity of seeing the Michelangelo artwork on the ceiling in the Papal state. Just a few steps outside the Sistine Chapel, I crossed the non-marked, non-patrolled and, quite frankly, largely irrelevant "border" back into Italy, where another city in this country bursting at the seams with tourists is Venice.

I visited Venice for New Year some time ago with my family and, aside from the completely unique setting of this beautiful city on the canals, I have very fond memories of ringing in the New Year with friendly, exuberant and passionate Italians who popped corks from bottles of prosecco all night long in Piazza San Marco, surrounded by my mum, dad and sister. Italians certainly enjoy a party, and the atmosphere was buzzing. There were sparklers and rockets going off across the square. Health and safety? Well, it didn't seem to be of grave concern in Italy. Just relax, enjoy yourself and hopefully it'll work out all right. What a way to bring in the New Year though, with a bunch of raucous Italians. It made the crowds on the famous Rialto Bridge and motorboat traffic down the Grand Canal seem minuscule in comparison. A must-do ride on a gondola across Venice's iconic waterways later, and I made my way to Bologna with the intention of visiting Italy's second country within its borders, San Marino.

I drove from Bologna to San Marino through the picturesque Italian countryside in a classic old Italian Fiat. After a quick stop at the top of San Marino to see the Palazzo Pubblico and the changing of the guard, I made my way back to Bologna. I stayed longer in Bologna than I had originally planned as this was my biggest surprise in Italy.

Bologna is a university town, steeped in history, and it provided a welcome break from the bustle of more popular Italian cities. Bologna is not the most popular destination in Italy, but what a find this was. The food in this whole region, Emilia-Romagna, is simply incredible. You can have balsamic vinegar on almost anything here, and I even tried it on Italian gelato. It was actually surprising how great the balsamic tastes, even on sweet food. Multiple museums aside, one of the coolest things I found to do in Bologna was to visit one of the world's oldest universities and take a tour through the wooden 17th century autopsy room; a remarkable sight showing how medically advanced they were at the time. I also climbed Italy's tallest leaning tower in Bologna, the Asinelli Tower. This is a heady climb up perilously old wooden stairs, so move aside the Leaning Tower of Pisa, you are not the tallest leaning tower.

Pisa is actually a fairly dull experience, and I luckily avoided having to stay a night there. It's a small town that doesn't have the same kind of soul as many other Italian destinations and, apart from the leaning tower, which, granted, does make for some fabulous photos, seemed to have little else going for it. After getting lunch here in one of the many restaurants, I found it more rewarding to move on, unless of course you're into being sold cheap leaning tower replica key-rings and a town that largely shuts down by 9 P.M. every evening.

Next stop was Italy's fashion capital, and arguably the fashion capital of the world. I found this a fantastic city for people watching. Spend a few euros on an espresso in one of the many coffee shops around the Duomo or the stunning Galleria Vittorio Emanuele and watch the people of Milan pass you buy. The incessant buzz of all the Vespa engines provided the soundtrack. I took regular trips around the city on my Vespa while there, which was an intense and stressful experience as Italians can drive like maniacs at times. But the Vespa made it easier to navigate the sights of Milan, and it was easy to find a parking space. I actually skipped Leonardo da Vinci's incredibly famous Last Supper painting. Instead, I avoided the balmy and long lines and chose to visit his summer house. This house is quite the mesmerizing masterpiece itself, hidden in the city and set in beautiful gardens, but with a very strict visitor limit.

As the evening drew in over Milan, there was nothing quite like swapping the Vespa for a Ferrari, and there was nothing quite like rolling up to the incredibly trendy and classy Principe di Savoia and Bulgari hotels for cocktails in a Ferrari convertible, which belonged to one of my Italian friends in Milan. The crowds here are simply glamorous, and many older Italians look completely timeless; maybe it's a Mediterranean thing.

There are some spectacular restaurants in Milan. There is the gorgeous location of Il Salumaio with its lemon tree-lined courtyard setting, which lays claim to being popular with the likes of Bernie Ecclestone's daughters, and La Terrazza, where I took Elena on a fairly impromptu evening. That evening, there was an open art gallery night in the six floors of the building below, and so we were actually several hours late to dinner because we latched on to this private viewing where the jamón and Italian red wine were free.

We seemed to have good luck and timing with events in Italy. When we traveled to Tuscany on a later trip, it was June 24, the feast day of St. John the Baptist in Florence. After a day of strolling around the stunning city of Florence with the intricately designed Santa Maria del Fiore, we were lucky enough to catch the fireworks and celebrations that lit up the city in the evening. Every day, Italians sat by the river and drank out of bottles in what was an incredibly friendly atmosphere. Florence is one of my favorite places in Italy.

We stayed in a villa when we visited Tuscany, which was quite the quintessentially Italy experience in summer. Lazy days by the pool in pristine weather, coupled with trips to vineyards for Italian wine and cheese tasting in a region that is so incredibly illustrative of the Italy I love. And there are still many places to see in this country. However, I have also hopped through Sardinia and Sicily on a cruise, and despite Sicily being home to one of the world's most famous volcanoes, Mount Etna, there is very little to do in the southern islands, I found, beyond eating and drinking, but hey, when it's this good...why not?

Most of my trips to Italy have been during summer, but, along with my New Year trip to Venice, I also visited Courmayeur in the Italian Alps in winter for my first experience of skiing, with my friends Rob, Jev and Alf, and what an awful skiing experience it was. I guess the people who know me would say that if I have given up with something, or am simply disinterested in something, I can be a nightmare to talk to about it, and this was the case with skiing. I know I have awful balance, and I had almost already given up hope before I started, despite the other guys I was with hiring a great instructor to teach me. The instructor was so incredibly confident he could get me skiing, but, one hour later, my infuriated ski instructor skied off into the distance after giving up and leaving me to my own devices. This initially seemed fine to me as I defiantly returned my skis and went to enjoy some après ski time, until I realized the restaurant we were eating lunch was halfway up a red (intermediate in Europe) ski slope. You can picture me holding onto the ski lift as it dragged me up while I was still wearing my skis, and then I tried to run in ski boots, which quickly turned into me being dragged up the mountain on my face. A few bottles of red wine later, and I was stumbling back down the mountain, into what surely must be one of the more stylish ski resorts in the Alps. It is Italy after all, and the Italian Alps attract many affluent Italians who certainly know how to dress.

I have shared memories in Italy with many people close to me, and due to its proximity to London and an increasingly interconnected world, I have several friends in Italy now as well. This is a country that, so long as I live in London, I will re-visit every year.

CHAPTER 32
Spain, Andorra and Portugal

From my favorite European country to perhaps my second favorite—Spain. There is something about Mediterranean Europe that will never lessen my desire to visit. While Spain holds similarities to Italy in its proximity to the Mediterranean, the culture, history and even the food varies greatly between them.

My paternal grandfather was Spanish and my grandmother was Greek, which is likely where I get my slight Mediterranean look from, so both these countries have family ties for me.

I first visited Spain when I took a cruise from Palma when I was a teenager, and I was instantly struck by the leisurely pace on the Spanish isles, where the cobbled streets were lined with pavement cafés. Although there are some incredibly nice Spanish islands, such as Ibiza, there are also a lot of incredibly tacky areas where mostly rowdy British teenagers head to some type of alcohol-fueled rite of passage. You can almost smell the chlamydia in the morning air after a Saturday night in

Magaluf. Many of us go to these Spanish islands, offering 50 cent shots on repeat until you are lying in a pool of your own vomit, but they are not places I will likely visit again.

I had this pre-conception of non-stop partying when I visited Ibiza, but contrary to my expectations, it is a multi-faceted destination. First things first, if you want to do Ibiza "properly", it is not cheap. Sure you can head to the cheaper bars around the town, and most evenings we ended up at a relatively unimpressive bar, called Sankeys, to close the night out, however the super-clubs of Pascha and Amnesia are going to cost you. That can mean anything north of 100 euros a ticket, depending who is playing, but it's worth going for the experience.

The hotels in Ibiza have also morphed into party destinations. I have stayed at both Pikes and the Hard Rock Hotel in Ibiza, and both regularly put on pre-parties, after-parties –

you name it. Without a doubt, my favorite place to go in Ibiza remains the beach club Blue Marlin. I went there with a group of my best friends and indulged in a boozy lunch on the beach while large swordfish are carved up for the table to share over bottles of rosé so large they have to be hoisted onto the waiters' shoulders. It is a fabulous way to spend a day in the Spanish sunshine. As the sun begins to set, you leave your beach bed behind and the dancefloor opens up, meaning through a whole day you don't have to move too far. Ibiza ticks all the boxes. Just be warned, even though you will get a more pleasant crowd in Ibiza than some of the other islands, you will encounter drugs at almost every turn here. For example, when we were around the hotel pool, my friend Laurie threw a piece of pizza at me, and my retaliation was to throw him into the pool, with his drink flying everywhere. As this unfolded, the beefy looking hotel security guard's radio started buzzing as he ran over to inspect the situation, but clearly seeing us drunken idiots larking around as an opportunity, his first question when he got to the scene was to ask us, "You want weed or charlie?"

Away from the Spanish isles, my favorite destination by far in Spain has to be Madrid. Unlike Barcelona, I feel Madrid remains authentically Spanish and, away from the world famous Prado Museum and cringe-worthy Segway tours that whizz around the city (I'm ashamed to say I was one of those people once), the main attractions of this city for me have always been the food and relatively leisurely pace of life. For example: I was enjoying a coffee in the Plaza de Cibeles when a fire broke out in one of the old buildings, but Spaniards were so laid back we all just watched it burn. Fire engines? Nowhere to be seen, apparently not necessary. People moving in panic? Not at all. Everyone remained and paid no more attention than an occasional glance.

As I already mentioned, the food in Madrid is delectable whether you get it from the food stalls, the colorful Mercado de San Miguel or a gourmet experience, such as on the top floor of El Corte Ingles where you can pick and choose your meal ranging from mini wagyu burgers to macaroons. Madrid is a food lover's paradise. There are tabernas dotted everywhere across the city and jamón ibérico is available almost everywhere, even in small cafés in the parks.

No trip to Madrid would be complete without spending an evening Flamenco dancing, and as the patatas bravas and amazing chocolate con churros get washed down with Rioja, you can sit back and watch the experts demonstrate how the Flamenco should be done.

There were two things that I preferred in Spain's second city, Barcelona. Firstly, there were less beggars in Barcelona; the sad state fact is you will even get beggars at the airport in Madrid as you exit. Secondly, Barcelona is home to Gaudi's sensational modernist architecture, which is on display throughout the city, such as the intricate Gaudi buildings abundant along the Passeig de Gràcia and the Sagrada Familia, which is Gaudi's unfinished masterpiece church with incredibly detailed carvings in the famous spires. However, generally, I much prefer Madrid to its Catalan counterpart as Barcelona doesn't have quite so many of the little tabernas and tapas bars. The choice of these is almost endless in Madrid. That doesn't mean Barcelona doesn't have more to offer beyond the Camp Nou stadium, home to the world famous soccer team, Barcelona. After a tour around the behemoth stadium, it was time to enjoy Barcelona's specialty: fresh seafood along the beautiful Mediterranean coast.

La Rambla is a road that has to be seen for any newcomer to the city, but I preferred to steer well clear of the Irish bar crawls that were constantly advertised down La Rambla. These immensely annoying bar crawls romp around the city at night with mostly exchange students. I felt they detract a little from Spanish culture. Instead, I chose more niche events like immense movie screenings on a Mediterranean beach with the city glistening in the background—now that was special—but beware of the section of beach near the highly recognizable towering W hotel. If you are taking a short cut through the beach here, you will have to strip down naked as it's a nudist beach. Paradise if you are an exhibitionist though!

From Barcelona I took a quick drive through the Pyrenees to the rather obscure nation of Andorra. A heavy duty free presence and lack of income taxes provide a strange dynamic in what is a very relaxed environment in Andorra la Vella. The local population seems to spend the majority of the time relaxing in cafés.

Unless you like hiking in summer and skiing in winter, neither of which particularly appeal to me, there isn't a lot to keep you occupied in Andorra. Therefore, I planned to make my way to Spain's more prominent neighbor, Portugal. First I had to drive back to Barcelona. After being given an upgrade from the rental car company in Barcelona, I was looking forward to the beautiful drive back through the Pyrenees. Before departing, I swung by the bus stop, red bull in one hand, music blaring out of the open window. I crawled by and said, "The bus takes four hours, I made it here in two without breaking the speed limit. Anyone want a free ride back to Barcelona? I'm just looking for some company." Predictably, this was met with a lot of head shaking and refusals, but I didn't drive a car in London, so I thought I was kind of cool. Looking back at it now, I can see how I may have looked a little creepy, but alas, I drove back (alone) and continued my journey to Portugal.

I had originally traveled to Porto several years earlier and, although a nice town, there is little to do in Porto to occupy more than a couple of days. The heart and soul of Portugal, however, is in the livelier city of Lisbon, the capital. I visited with Elena. This is a small but pulsating city that has the perfect combination of fantastic tourist sites such as the Jerónimous Monastery and the UNESCO World Heritage Site of Belém Tower, a beautiful Gothic structure at the entrance to Lisbon harbor that dates back to the 1500s.

There is also a great eating and drinking scene in Lisbon. The dining options range from the sublime table service with gorgeous views over the city from the hills above to the equally glorious and casual pick and choose options, at Mercado da Ribeira, for example. Lisbon had already grown on me immensely by the time we had become highly accustomed with the bar hopping scene in the cobbled streets of Bairro Alto.

There is a very retro yellow trolley car that takes you to the very top of this hill. This was a fantastic novelty for us, but after many Sagres beers and rum, good luck finding your way back down. However, there is more to the nightlife in Lisbon than Bairro Alto, and there are many cafés to watch the city pass before you, particularly in the well-manicured Praça do Comércio. It was here that we passed a beautiful old building and upon asking what was the event inside, we were invited to take a look—it was a Hendricks gin party, and possibly the coolest thing I did in Lisbon. They had gas masks where you could inhale gin gas. They even had a hot air balloon rising inside the grand hall that you could ride on. The gin was flowing freely and random men and women in top hats and waistcoats rode unicycles around the event. It felt like the 1920s, but was illustrative of the types of quirky episodes that are commonplace in a city such as Lisbon.

CHAPTER 33
Greece, Cyprus and Malta

Greece is another of my favorite Mediterranean destinations, largely because I am also one-quarter Greek. My grandmother was from Greece, but depending on how she felt about her fellow Greek people, she would be Cypriot on any given day. Greek-Cypriots are very passionate and opinionated people, and my grandmother always vocalized her opinion. I witnessed that once when she took me to stay with my uncle in Athens for the 2004 Olympic Games. This was my very first taste of the Mediterranean, and my first impressions were not positive, as I remember. Things seemed extremely foreign to me here, riding on packed trolley cars where Athenians would be wearing vests in the scorching Greek summer heat, forcing their armpits in my face. I was not used to this in Western Europe, at least not to this extent, but I was relatively young at the time. Also, it seemed to me that the buildings were crumbling and the people were aggressive. But, by the time I left, my passionate obsession with the Mediterranean had begun and the crumbling buildings were now gorgeous through my eyes, the aggressive people were passionate, and well, everything else that may have seemed slightly undesirable at first was brushed aside to be accepted as Mediterranean culture.

Athens was a historical capital as far back as 500 B.C., and widely regarded as the birthplace of democracy around this time. This city is a history and architectural enthusiast's playground. The pedestrian zone around the key archaeological sites of Hadrian's Arch and the sacred rock of Acropolis which holds the Parthenon is especially interesting. There is nothing quite like having an al fresco meal in the height of summer overlooking the Parthenon lit up beautifully at nighttime.

We made regular refreshment stops at the iconic and magnificent Grand Bretagne Hotel in the city center that is a landmark in its own right. We then witnessed more ancient architecture at an Olympics that was a surprising success to the watching world. Old venues, such as the Panathenaic Stadium, which was used for archery, was quite an experience to observe. This historic oval shaped stadium was used for the inaugural modern Olympics as the finishing point for the marathon, the Greeks were very proud to explain. In a largely forgotten event, I saw the Iraqi soccer team progress all the way to the semi-finals. It was such a fairytale story that it seems it will be near impossible to ever replicate. The atmosphere at the quarter-final match against Australia was amazing; with almost every neutral fan supporting Iraq. It was then on to the main Olympic Stadium and, despite there being large sections of empty seating, the evening's atmosphere was electric, and this certainly carried over into the city center. Fans from across the world wore their home flags in a cape fashion across their backs in what felt like a truly global event played out in an extremely friendly setting. It felt as though I was on a global tour in a melting pot of people and culture all in one place. Perhaps this was another early memory that infused my love of travel, but how was I to know what I wanted to do at this point.

As I said, not only did my grandmother claim to be Greek, she also claimed Cypriot heritage at times. I therefore really wanted to visit the nearby island of Cyprus with an open mind, despite having negative pre-conceived ideas of what to expect. The birthplace of Aphrodite has long seduced travelers. Cyprus's idyllic beaches and strategic location have made this island an area of great interest for centuries. The food is delectable, and the people are passionate, as I was obviously already aware of from my upbringing as I would get chased around the house by my grandmother as she waved a flip-flop at me! Cypriots seem to be located almost everywhere across Europe and are certainly well travelled, so the people here will always have a story of someone they know, and the ability to establish some form of common ground with you, which was quite simply paramount for them.

However, despite all these positives, Cyprus has positioned itself to cater for mass tourism. Cheap flights and ever-cheaper alcohol has meant that hordes of tourists and stag dos descend onto the shores every year, which means, it has become nigh on impossible to find your own little piece of this island. Every year, more all-inclusive hotels spring up, and a trip to Ayia Napa was potentially the biggest mistake I made. Scantily dressed tourists wander the streets where shots of alcohol are cheaper than water in many bars, and the average age of revellers struggles to push far past 18 on certain nights. This is largely what a vacation to Cyprus has now become. Marketed as sun, sea, sex and booze, there are many more beautiful islands in the world where I would rather spend my time, even though the word Cyprus still resonates warm images for me.

I later passed through another Mediterranean island on my way to Libya. I landed in Malta during what was possibly the worst storm I have flown in. The pilot had aborted two earlier landings and the plane shook violently from side to side. Eventually, we touched down to the sight of palm trees being violently pushed to seemingly impossibly angles by the strength of the wind and ginormous waves that continually pushed up through the Grand Harbour. Even this violent storm could not dampen my joy at arriving in Malta, as I knew that these few days would be a brief touch of paradise before delving into the unrest in Libya. The very next morning I awoke to clear blue skies and sunshine. And, oh my, does the city of Valetta look divine at sunset too, with the sun reflecting off the striking red and brown brick colors that make up the majority of the buildings across the city.

Malta is often described as an open air museum, and it was easy to see why. Impeccably preserved forts, that were way beyond their time in terms of engineering prowess, enclose this city where I could not stop taking photos. I headed to Sliema seafront for the most spectacular view of Valletta and the golden bay that hugs this rugged coastline. Not only is this country beautiful, the people of Malta radiate happiness. With great weather and beautiful surroundings, wouldn't you be that happy? Combine this together with great Mediterranean food and a lively nightlife, where the Maltese love to drink on the old cobbled streets of Valetta, and you have one of the most desirable cities in the Mediterranean.

CHAPTER 34
France, Monaco and Luxembourg

From one of the most beautiful Mediterranean cities to one of the most visited Mediterranean areas—the French Riviera. Running from Cannes and Nice all the way down to the country of Monaco, it is an area that often divides opinion. Whether you love it or hate it, this area is fairly unique. It is a playground for the rich and famous, and as long as you know what to expect, you can enjoy the spectacle around you. It's not too dissimilar to a visit to Dubai, for example.

In Monaco, away from the sights of the infamous Monte Carlo Casino, the changing of the guard at the palace and the perfectly maintained fountains at the Hotel de Paris that is never short of supercars out front, this principality displays a plethora of unashamed pretentiousness and wealth. While sipping champagne, looking out at the increasingly boastful megayachts that hug the marina, you're never too far away from references to the Formula 1 street race that brings an even greater number of the rich and famous to Monaco every year. I happened to quite like visiting Monaco, but was sure not to spend too long there after overpaying for a few drinks and leaving some money in the casino. I left it behind and headed just a few miles down the road to visit France.

I had visited one of the most uninteresting places in France quite a lot as a child—the border port town of Calais. My mum used to get day trip tickets every so often, and we would go on the ferry across the English Channel, surrounded by duty free shoppers who would bring back cart loads of cheap alcohol from France. Beyond that, there was almost nothing to do in Calais. When I was older, the Eurostar rail link had been constructed and that meant journeys to Paris became a feasible option for day trips from London, with a travel time of under three hours from central London to the center of Paris.

Stepping out of the Gare du Nord doesn't inspire much confidence in one of the most visited cities in the world, but not far from this dismal area of Paris you can find some of the most iconic and beautiful sights in Europe. The Eiffel Tower is obviously one of the most recognizable structures in the world, although I wouldn't suggest taking the stairs to the top. I did this when I was younger, and I was sweating so profusely in the Parisian summer heat that I could barely grip the handrail when my legs begun to give up on me. The way the Eiffel Tower is now lit up at night is simply spectacular, and combine this insatiable view with the sights of Notre Dame cathedral and the instantly recognizable Arc du Triomphe and it becomes easy to see why so many people fall in love with the city of love.

There are quite possibly some of the best art galleries I have ever visited in my life here, but beware of the long lines, and indeed the unabating crowds around the Mona Lisa at the glass domed Louvre Gallery. The nearby Musée d'Orsay is equally as famous among art lovers and set inside a beautiful old train station, yet you avoid the unseasoned tourists who head straight for the Mona Lisa. There are often such great expectations in this city that garners grand romantic images for the intrepid traveler. Yet, because of these high expectations, Paris can sometimes disappoint. I do like Paris, but now that I have been several times, I find much greater pleasure avoiding the main tourist sights and meandering ever so slightly off the beaten path. I would avoid the Champs-Élysées, with its jam packed streets of eccentric and unrelated shops, such as the Renault and Peugeot stores that simply sell original merchandise like pens and pepper shakers but not cars.

The padlock bridge at Pont des Arts is a beautiful setting, but beware of people trying the "gold ring" trick round here. They tried it on me several times. This is where someone will bend down by your foot and give you a cheap worthless "gold" ring they will claim you dropped, but then demand money as a reward. This scam never seems to get old.

I like to spend time in the beautiful cobbled streets of Montmartre, where you can find the incredibly popular church of Sacré-Coeur, which is worth seeing. Pick out a table in one of the many sidewalk brasseries and watch Parisian (and tourist group) life pass you by, while street artists paint the bustling scene.

Further off the beaten path, the Sainte-Chapelle with its Gothic architecture and gorgeous stained glass windows that date back to the 13th century was perhaps the standout attraction in Paris for me, along with the more popular and long running Moulin Rouge cabaret show. My excitement built for the Moulin Rouge show as I saw the spinning windmill and neon lights in the city's original red light district, but just be careful not to visit during a fairly common taxi strike like I did, otherwise navigating Paris will become incredibly more tiresome at night.

From Europe's most visited countries, to one of the less visited nations—Luxembourg. Poor Luxembourg City lives in the shadow of so many great European cities, such as Paris, Brussels and Amsterdam, not to mention nearby Germany, that it often gets overlooked in tourists' itineraries. Granted, there is not much to do here, and a flying visit is all this tiny landlocked country requires. But that doesn't detract from the fact that Luxembourg is extremely beautiful.

There is an incredibly high quality of life in a city filled with the young children of bankers and E.U. workers, and this variety meant that, at any given time, you can hear multiple languages across different conversations in bars and cafés. I was lucky enough to visit Luxembourg during the national day, where spirits were high and food and drinks stalls line the streets that exude a lively atmosphere. Luxembourg Day is, to be honest, an excuse for the majority of the population here to have a bit of fun. There is a large number of people walking around with the Luxembourg flag painted on their cheeks and waving flags of celebration who are not from Luxembourg. A group of people explained, "It's just an excuse to get pissed really," before I witnessed them climb streetlights to get a view of the celebratory fireworks show. This was certainly a different perspective on some of the more passionate national holidays I had witnessed in other parts of the world, but an interesting experience nonetheless.

CHAPTER 35
The Netherlands and Belgium

Near to Luxembourg is the incredibly friendly and flamboyant nation of Holland, otherwise known as The Netherlands. Amsterdam was more or less closed for renovations when I visited, as it transformed its image to focus more on its museums, which were consequently mostly shuttered and, despite re-opening now, the concentration of visitors remains in the city's seedier underbelly. Amsterdam's red light district has become synonymous with stag dos and backpack-wielding travelers looking to get stoned. In Holland, you can smoke weed in what are referred to as "coffee shops," and they are abundant across the city. Stepping into the red light district is a tourist attraction in itself. Uncensored porn lines the majority of shop windows where impossibly large dildos and quite obscure sex dolls are the secondary merchandise, after the popular peep shows, which is like a real life vending machine. More of a naked woman is revealed as more cash is slotted in, and the strange part was that by strolling through this part of Amsterdam, I felt quite voyeuristic anyway.

Amsterdam is an experimental city with a strong Bohemian rebel vibe. With its insane population of bike riders and skaters, this is a youth paradise destination. However, this city, and indeed Holland, is not just a crazed sex show fueled by weed on steroids, there is so much more this destination has to offer.

Within the city, the cultured mind can visit the Van Gogh Museum and the equally famous Rembrandt House Museum before a sobering tour round the Anne Frank House. If you're looking for something a bit livelier after this, then check out Holland's favorite export at the Heineken Experience where they have interactive tasting rooms along the tour. But to see the real Dutch beauty, head outside the city.

A short drive took me to the Zaanse Schans windmills that are flanked by old wooden houses in the beautiful Dutch countryside. Historical engineering is one thing, but I wanted to see the modern day Dutch engineering, so I passed by the polders which is land that has been reclaimed from the sea through a quite simply ingenious feat of engineering, which results in a significant portion of the population living below sea level. After a quick stop to see and, of course, taste some particularly smelly Dutch cheese, the grandiose encore of this small but vibrant country was without a doubt the tulip fields. The incredible purple colors canvassed on an orange background at sunset was absolutely incredible, although I fear I may not have appreciated the immense spectrum of colors as much as others, as I'm color blind. That doesn't mean I see the scenery as black and white; I see everything in full color, it's just that sometimes faint and similar colors blur slightly. I've found this often happens during spectacular sunsets where others point out the pretty shades that I can't really make out, but needless to say, this was spectacular, whatever colors I saw!

Just a short trip from Amsterdam, and London lies Belgium. I first visited Belgium when I went to the "I Love Techno" music festival with my friends Alex and Chris from university, which was quite an experience. The crowd was mostly comprised of students who wore all sorts of strange attire in a ginormous sweaty disused factory. After throwing off the shackles, I too found myself somehow jumping up and down to the music wearing a "wife beater" and a gas-mask. But don't ask me how that came about because, quite frankly, I don't remember! The smell of hops wafted through the air from the nearby Stella Artois brewery, and this encouraged us to visit the infamous Delirium Café in Brussels. This is a three-story behemoth bar that boasts the largest selection of beers in the world, no less than 2,400, in fact. After having their trademark beer, Delirium, and the President Bush drink, which is a concoction of Bush beer which has an alcohol content north of 20% (similar to some weaker liqueurs) mixed with all sorts of liquor, such as vodka and brandy. I could barely stand straight so went to scoff some Belgian waffles and fries with mayonnaise. Just to be clear, the President Bush was one of the most disgusting drinks I have ever had, and it was clearly more of a novelty menu item. But Alex said everyone had to do it once. It tasted so abysmal that I could not sip the pint; I so had to be drunk in one go, so you may understand why my subsequent view of Brussels from Mont des Art may have been slightly blurry. The night was topped off by seeing an even drunker man being arrested urinating on the famous Manneken Pis statue of the little boy pissing into the fountain in the center of Brussels. Immense amounts of Belgian chocolate aside—which seems to have been crafted into continually pioneering new structures, such as 6 feet tall detailed chocolate models of the Eiffel Tower—Brussels is a very picturesque city, and the Grand Place has to be one of Europe's most strikingly beautiful squares.

CHAPTER 36
Germany, Switzerland, Liechtenstein and Austria

Neighboring Germany awaited me next. The economic and famously efficient powerhouse of Europe. I first visited Germany as kid when my dad took me with him when he was flying to Cologne. Beyond the pancakes in the city, I remember very little about Cologne, but nearby Dusseldorf holds fond memories. Despite being a relatively small city, as most Germany cities are in comparison to the likes of Paris and London, I visited Dusseldorf during carnival which was an electric affair. Fairground rides and stalls occupy the island in the city that can only be accessed by a short ferry ride about 50 meters long. Beer and Jaeger flows freely and, minus the exuberant German dress-code, this feels like Dusseldorf's own version of Munich's Oktoberfest where lederhosen are worn aplenty in gigantic beer tents.

From here, the highly efficient and speedy Deutsche Bahn train takes you to Frankfurt. The financial center of Germany is home to a cluster of skyscrapers, and the incredibly charming and elegant Römerberg town square, which charms at Christmas time with its sizeable and gracefully decorated Christmas tree and appealing food stands serve delicious bratwurst and mulled wine. There was, however, not a huge amount more for me to discover in Frankfurt, so I headed to the much livelier Berlin.

I had taken my grandparents to Berlin a few years before, and my grandad had not been back there since he lived in Germany, which was before the Berlin Wall fell, so it was interesting to hear his stories of how life in Berlin used to be. This city was torn apart during the Cold War after extensive bombing during World War 2. Largely as a result of difficult times, Berlin has become one of the most tolerant and experimental cities in the world. The differences in architecture between the west side of the city and the incredibly Sovietlooking East Berlin are striking and can be seen from the top of the TV Tower.

After seeing the strikingly lit Brandenburg Gate and the unique parliamentary Reichstag building with its old façade contrasting with its modern dome, we toured some of the meaningful and sobering sights. First was the Memorial to the Murdered Jews of Europe in central Berlin, where 2,711 blocks of concrete erected at various heights pay homage to those who lost their lives during the Nazi occupation of Germany, mostly in callous concentration camps. We went out to one of them, the nearby Sachsenhausen, where the guide explained that it was strangely rarely sunny there. As predicted, the weather was dreary and very reflective of the somber atmosphere. Sachsenhausen remains to demonstrate the atrocities that occurred here, in the hope that they will never happen again, and never be forgotten. On the pensive drive back to Berlin, we passed Checkpoint Charlie, but the day of learning of the atrocities throughout World War 2 and the Cold War gave a sense to how Berlin had developed since, into a tolerant and speculative city.

This lenient city comes to life at night, where the parties often go well into the next day. I went out to Panorama Bar, which was inside a former factory, where the partygoers would only occasionally stop to refuel on currywurst from the surrounding food vans. From parties inside disused factories, to underground raves, the options in Berlin seem endless, where multi-level clubs are like adult playgrounds that provide different and varying degrees of debauchery as you explore. However, the nightlife scene in Berlin does not just revolve around raves. Despite the immensely young, single population in this city, the Berlin Philharmonic Orchestra is always sold out when they regularly perform at Charlottenberg Palace. I took my grandparents here, but not before visiting the unique and quirky Hall of Mirrors at Clärchens Ballhaus, a beautiful restaurant with long communal tables and dim lighting and populated with abundantly large mirrors. This place was completely full, and with young people as well, showing that Berliners have a multi-faceted perception of nightlife that certainly runs thick through the veins of this city.

I later visited Munich and saw the Bavarian way of partying was quite different to Berlin. The crowd in Munich is older and arguably much more boisterous, as the steins of beer get knocked back at Hofbräuhaus. This multi-floor beerhall is a city landmark, and you feel like you are soaking up the German culture as lederhosen clad beermaids serve liter upon liter of beer and Bavarian bands play the soundtrack.

From raucous biergartens, I headed to the very sleepy nation of Switzerland. The largest city, Zurich, is very charming. It is penned in by the Alps on one side and a lake that glistens in summer on the other. The quality of life here is extremely high, and I could certainly see why Zurich is consistently voted one of the most livable cities in the world. Yet this famously neutral nation that has not involved itself in military conflict for over 200 years, was a little too sleepy for me to remain for too long. The old town was indeed picturesque, but with little social happenings after 9 P.M., it began to feel slightly more like a ghost town. The lack of nightlife is compensated by some of the views that Switzerland offers. I took a steep mountainside train up to Dolder Grand from Zurich, and ate at the incredibly famous Zeughauskeller restaurant, which was built in the 15th century and looked like a castle from a fairytale. If I was look- ing for a change of pace from here I was not going to get it from my next destination—Liechtenstein.

After a predictably efficient bus and train journey, I arrived in this tiny nation with a population of only 40,000 people. Liechtenstein is very prosperous and, in terms of landscape, you would be forgiven for thinking you were still in Switzer- land. But what is there to see here? The short answer is banks. Lots and lots of banks. Many of which you may never have heard of before. A lunch stop was about all I could stomach as a lone traveler in the sleepy town of Vaduz. After a quick peek at the castle, I headed to Austria for my sanity, if nothing else.

I had visited Salzburg when I was much younger, and don't remember much beyond a city dedicated to the great com- poser Amadeus Mozart and the rather eerie secret war bunkers of Adolf Hitler buried deep within the hills. But it was a trip back to the ski slopes of Austria's beautiful Alpine ski resorts this time. You may be wondering why I keep putting myself through the embarrassment on the ski slopes, but this time it was my wife Elena who wanted to go. With her being a great skier, I was more than happy to give it another shot.

We traveled to the scenic Kitzbuhel and stayed in a lovely hotel in the mountains that had a wonderful spa and a sauna where the German guests who were already staying at the hotel got extremely angry if you weren't naked. They actually demanded that we strip off, but in a very aggressive manor. Sauna aggression aside, the hotel called A-Rosa was so beautiful and encompassed the aspect of ski resorts that I love so much, cozying up to a huge fireplace drinking warm hot chocolate with a generous portion of brandy.

However, and unfortunately, as day broke, it was time to take the terrifying lift up to the slopes. After actually mastering the children's slope (with a lot of Elena's help), she pushed me to try the steeper slope, which ended in tears as skis flew off at all angles and I threw a tantrum. I told Elena to enjoy herself on the fun slopes, and she agreed as long as I promised to keep practicing on the children's slope. However, upon crashing into another snow covered wreck at the bottom of this slope as I attempted a simple turn, I found the greatest part of the slopes. There was a pop up schnapps bar made from ice advertising a new social networking app. Within no time the skis were off and the poles were resting in the snow as the party began. Several hours later and a plethora of schnapps between, Elena returned and knew instantly that I hadn't been practicing skiing. This was made worse when a promotional video for the app was played on their projector screens at possibly the worst time with a compilation clip of highlights from the day. Most of the time lapse video showed seasoned skiers taking a shot, and skiing past to get onto the slopes, yet the one constant seemed to be me. Worse still, there was a video drone flying around the makeshift bar that had slow motion clips of me having shots holding my ski poles aloft to the beat of the music. The look on Elena's face summed up her thoughts, and with a little smile we continued to drink schnapps together, accepting that I had not really improved my skiing ability that day.

CHAPTER 37
Eastern Europe

After my trip to Austria it was time to explore Eastern Europe. Slovakia was my first destination, and I traveled there with my childhood friend George. The capital, Bratislava, was a destination that rarely featured on European itineraries a little over a decade ago, but a combination of an alluring Old Town, cheap prices and beautiful women has enticed more adventurous travelers and stag dos to this beautiful town. Austria's capital Vienna lies close to Bratislava, and we got a good view of both countries from the rather strange U.F.O. Bridge.

The architecture in Bratislava is similar to that in the Baltics where the famous Bratislava Castle, which has existed since the 9th century and now with its pristine white façade, towers over a multitude of old town pubs. Unusual statues, that range from sculptures of men climbing out of drainpipes to pairs of open female legs, were recently constructed across the city to brighten the bleary original communist constructions. In among boats drifting down the sleepy River Danube, it's worth keeping your eyes open for other unconventional features in

Bratislava, such as the narrowest house in the city that is only just over one-meter-wide and sits above the kebab shop near the old city gate.

A short bus ride away takes the overlander to nearby Budapest in Hungry, which is also easily accessible by boat down the Danube too. I traveled to Budapest on a separate trip with my grandparents during the weekend that the city played host to the Hungarian Formula 1 Grand Prix, which produced an electric buzz in Budapest. The two cities of Buda and Pest have combined to create the namesake that could lay claim to the most beautiful city in Eastern Europe. The iconic stone chain bridge lays the pathway toward to the ginormous Hungarian parliament building that was best viewed lit up at night from a boat on the famous river. I personally found the highlight of the city to be the Buda Castle, which I think is the most exquisite fortress I have seen. The Fisherman's Bastion allows a panoramic view across all of these alluring sights, but beyond the picture postcard city lays so much more. Ruin bars are scattered throughout the city that are essentially converted houses that convey a relaxed atmosphere that range from Hungarians and tourists congregating to play table football to more grungy graffiti-ridden watering holes. You have to try Hungarian goulash at the Opera House, but the best treat in Budapest's drinking and eating scene is at the New York Café at the Boscolo Hotel, which I believe is the very best café in the world. I sat at old wooden tables, sipping coffee and looking up at beautifully crafted ceilings in a mesmerizing theater-type setting that is incredibly difficult to describe in writing or even pictures.

If you're looking for a city as beautiful as Budapest, then Prague gives it a good run for its money. I travelled here with my sister and had an incredible long weekend watching this picturesque city in all its glory during summer. The Gothic architecture is a rich contrast to the folk designs found in the Baltics and, as with many Eastern European cities, the charming Old Town provides the most alluring scenery.

Prague's Old Town has the very unique feature of the astronomical clock that is splendidly and intricately designed and performs hourly. The windows to the clock's building open and dancing ensues. The Charles Bridge continues the theme of Gothic architecture with its eerie statues. And, in a city that seems to have a penchant for the otherworldly, it's worth stopping by the museum of alchemists and magicians, which is something of an interactive creep-show attraction. I found that Prague was best observed while dining at Zlata Praha at the InterContinental. This gave a sunset view of the Prague Castle with the sun reflecting off the beautiful colors of the exterior, while I smoked a cigar. Granted, by this point there were many aspects of Eastern European cities that were overlapping. Old squares, small cafes, and at times it felt as though a lot of these destinations were all too similar. But then again, can the same not be said for Mediterranean islands for example, and to be honest, I love both, so despite the similarities, why not continue to indulge and recognize the variation in places you enjoy? On this note, it wasn't long before that I took a trip to the Czech Republic's neighbor, but at this point the similarities began to fade slightly.

To the east lies Warsaw in Poland. Warsaw doesn't compete, lookswise, to Budapest and Bratislava. It is more spread out with bulkier, less aesthetically pleasing buildings. There is, however, a lot more open space and Lazienki Park is beautifully manicured in the middle of the city. The palace on the water glistens in this massive patch of tranquility where dogs run around off their leads, seemingly content. Chopin's Warsaw seems a far cry from the current attractions of this city that range from the ludicrous neon museum that pays homage to the bygone era of the 1970s to the incredibly fun range of bars in Nowy Swiat.

There are many particular establishments in Warsaw, including fairly unique milk bars, which are quite standard in Poland. Contrary to what the name may suggest, they don't serve milk but mostly dairy dishes. However, I would happily take these peculiar outlets over the boorish options offered in neighboring Belarus. After our airline—the immensely annoyingly named Wizz Air—canceled our departing flight due to apparent fog, and we could only fly out of Warsaw the next day, I began to plan my journey to the most secretive and closed off nation in Europe.

The arduous process of obtaining my entry visa for Belarus with the dreaded letter of invitation that costs a small fortune and consumes huge amounts of time, was not the best introduction to a country that feels like it got lost in time when the U.S.S.R. broke up. Minsk conveys heavy communist vibes that are distinctly visible in the architecture around Victory Square and the Belarusian Great Patriotic War Museum, but it was nowhere more visible than the communist propaganda around the Belarussian State Circus. In a city that has been completely burnt to the ground multiple times and that had to be rebuilt after World War 2, it seems the bulky but endearing Soviet designs will remain here now. Time seems to drift slowly in this city that has remained largely forgotten to the rest of Europe, despite its proximity to such regularly visited capitals such as nearby Warsaw. Many lazy days are spent in Gorky Park, where there is a rather dilapidated looking Ferris wheel that creeks around in the wind and is reminiscent of the infamous image of the abandoned town of Pripyat in Ukraine.

Unfortunately, I wasn't only traveling around the European continent during summer. I voyaged to Ljubljana in Slovenia in the middle of winter. This is a very picturesque sleepy town without the hordes of tourists. Gothic architecture remains popular here, and is illustrated on the Dragon Bridge that passes over the frozen (at that time) Ljubjlana River where three bridges connect the old town. Across the bridge, is the iconic pink Franciscan church. The snowcapped castle sparkled above the Old Town and lit up the city below. It's hard to describe the charming and arresting nature of this town in words, but it was worth bearing the extremely cold temperatures to discover the capital of Slovenia.

I took the onwards train to Zagreb in Croatia. I have long heard how attractive Hvar and Dubrovnik are on Croatia's coast, but with winter in full swing, I went to the often by-passed capital city with its raving arts scene. A new initiative here called "Pimp my Pump" has rather imaginatively pioneered brightening up Zagreb through art. Old disused water pumps are transformed with bright and innovative paintings. Zagreb is another relatively small city and Trg Bana Jelacica is the focal meeting point where people-watching familiarized me with the city. Trolley cars rumble past as vendors sell a variety of goods around the famous statue of Jelacic on the back of a horse in a macho pose. Interestingly, this very same statue that had stood here for many decades was removed and placed in storage to be returned in 1990 after it was no longer deemed too nationalistic anymore.

To the east of Zagreb, I ventured toward Serbia on the night train, and what a treacherous journey this turned out to be in mid-winter. The windows to the dark train cabin were jammed open and the temperature outside must have been minus 10 degrees Celsius. The bed bug ridden triple bunk bed provided little respite from the grinding rumble of snow beneath the train on the tracks. Shivering and tired, the journey became a lot worse as I crossed into Serbia, and passengers were asked to get out to clear snow from the tracks if they were willing and able. The conditions were atrocious and our train had become stuck in the snow, but after hours of delays and periods of ploughing through the snow (for which I should have probably got a partial refund on my ticket), I reached Belgrade.

There are just a handful of sights to see in the capital of Serbia, such as the spotless white Church of Saint Sava, which I could barely distinguish from the snow covered surrounds. But it was the exhilarating nightlife in Belgrade that was the positive surprise. This city likes to party and feels a touch hedonistic after such tough times, very similar to how Berlin has transformed into a carefree and experimental city after the fall of the Berlin Wall. In the 1990s, civil war led to the breakup of Yugoslavia, and sanctions meant that Serbia is a fair way behind European peers in terms of economic development, but Belgrade is certainly one of the most developed in terms of its nightlife despite these setbacks. Some of the colossal clubs here are similar to the super-clubs of Las Vegas and Ibiza. There were attractive dancers on poles, platforms and cages in behemoth clubs that have sprung up just about anywhere they could in this city that was bombed by NATO in 1999. Locals told me about the splavs in summer time, which are monumental floating clubs on the river. In the midst of winter, I was only able to frequent the clubs capable of handling harsh winter conditions. The splavs may not have been able to handle the subzero temperatures, but Serbian women certainly could. It didn't seem to matter how cold it was, they continued to walk around in heels and condition-defying dresses.

I took a bus ride south from Belgrade to Kosovo, which, although not a U.N. country, seemed worth a visit. This patch of land has divided opinion across the world and, although still part of Serbia, I was unable to re-enter the non-contested part of Serbia after crossing into Kosovo. The Serbian authorities claim you have illegally left their border if you get a stamp from the Kosovan authorities. The U.S. supported Kosovo in the late 1990s, and so, in addition to lots of street art in the capital city, Pristina, there are many monuments and murals paying homage to Bill Clinton. There are not many nations across the world that have statues of former U.S. presidents with their hand in the air, but the majority of Kosovans love the U.S.A. for the support they provided, and they are not afraid to demonstrate it.

My only way out of Kosovo therefore was to head Bosnia and Herzegovina. Sarajevo is incredibly culturally diverse and has been for hundreds of years. Nowhere was the diversity more evident than when taking a stroll through the old town bazaar where the demographic is varied and the prices were cheap. The Sebilj landmark in what is known as Pigeon Square is an image of peace in this city, but oh my goodness the pigeons. If I thought that the number of pigeons was excessive in some squares of the world like Trafalgar Square, then the aptly named Pigeon Square is inundated with them. There are even vendors selling pigeon food, which compounds the problem as locals feed these flying menaces in what appeared to be a relaxing pastime for some.

A stroll across the frozen river took me to the infamous but seldom recognized sight of the Latin Bridge, which was the exact location where Franz Ferdinand, the heir to the Austro-Hungarian empire, was assassinated by a Bosnian-Serb; an act that led to the start of World War 1. More recently, there have been greater tensions and unrest in this city that saw peace for so many years. There was no better way to get an understanding of the atrocities in Sarajevo that was besieged for years in the 1990s than to climb through the tunnels that were dug under the city, which helped to save hundreds of lives.

After Bosnia and Herzegovina, I returned back to London and waited until spring to go to Montenegro. This is on the Mediterranean coast and looks more enchanting in the warmer months when the sun is shining on the red roofs of the venerable town of Kotor. Beyond the brick masonry of the fairly dowdy clock tower in the capital Podgorica, there was not much to see here, but the nearby beaches in Budva felt more like the Italian Riviera. Outdoor cafés pose within palm tree-lined cobbled streets that lead toward the calm sands of the Mediterranean. A trip to adjacent Sveti Stefan was the prize along this sumptuous stretch of coastline. This picture postcard fort town is just off the shore, and lazing on the nearby beach with this stunning perspective was a fantastic way to say goodbye to Montenegro before heading to Albania.

When I arrived in the capital Tirana, I instantly noticed that this seemed to be a city under construction. When I asked people why most roads and squares were blocked off, they told me that there had been a big effort in recent years to make the capital seem more appealing. Hence, when I visited, it was distinctly unappealing, as building works closed off large swathes of the city. The main attraction of Skanderbeg Square was among those being excavated so, after a quick stop by Mother Teresa Square and some tranquility in one of the many lounge cafés here, away from the sound of heavy construction machinery, I moved on toward Macedonia, which was in fact where Mother Teresa was born.

Her birthplace of Skopje is a city where the main attractions are memorials and monuments and the marvelous view from the Kale Fortress. There is a monument to Alexander the Great and, predictably, a memorial house dedicated to Mother Teresa in a city that tends to feel more like Turkey at times with an eclectic Balkan mix of people and cultures.

By the time I had delved this far into the Balkans, some of the more unusual sights began to seem perfectly normal. A guy bringing his dog to a nightclub? Sure, why not, it happens. But in a place where the food is cheap and the Macedonian wine was great, this country made for a satisfying trip.

From this landlocked Balkan country to the last remaining Balkan state, a short flight took me to Sofia, the capital of Bulgaria on the Black Sea coast. Although I never made it to the celebrated resorts, I was able to garner a good if only brief understanding of this country in Sofia. The modern day peaceful stature of Bulgaria is best summarized at the Kambanite, which is a monument of a hundred bells from countries all across the world that represents peace with these nations. You can even go and ring the bells. At any time of the day you can find this place by listening for the sound of bells, even from what seems like miles away. There are some beautiful buildings in Sofia, not least the old and cozy looking but beautiful National Theatre. But the real showpiece of the city is undoubtedly the Alex-

ander Nevsky Cathedral with its many sides and uniquely recognizable gold domes.

Away from the monuments, cathedrals and strange puppet
shows that Bulgaria seems to have a rather obsessive penchant
for, a stop in Sofia wouldn't have been complete without visiting a:part:mental after dark. This incredible club was like nothing I had seen before, with fairly small but differently themed
rooms in one large building, giving you the feeling that you
had stepped into one big, wild house party. One of my former
colleagues, Alex, is from Bulgaria, and I later traveled with him
further north around the Black Sea to Ukraine.

The nightclubs in Ukraine were also pretty insane where
well-heeled women trekked through any depth of snow to
make it to clubs that appeared to be severely lacking male revellers. Multi-floored venues came to life at night across the
city, anywhere and everywhere it seemed, even tucked away in
the middle of snow blanketed parks. There was a very unique
mix of the newly acquired wealthy and the older, perhaps
wiser, population in the capital Kiev. Although the older population who have seen so much change in Ukraine would
probably be used to the sight of people drinking beer in the
incredibly beautifully lit Independence Square, they were
probably less used to seeing the nouveau riche that seemed
abundant in Kiev.

This aside, there were many aspects of Kiev that felt like
mainstays in this city, from the outgoing people—best witnessed by the multitude of street performers (and small demonstrations) along the main Khreshchatyk street—to the Russian Byzantine architecture of yellow and pink cathedrals that
is best observed in one of Kiev's many city parks. Grandiose
designs look down from strategic positions on hills. There is

the Mother of the Fatherland monument at the Museum of the Great Patriotic War where, rather nationalistically, you can take a tank ride. This seemed to stir emotions among the children, which I guess was the aim. However, the showstopper in Kiev was undoubtedly Saint Sophia's Cathedral. This UNESCO World Heritage Site, constructed in the 11th century is instantly recognizable with its unique green and gold domes that shimmer across the city. From a congregation of famous sights and a lively buzzing city, I was off to neighboring Moldova.

I actually took the inaugural flight from London to Moldova on the rather lackluster Air Moldova. Predictably, the flight was delayed for many hours, and the delay only came when we were moments from taking off. We had to spend this excruciating amount of time crammed into our seats in a maintenance bay. This was in the middle of the night, so by the time I landed in the capital Chisinau, I wasn't in the best mood. And this relatively small nation wedged between the behemoths of Ukraine and Romania had relatively little to offer. Apart from seeing the Soviet designs of the Chisinau Water Tower and the admittedly spectacular Victory Memorial with its eternal flame (also the place where everybody gathered in the city), Chisinau had precious little more to offer, and so I made my way to Romania.

I arrived in Bucharest during Halloween, to a city that knew how to dress up for the event. But what else would you expect in the "Birthplace of Dracula?" Dimly lit bars and intricately carved pumpkins adorned the entire city where people took dressing up very seriously, so I certainly looked out of place in jeans and a tee-shirt. Transylvania is synonymous with vampires, and I was able to see the final resting place of the infamous Vlad the Impaler near the Bucharest monastery, in the middle of the eerie Lake Snagov. Vlad was the bloodsucking prince that was the inspiration behind Dracula, and this was a quirky but interesting trip outside the city.

Back within the confines of Bucharest, I saw vague glimpses in the Old City as to why the capital had previously garnered the nickname "Paris of the East" before large swathes of the city were destroyed in World War 2. Victoriei Avenue was the best way to become accustomed with the diverse architecture of this seldom visited city. I was completely unaware before I visited Bucharest of the immense structure that is the Palace of Parliament building. This is the world's largest parliamentary structure and displays the grandiose communist designs on a construction that was so controversial when such large parts of Romania were starving. Interestingly, this is the second largest administrative building in the world, only to be bettered by the Pentagon in Virginia. The building is clearly of a different time period, for this now incredibly progressive nation. A tour around parliament only allows you to view some of the immense 1000 rooms.

With my visit to Romania, I had visited all the countries on a traditional map of Europe, but the ambiguity of recent history now places the Caucus nations of Georgia, Armenia and Azerbaijan in Europe as well, with their locations wedged between the Black Sea and the Caspian Sea.

I visited Tbilisi in Georgia with my father. He was flying the plane out there, which was an incredible experience for me as I mentioned before, but this never seemed to wear on me how awesome it was. The geographical location means that there is a tremendous mix of people in this part of the world where petite alleyways and streets comprise a city populated with old men who leisurely play chess outside cafés and there seem to be more churches than anything else. Everywhere I walked I found yet another church, from the beautiful Rustaveli Avenue, which is spectacularly lit up at night, to random enclaves in the mountains, there was more often than not a church in sight. But nothing compared to the spectacular Sameba Cathedral, which is the most sensational building in the Caucuses in my opinion. This breathtaking Orthodox Church comprised of 10 smaller churches, and I only saw it on my last day before I bade farewell to my father as he flew home and I caught a minibus through the rugged Georgian landscape toward Armenia in the south.

When I arrived in the capital Yerevan, I was instantly mesmerized by how friendly the people are here. Armenians are incredibly humorous too, and the friendly nature often developed into cheeky banter. The prices here are reasonable and Armenian women are very beautiful. Mix all of this together with dazzling architecture, and Yerevan certainly becomes a city that I remember fondly.

The capital had a very small population at the beginning of the Soviet era, despite such a long history. City planners attempted to create a neoclassical jewel in Armenia, and they succeeded. In contrast to other nearby cities, especially those of the former Soviet republics to the east of the Caspian Sea, Yerevan looks distinctly different, with more beautiful and intricate designs rather than traditionally large and bulky Soviet architecture. There are so many showpieces in this city that I would struggle to choose my favorite, but high on the list would be the beautifully lit Republic Square, which is adorned with luminous buildings around central fountains and an incredibly unique cascade staircase. This grandiose set of stairs links the city to the hilltops, with garden courtyards on each ascending level. From afar, the structure looks immense, and at the top lays Victory Park and the Mother Armenia statue with its rather unfortunately creepy amusement park and Pripyat-esque Ferris wheel. For more unique architecture I headed out of the city to the Monastery of Geghard which is carved into the mountainside in a manner that was reminiscent to the Valley of the Kings in Luxor.

Due to the lack of diplomatic relations between Armenia and Azerbaijan—the two countries are actually technically still at war—I was unable to travel to Azerbaijan directly from Armenia. Instead, I took a slightly longer route to visit my final country in Europe. Azerbaijan is an incredibly oil rich nation that combines a unique mix of ginormous seafront skyscrapers next to the old town city walls, which you can partially see from a boat on the Caspian Sea. This is a nation that seems to have a love affair with all things related to Europe: black cabs prowl the streets of Baku and European restaurants are everywhere. I sat down at the 360 Bar on top of the Hilton hotel for a celebratory and reflective drink, knowing that I had traveled to every country in Europe. Around me, the other guests continued their conversations, mostly about oil.

Despite the geographical borders of Europe being more loosely defined with regards to where the continent starts and ends, the broad spectrum of cultures, architecture and climate—all the way from Iceland to Greece and beyond that—made this one of the most diverse continents to visit. Some of my favorite countries in the world are in Europe, such as Italy and Spain, and, if for nothing more than incredible and varied food combined with passionate people, I'm incredibly lucky to call this continent home. I have been blessed enough to travel around this relatively small but vibrant continent with many of my friends and family. Some are no longer with us, but the proximity of so many incredible destinations to the city I call home, has meant that unlike most other places around the world, I will always have the greatest amount of shared memories with the people closest to me across this continent. No matter what happens in the future, no one can take away the memories we have created, and Europe has been great for that. Although my grandmother recently passed, I will always have memories such as that of her challenging the locals to drink a stein of beer in Budapest. Of course, my gran won, she always did, but even writing this now, although with a tear in my eye, I have a big smile on my face remembering the happiness shared.

CHAPTER 38
Australia and New Zealand

I was on to the home straight in my adventure, and my final untouched continent of Oceana and the surrounding South Pacific islands awaited my final journey. After nearly 24 hours of flying, with a brief stop through Hong Kong, I reached Melbourne, Australia. It is still quite remarkable to think how far travel has come that we can go to the other side of the world in such a relatively short space of time. The world is a huge place, and there are still so many destinations I haven't been to, despite visiting every country. But regardless of the sheer magnitude of places to visit, flying across the globe in that period of time also conveys how small the world can be.

Melbourne is certainly one of the more enclosed and cliquey cities in Australia. There were a multitude of cool bars and restaurants, and it was easy to see why the quality of life is so high here. However, people remained very much in their own groups. Melbourne was perhaps not the best introduction to Australia, but this could also have had something to do with the fact that I was there over Christmas, spending Christmas

Day in my hotel room, eating a sandwich and cheese from the local 7-Eleven. It was not ideal.

However, after Christmas Day, the city quickly livened up—just as I was leaving. I just about had time to witness the bustle around the brightly yellow colored Flinders Street railway station and to relax on deckchairs in the parks where big screen projectors screened the Boxing Day cricket test match with England. I then made my way toward the Great Ocean road to get a peek at the magnificent 12 apostles rock formations, which was quite a sight. This is actually now listed in some places as one of the seven wonders of the natural world.

Shortly after, I took off for Alice Springs which was, to be honest, one of the more depressing places in Australia. However, I had come to the outback for the sole purpose of visiting Ayers Rock, or Uluru as it was named by Aboriginals. I took the six-hour bus ride from Alice Springs to see the geographical and cultural center of Australia. Uluru is an iconic symbol of Australia, as much as the man-made Sydney Opera House, but this unique rock has more to offer than just a quick photo and a subsequently long journey back to the east coast. The route around the rock is six miles long, through caves and gorges, where you pass intricate Aboriginal paintings on the side of this spiritual rock. It's clear you're in the outback as the sun sets and the traditional Aussie BBQ is lit, accompanied by abnormal sized insects that fly around you and the food. You're a long way from any major civilization here, but it was truly magnificent. I tucked into barbecued ribs and shrimp, and the tremendous array of reds and oranges reflected off the rock as the sun went down on Australia for another day.

I left the outback and headed for the rather tropical destination of Cairns in Queensland. This felt like small town Australia, and I was fairly bored the few nights I spent in Cairns. Granted there are a handful of adventure activities around Cairns, but I had not come for that. I had come to visit the main attraction of the nearby Great Barrier Reef, which needs no introduction as the world's largest coral reef. This was a once in a lifetime activity for me, as I didn't really envisage myself returning to the rather depressing town of Cairns, so I chose to take a helicopter to the outer reef and land on a pontoon, which was one of the best spots for diving and snorkeling. Unfortunately, a large storm had passed over the reef a few days earlier, so the water was choppy and violent, and the reef had been stirred up by large waves that meant visibility wasn't great. Therefore, I didn't get the best diving conditions, and although it was still an amazing adventure, the Great Barrier Reef is famous for being the largest reef and not necessarily the best for diving. I'm sure that most seasoned scuba divers would tell you that there are many better places to view marine life than this vast reef off the Australian coast. I personally didn't think it compared to some of the strikingly beautiful areas of the nearby South Pacific islands.

My last stop in Australia was in the largest and liveliest city of Sydney. I stopped in this city many times on my travels around the South Pacific as it seemed most flight routes annoyingly and inefficiently took me back through Sydney. The aviation industry is so immensely under-connected in the South Pacific, not to mention excruciating expensive. A one way flight that could have been as little as 2 hours in duration occasionally put me back as much as $500, even way in advance in the Pacific. Sydney is one of the southern hemisphere's landmark cities, and seems to be blessed with all-year-round good weather. I was lucky enough to visit Sydney during New Year, where the city puts on its world famous fireworks display over the Harbour Bridge. It's often televised globally as one of the first displays of the New Year, after Auckland, New Zealand. I grabbed my patch of grass on one of the many fabulous viewing points around Darling Harbour, and celebrated the New Year in a fabulous atmosphere. Thousands of boats filled every bit of water to navigate the best view for one of the greatest fireworks displays I have ever seen.

Beyond the annual celebrations that are conducted so brilliantly in this city, there are many activities to keep you occupied in this gateway to Australia, from climbing the Sydney Harbour Bridge to relaxing on the surfer shores of the famous Bondi Beach. There are also multiple options for viewing Australian wildlife. I ventured to Featherdale petting zoo where I was able to play with and even feed wallabies and kangaroos and get up close to a koala bear. I even had my picture taken with a quokka. These are the familiar animals that seem to always be smiling and make for fantastic photo opportunities.

Back in the city, and I spent leisurely days taking a boat around the harbor for gorgeous views of the skyline with the sail shaped Sydney Opera House ever prominent. Not only is Sydney a friendly city where the quality of life is great, but there is a diversity across the modern architecture that gives a certain presence to the city, from the views below the revolving restaurant perched on top of the Sydney Tower, to the older and beautifully constructed Queen Victoria building on street level. As night drew in, this city exploded further into life with bars dotted all around The Rocks area, where the popular choice seems to be delicately constructed prohibition type bars with live music. But mind your wallet, this city is extremely expensive, and even a packet of cigarettes will set you back a mind-boggling AUD $35.

My next stop was New Zealand, and Christchurch to be precise. This sleepy, laid back town in the South Island didn't feel too dissimilar to stepping into a quaint English town. There are many parks in this city that was devastated by an earthquake after my visit in 2011. I was lucky enough to see the beautiful Gothic cathedral in its glory before it was largely destroyed. Although there are a handful of activities to keep you occupied here—like the International Antarctic Centre where you can play with penguins in freezing cold Antarctic like conditions and learn about this nearby frozen continent—the real beauty of the South Island was best seen by driving out of the city. I visited nearby Mount Cook, New Zealand's highest mountain, with its beautiful snowcapped peaks. The drive took me through some of the South Island's fantastically beautiful natural scenery, where much of The Lord of the Rings movies were filmed. Similar to Australia the quality of life in New Zealand seemed very high with the major difference being the stereotypical, but realistic abundance of sheep here. The countryside was awash with these furry little white creatures munching on grass in a country where the sheep population outnumbers humans by many multiples. I was even invited to watch a predictably strange sheep shearing demonstration when I visited the similarly sleepy town of Wellington on the North Island.

Riding on the Wellington cable car and watching a cricket match with a picnic on the grass banked stadium in Wellington aside (which was an incredibly different affair to the cricket match I watched in Bangladesh remember), I moved on to the only destination in New Zealand that truly felt like a lively city, Auckland. Despite this, I only used Auckland as a base to explore the extensive natural beauty of the North Island, from the Waitomo Caves with their incredibly unique sight of thousands of glowworms on the ceiling of the pitch black cave, to the volcanic landscape of Rotorua. I spent time exploring Kiwi Maori traditions on a day trip that also included spotting the highly endangered Kiwi bird and concluded with a visit to the weird landscape of bubbling hot mud pools and extremely pungent Sulphur springs. Without question, the most prodigious sight was the Pohutu Geyser which intermittently burst hot boiling water and steam as high as 100 feet as the build up of gas broke the equilibrium.

Maori and similar tribal traditions run deep through this part of the world, and I stepped off the larger land masses to begin island hopping around the South Pacific to witness more of Polynesian and Melanesian culture.

CHAPTER 39
South Pacific and Micronesia

My first stop was the most populated Pacific island nation of Papua New Guinea. The capital Port Moresby is simply referred to as POM by locals. Although this would likely be the last of vaguely developed civilization I would see over the next few weeks, I was eager to move on. This is not the nicest city, and the number of signs saying, "No guns, no chewing betel nut," were all too regular. To be honest, I didn't have a great pre-conception of Port Moresby from what I had read and heard. For the first day I thought that red stains across the sidewalks and strewn up the sides of the walls were the scenes of earlier street fights. I soon found out that this was the red juice from betel nuts that people spit out anywhere and everywhere as the nut is chewed. Petty crime is likely to be the only real danger faced by tourists in Papua New Guinea, and unless you are traveling to some of the most remote jungles on Earth, which it is said, still house tribes that have never encountered modern civilization, then you are not going to be affected by cannibalism, contrary to popular belief.

I was in a rush to move on from the polluted and congested city of POM, but not before visiting PNG Art, which was like an art gallery but you could buy any of the displays, from spirit masks to spears. Fancy buying a penis gourd? Then head here. If it's just the natural beauty of the islands you're looking for, head out to Loloata for some beautiful snorkeling, or move on to the Solomon Islands as I did.

The Solomon Islands was massively underdeveloped in comparison to Papua New Guinea. This was evident as soon as I landed and we pulled up to the airport "terminal," which was not much more than a small shack. I would have to get used to this; this was a common theme at the airports across the South Pacific, with the sole exception of the much more developed Fiji. However, by the time I left the Pacific islands, I would come to miss these endearing little airports and the laid back way of life here.

Solomon islanders regularly use the term, "We don't put on makeup," referring to the landscape around the country that is largely untouched and undeveloped. There is barely any tourist industry here, and my guide wasn't even aware of the very few tourist sites on the main island of Guadalcanal. He had explored so little of it, seemingly. Apart from countless rustic villages that populate the majority of the island and retain a chief, a large portion of the population is made up of expats. Tourists are few and far between. With a booming mining industry and significant peacekeeping still in place after the widespread civil unrest in 2000 between islanders, expats remain a fairly common sight, ostensibly hopping between the nice cafés in the capital Honiara, and drinking throughout the majority of the day.

The civil unrest that bordered on genocide in 2000 saw such extreme measures as bullets being taken and used from the World War 2 museum, and kept tourists away from this ruggedly beautiful island. But you would be missing out if you didn't visit the Solomon Islands. Granted, it is a place that can quickly get boring, but the island of Guadalcanal saw some of the bloodiest fighting during WW2, between Japan and the U.S.A., which has led to large swathes of the island being comparable to one big giant outdoor war museum. Shipwrecks stick out from the water's edge just meters from the shore, and diving toward the west of the island provides a fascinating look at sunken submarines and fighter planes. I ventured to Vilu Open Air War Museum, which was awash with damaged tanks and planes submerged into the forest. Some are better preserved than others, but what a unique sight this was. If anything, come and visit the Solomon Islands to witness the atrocities that occurred here, not least symbolized on Tetere Beach, where the man who runs the tank museum will explain how his grandad fought in the war, and how he himself uncovered the mass grave filled with over 3,000 Japanese troops.

I continued my journey east and landed in Port Vila, Vanuatu. This is a country that had an attempted political coup in the 1990s and was not shy of a protest, yet has developed its tourist industry immensely and is now a very safe country. New resorts spring up regularly here and, although not developed, like Fiji, this produces a charm that is unique to Vanuatu. I stayed in an overwater villa in a lagoon that allowed for fantastic sunrises in the tropical environment.

Despite being innovative in their development here, with activities such as zip-lining though the Vanuatuan jungle and even delving the depths of the ocean in a mini submarine, this country still retains many of its tribal heritage roots. Before I explain that, I just want to say what a unique experience this submarine was. It dived to 50 meters below the surface to give a clear viewing of marine life through the crystal clear waters of Vanuatu. Although safety never seemed an issue, it was immensely cool how the captain even allowed me and Elena to press certain buttons to assist with submerging, an experience that would be incomprehensible to even fathom in the safety conscious Western world. Granted it was only us on the submarine, so we only had ourselves to blame if it went wrong. Luckily, we resurfaced and explored the marine life on the surface of the lagoons, where baby turtles were abundant, with some no larger than my fingers. This was in stark contrast to the 140-year-old humongous peaceful turtle that ate papaya out of our hands.

As I said, Vanuatu is certainly more commercialized than some of the other islands, and there are even pioneering restaurants, such as Stone Grill that provides a boiling hot slab of granite on your plate to cook whichever fantastic cut of meat you ordered, however you like—you become the chef and don't even have to leave your table. They even serve the gruesome looking coconut crab with its gigantic purple pincers. It can grow to the size of a soccer ball, and looks truly terrifying, yet tastes delicious.

Large portions of this country remain untouched and rival anywhere in the Pacific islands. We took a trip away from civilization to witness a local tribe who jokingly threatened to kill and eat us at first, before welcoming us to their village. This was not a tourist fad in Vanuatu, this was a real tribe and this was how they lived, demonstrating everything from their animal traps and the pigs they had caught to their traditional dances. We sat and drank the rather earthy tasting kava with the local chief, just miles from the pristine lagoons where we had earlier been sipping water from coconuts on the beach. Granted, much of this exists in other Pacific nations, but Vanuatu was where I truly embraced it and this gorgeous country will hold a special place in my heart.

All roads in the South Pacific seem to either lead to Sydney, Auckland or Fiji, and Fiji was my next stop. I ended up crossing through Fiji many times to reach other islands around the region, but whenever I did, it was always nice to have windows that closed in my hotel room and a hot shower. Fiji always meant a little dose of luxury for me, and there was no place like Denauru Island for rest and relaxation. Fiji has developed a major tourism industry, similar to that of Hawaii, and it's as common to hear their welcoming, "Bula," here as it is to hear, "Aloha," in Hawaii. Away from overcrowded tour boats that take groups out for diving trips, I truly embraced "Fiji time," enjoying the sun, sea and a very mature and varied gastro scene. There are ample opportunities for enchanting perfect postcard type pictures here, but because this is the hub of activity in the South Pacific, I was always keen to take a short flight to other nearby islands after getting my little dose of five-star luxury.

A few short hours from Fiji on a tiny turboprop propeller aircraft took me to the Kingdom of Tonga. Yes, the kingdom. This tiny cluster of islands with one of the smaller populations in the region, has an actively serving king. One of the first things you will notice about Tonga, after the stunning scenery and abundance of palm trees, is the subtle economic competition for dominance occurring between China and the U.S.A. on this tiny strategically located island. There are many Chinese people living here, and they are contributing with the construction of roads, whereas the U.S., or Utah specifically, has constructed a plethora of Mormon churches across the island that seem to supply free education to the majority of Tonga children. There is even a street that Tongan's refer to as "Mormon-ville," which houses the Mormon headquarters. After a day or so familiarizing yourself with the beautiful lagoon nestled into the middle of Tongatapu island you stop noticing symbols of this Chinese-US tussle and it just becomes the norm.

I have visited Tonga a couple of times and, on the most recent occasion, I actually stayed on another island called Fafa. It is stunning. Elena and I had our own log cabin nestled in this wildlife reserve and, although we shared our dimly lit solar powered cabin with an entire family of giant lizards, it was a truly fantastic experience, especially being able to roll out of bed onto our own stretch of private beach. Not only that, but we had regular sightings of ginormous whales frolicking in the water as we traveled with the sailing boat to the mainland each day. One whale came right up to the boat before splashing into the water in a display that alone made the tour worth it.

The main island had an abundance of sights, ranging from the flying foxes and fishing pigs—they stick their snouts in the ocean to eat fish—to the standout sight of the blowholes that spray water 80 feet into the air. You can see these air inlets along the coast for as far as the eye can see. We witnessed ungodly rocks on the shore that was aptly named Tsunami Rock, which remains an inexplicable formation, and swam in near pitch black freshwater caves. All this in a country where the people are incredibly friendly and the food is abundant. Tonga is without doubt one of my favorite countries in the South Pacific.

When I first visited Tonga, the international dateline ran straight through the middle, meaning that working out itineraries flying to and from neighboring Samoa was complex. This was ever more difficult by the fact that the majority of the very few flights flew over midnight. That meant there were occasions where there was just a one-hour flight from Samoa to Fiji that would take off at 11:30 P.M. and land in Fiji two calendar days after it took off. The dateline has since, and sensibly, been moved and now places all these nations in a similar time (and date) zone. The dateline is no longer a line but more of a squiggle that looks as though a child has taken a crayon to a global map.

Nevertheless, I made it to Samoa, which in many ways was similar to Tonga. The people were big, the food was great and the smiles seemed never-ending in another stunning and friendly Melanesian country. The palm tree green and sky blue backdrop welcomes visitors at the airport of this stunning natural paradise. There are more resorts here than in Tonga, and there is a certain infectious energy about Samoa that is no better encapsulated than by the world famous Sua Ocean Trench. This is a volcanic pool on the east of the main island that looks like something straight out of paradise, but then again, I was in paradise. I took the steep and rather slippery wooden ladder all the way down to the crystal clear waters below. The best part was, it was almost empty. The more adventurous swimmers and divers can actually swim all the way from this water-filled trench through an extinct lava tube all the way to the ocean, but this seemed like suicide for an intermediate swimmer. The natural beauty of Samoa didn't stop there, as sapphire colored seas flank an immense number of waterfalls in the middle of the island. A trip to Fuipisia Falls and the magnificently fun sliding rocks mini-waterfalls provided endless hours of fun.

As with Vanuatu and Tonga, the people are what really encapsulate and affirm the overall beauty of this nation, and it was a great encore watching the Fiafia traditional fire dancing at night. I rather embarrassingly joined in, hopping around on the sand to avoid getting burnt.

After another transit through Fiji, my next stop would unfortunately be the rather soulless island of Nauru. Unlike many of the other nations in the Pacific that are made up of dozens if not hundreds of smaller islands, Nauru was just one small dot on the map. One solitary island that you could drive around in one hour. In contrast to Tonga and Samoa, arriving visitors are greeted with a view of the port and an abundance of shipping containers. There is a large Chinese population on this island too, and the only real restaurants are Chinese fast food. The availability of fresh local produce there was almost non-existent. Nauru is one of the world's smallest independent republics and phosphate exports account for the majority of income in a nation that claims rather unflattering statistics of 90% unemployment and 95% obesity. Fortunately, my time here was brief and I continued my long and protracted journey on to Kiribati.

I visited Christmas Island, or Kiritimati as it's otherwise known, which is a raised atoll in one of the most remote locations on Earth. The island's name is derived from the fact that Captain Cook landed there on Christmas Eve in 1777.

There were just two flights a week here and, although beautiful, a week would have been too long to spend on this coral reef, so I was lucky that the two flights were only a day apart. The flight that dropped me off in Kiribati continued on to Hawaii and returned the next day.

This entire island is a wildlife sanctuary, and one of the first things I noticed was the plethora of birds flying around this obscure atoll. But then the next thing I quickly noticed was without a doubt the most incredibly beautiful clear water lagoons I have ever set my eyes on. The islands surrounding Christmas Island were unfortunately the location of extensive nuclear testing, including the nearby Bikini Atoll, from where all the inhabitants were moved, but that hasn't prevented people in the region repopulating and rebuilding, albeit slowly. The government was building a new runway when I visited, and the construction workers were quick to buy me a drink when I landed, explaining that it was because of me that they got this one day off a week, when there was a flight!

Undoubtedly, as I approached the last handful of countries in the world, the most incredible sight in this country was that of the sunrise. Christmas Island's location just to the west of the international dateline meant that this is the very first inhabited island in the world to see the sun rise each new day. This attracted quite a bit of tourism in the year 2000, especially among those from the left-field school of thought that believed the world would end. What a disappointing return flight that must have been. So there I was, sitting on a beach all to myself, knowing that I was the very first person in the world to watch the sun rise that particular day. Simply amazing.

My next stop was my favorite island in the South Pacific, Tuvalu. This just pipped Tonga to first place (if I had to rate them, of course). Tuvalu is one of the smallest and most remote countries in the world, and one of its main exports is the selling of their ".tv" internet domain. By the time I reached Tuvalu, I was about as far away from home as I could get. The aptly named FUN airport on the island of Funafuti had just two flights a week, and we flew in on an incredibly old Hawker Siddeley propeller plane with rust on the wings and which still had pulley and lever controls. This has to be one of the oldest commercial planes flying in the world, and if baffled me as to why Air Pacific used just this one plane on the route. But, my goodness, did it make for incredibly stunning photos as we landed on this obscure patch of sand. When we touched down on a runway that occupied nearly half the land mass of this island, everything seemed extraordinarily laid back here. The sole prisoner (I later found out) in the tented "jail" next to the runway, was waving at the disembarking passengers, and, just to give you an idea of the sense of small island community on Tuvalu, he was actually free to walk out of the prison if he chose to. The only hotel on the island was described as just 50 meters from the airport terminal, and as per the description, it actually was, so small is this beautiful little paradise. This place is simply incredible. There were perfectly situated shallow corals right outside my hotel window and the sashimi, caught fresh by fishermen with spears each day, was divine.

The only vague danger I encountered was when I was in the ocean and was told by a nearby local to clench my fists. Just meters away from me was a small black and white stripped snake swimming. Later, the man told me it was the most poisonous snake in the world, but its mouth was so small it can only bite the webbing of your hands. Still, if it did, I would almost certainly have died. However, passing without event, I got back on to land and rented a motorbike, from a lovely woman for just $10 a day, to explore the island. Such was the intricate community in Tuvalu that I couldn't find her house the day of my departing flight to return the motorbike. After driving up and down the length of the island several times looking for her house, a very kind lady said she knew her and that she would return it for me. Elsewhere, I would think twice before handing over someone else's motorbike so easily, but in Tuvalu I barely gave it a second thought. I spent hours driving this little bike up and down the one road on this island right to the tip where the country is just a matter of meters wide from east to west. It was just the width of the road with a minuscule beach, that was more a deposit of sand, on both sides. As is the problem with such small remote territories, at the very end of the island was a gigantic heap of garbage waiting to be burnt piece by piece. Yet this was the only unsavory, although necessary, sight on such a perfect island.

On my ride back to town, that realistically was only a small grouping of houses and a corner shop, I was invited into a local's house for dinner and afterward the family showed me the most remarkable sight in Tuvalu. The runway is only used for brief periods twice a week, yet occupies a large proportion of the country, so the people here have not let the land go to waste. On my return past the airport, as I rode my motorbike up and down the runway, I witnessed what must have been half the country playing volleyball and soccer on it. And then I joined in. If this wasn't remarkable enough, a huge proportion of the population drag their mattresses from their homes and sleep on the runway at night. In a country that can experience stifling tropical heat north of 40 degrees, the coolest place to sleep was the open space that attracted a cooling breeze across it. On my last night here, I did the same, falling asleep on the commercial runway, looking up at the clear sky above. What an incredible adventure that was, and certainly one to tell the grandkids.

My final stretch of countries would take me slightly more north in the Pacific, to what would more accurately be described as the mid-pacific, geographically speaking. I returned to the city of Manila to catch one of many United Micronesia hopper flights through the final three countries. Palau was my first stop.

My initial impression when I landed in Koror was surprise at the multitude of resorts here. Palau has the most developed tourism in Micronesia by far. There was an abundance of clear blue water as we left the airport, on all sides. Despite checking out the lively bar scene, Palau unfortunately remained but a stepping stone toward my final objective at this point. I hopped over to Guam, and although not officially an independent country, I did have enough time to explore some of the beautiful beaches. It was also a relatively simple hike to reach the tallest mountain on Earth, Mount Lamlam. The peak of this mountain barely reaches more than 1000 feet, however, the mountain submerges into the deepest part of the ocean in the Marianas trench. To put the tip to base height of this mountain into perspective, if Everest were to stand here it would still be 7000 feet below sea level.

From Guam I moved on to my penultimate country, the Marshall Islands. I must admit, by this point I only had the finish line in sight, so to speak. The capital Majuro was little more than a singular strip of sand in the Pacific, intended to house U.S. servicemen for rest and recuperation purposes. Tacky neon lights advertised bars all along the strip, and what a difference this patch of sand was compared to Tuvalu with its singular road one of the only similarities. Most areas in the Marshall Islands were difficult to reach and off limits due to military activity and previous nuclear testing, and so, after spending as little time as possible here, I boarded a plane for the last time on this epic adventure to head to my very last country in the world, and what an amazing country it was.

There I was, standing at the immigration desk for the very last time on this epic journey to over 196 countries and a handful more territories. It had taken me over five years. The stamp came down on my passport for the last time, and I walked through the perfectly placed sign: "Welcome to the Federated States of Micronesia." This moment that I had been striving toward as a clearly defined goal for the last couple of years of my travels actually passed me. At the time, it didn't really hit me what I had achieved. Elena was hugely supportive. She was there with me to cross into the final country, but it wasn't until after a few days in Micronesia that it dawned on me that, once officially recognized, I was the youngest person to travel to every country in the world. For the last time in a new country, I snorkeled. It was from pristine Micronesian beaches, and the boat trip to the archaeological ruins of Nan Madol near Pohnpei (which is sometimes referred to as the "Venice of the Pacific"), was a very reflective moment for me. We were quietly meandering through the canals between the stone ruins and there wasn't a tourist in sight. I stopped for a minute, for a moment of nostalgia, thinking back and comparing this to the other destinations in the South Pacific. And that brought a big grin to my face. Earlier on that trip, I had dived to the shallow ocean floor and come across truly unique statues in perfectly formed circles in what was an almost cult-like setting. I realized that day that I had never seen anything like that in the Pacific or anywhere else the world.

This is where it dawned on me, that far from the journey being over, it was only just beginning. Sure, I have traveled to every country in the world, but what is a country? Human drawn lines of territory that don't define the absolute exploration of everything within those lines. I guess I was initially feeling a little melancholic, but it took until discovering something completely new in the very final country, something I had never experienced before, to make me realize that there would be so much more for me to see from here on out. What if the borders of separation had been drawn up slightly differently by the powers that be, and hypothetically, the Marshall Islands and Micronesia were a group of islands under just one nation's flag? Well, then I may have never discovered what I like to call the underwater terracotta army.

EPILOGUE

There are so many more things to discover in this world, for all of us, even those who think they have traveled far and wide. We don't just visit places and consider ourselves experienced. We are an evolving species, and the landscape that we find so marvelous and beautiful has also evolved over so many millions of years. We are an amazing race, and people have provided the most enticing part of my traveling. The memories I have and call my own are unique in themselves, and some of these memories are immensely personal and mine alone. I have looked out across oceans and deserts alone. I have been the first person in the world to watch the sunrise one day, where there was not another soul in sight. That memory will stay with me forever, until I'm old, and it is mine to cherish. I cannot reminisce about this with anyone, and that is beautiful in itself. But memories are best cherished when they are shared. Sure, some of my adventures were that bit more touching where the landscape felt like it belonged to me, but the time you will see me smiling the most will be when I recollect the exploits with my family, my wife, my friends, and everyone else I met along the way. You all know who you are, and

I can truly say that every single person along the journey, even the ones who may never get to read this book, and especially the ones that made my life a misery, were a part of my story, and won't ever be forgotten. I have created memories throughout our magnificent world, both good and bad, solitary and shared. My happiest thoughts are those that are shared, and I am incredibly nostalgic even writing this, toward my family, friends, and everyone I didn't mention that was along the way with me every step of the way, even when you weren't physically present.

We all see the world through different eyes, and all have different tastes, and what appealed to me may be your idea of hell on earth. Don't follow anyone's footsteps, carve out your own path, and don't let anyone tell you how to explore, travel and live. All we will have left will be the memories we make, so cherish the precious time we have.

We're all inspired by different things, people or stories. I was always astonished by the articles I read in National Geographic and wanted to visit the immensely beautiful places illustrated in their magazines, and so off I went, armed with my Lonely Planet guidebook, the staple bellwether for so many backpackers. Everyone should set their own goals and objectives, and this became my goal. Regardless of whatever else happens in life, no one can ever take this away from me; that I have traveled to every country in the world. World records will come and go, and likely a younger person will beat my record at some point, as the ability to travel in a more interconnected world becomes ever easier through booking sites which have become so widespread now compared to when I first started.

Not only will the world record likely change hands, but in our ever-changing global landscape, countries will come and go. So, although in terms of segregated human-made borders I have been to every country in the world, realistically, I'm only just getting started. The one constant are the lifetime of memories I have and will share through this journey, and I'm truly grateful to all those who let me be a part of their journeys as well.

So what are you waiting for? Pack your bags, book a flight and travel. Explore the world in which we live. Push your own boundaries and see what you are capable of. Laughter, happiness, anger and likely tears. Let all the emotions encapsulate your senses, and I promise you, it will be the best thing you will ever do. What's stopping you?

51298858R00161

Made in the USA
Middletown, DE
01 July 2019